University of Cambridge Department of Applied Economics

OCCASIONAL PAPER 55

POLITICAL ASPECTS OF THE ECONOMY

DAE OCCASIONAL PAPERS

25 Soviet Planning Today: Proposals for an Optimally Functioning Economic System *by Michael Ellman*

28 Economies of Scale in Manufacturing Industry *by C. F. Pratten*

39 Company Finance and the Capital Market: A Study of the Effects of Firm Size *by E. W. Davis and K. A. Yeomans*

41 Exporting Workers: The Turkish Case *by Suzanne Paine*

45 Development, Income Distribution and Social Change in Rural Egypt (1952–1970): A Study in the Political Economy of Agrarian Transition *by Mahmoud Abdel-Fadil*

48 Domestic Monetary Management in Britain 1919–1938 *by S. Howson*

49 The State and Economic Development: Peru since 1968 *by E. V. K. FitzGerald*

50 Labour Productivity Differentials within International Companies *by C. F. Pratten*

51 Disappointing Marriage: A Study of the Gains from Merger *by G. Meeks*

52 The Political Economy of Nasserism: A Study in Employment and Income Distribution Policies in Urban Egypt, 1952–72 *by Mahmoud Abdel-Fadil*

53 Effects of the Temporary Employment Subsidy *by D. M. Deakin and C. F. Pratten*

54 Labour Market Structure, Industrial Organisation and Low Pay *by Christine Craig, Jill Rubery, Roger Tarling and Frank Wilkinson*

DAE PAPERS IN INDUSTRIAL RELATIONS AND LABOUR

2 Do Trade Unions Cause Inflation? *by Dudley Jackson, H. A. Turner and Frank Wilkinson* Second Edition

4 Africanisation, Nationalisation and Inequality: Mining labour and the Copperbelt in Zambian development *by Philip Daniel*

5 The Last Colony: But Whose? A Study of the Labour Movement, Labour Market and Labour Relations in Hong Kong *by H. A. Turner et al.*

6 The Active Trade Unionist: A Study of Motivation and Participation at Branch Level *by Patricia Fosh*

Other titles in both series may be obtained from:
The Publications Secretary, Department of Applied Economics,
Sidgwick Avenue, Cambridge, CB3 9DE

Political aspects of the economy

VANI K. BOROOAH

and

FREDERICK VAN DER PLOEG

CAMBRIDGE UNIVERSITY PRESS

CAMBRIDGE
LONDON NEW YORK NEW ROCHELLE
MELBOURNE SYDNEY

Published by the Press Syndicate of the University of Cambridge
The Pitt Building, Trumpington Street, Cambridge CB2 1RP
32 East 57th Street, New York, NY 10022, USA
296 Beaconsfield Parade, Middle Park, Melbourne 3206, Australia

First published 1983

Printed in Great Britain at the
University Press, Cambridge

Library of Congress catalogue card number: 83-7738

British Library Cataloguing in Publication Data

Borooah, Vani
Political aspects of the economy. – (Occasional papers/
University of Cambridge Department of Applied Economics; 55)
1. Great Britain – Economic conditions – 1945–
2. Great Britain – Politics and government – 1964–
I. Title II. Ploeg, Frederick van der
III. Series
330.941'0858 HC256.6

ISBN 0 521 25841 3

Contents

Tables

Figures

Preface

This book arose out of our dissatisfaction with the present 'state of the art' of economic forecasting and by implication with the models of the economy on which such forecasts are usually based. Typically, forecasts which attempt to chart the course of the economy five to ten years hence (known in the trade as 'medium to long term' forecasts) have to make assumptions about the likely economic policies that would prevail over the forecasting period with the consequence that the predicted outcomes are crucially dependent on the assumed policies. In preparing forecasts we felt it increasingly necessary to say something about the political aspects of economic policy formulation. For example, in preparing a forecast for the years 1980–1990 we realised there would be an election in 1983 or 1984 but found it difficult to predict which political party would win the election, what kind of policy would be adopted prior to the election by the incumbent political party and what kind of strategy would be adopted by the (unknown) victor after the election. The great drawback of most existing economic models (and of the forecasts they generate) is that they do not embody any mechanism which would provide an indication of the likely fluctuations in voter behaviour which in turn might induce changes in economic policy.

This prompted us first to analyse the link between economic performance and political popularity and subsequently to investigate the link between popularity and economic policy. We found that issues of social class and representation of different interest groups featured prominently in our analysis and this led us outside the domain of our 'conventional' economic background. We rejected the view of a government as a benevolent dictator promoting social welfare, familiar in the normative theory of economic policy, and instead modelled the government as a political animal promoting its own ideology and re-election interests. Our findings belong to the field of political economy and form the substance of this book.

The material presented here is, in our view, of interest not only to economic model builders, but also to general economists, political scientists, public administrators and interested lay-people. Some of the readers may however be less interested in the detailed technical arguments underlying our theories. It is for this reason that Chapters 3, 8 and 9, which are more technical than the others, may be omitted at first reading.

As will be obvious throughout the course of this book, we owe a vast intellectual debt to the writings of David Butler and Donald Stokes. The work embodied in this book is part of the larger research programme undertaken by the Cambridge Growth Project, and financial support from the Social Science Research Council is gratefully acknowledged. We are also in considerable debt to our colleagues on the Project: their comments and encouragement have assisted us greatly in the preparation of this book. Thanks are also due to the participants of seminars at the Universities of Edinburgh, Liverpool and Zürich, Queens' College and Churchill College, Cambridge, the 1981 European Meeting of the Econometric Society, the 1982 Meeting of the European Consortium of Political Research and the 1982 Meeting of Dutch Economists for discussing our work. We are also grateful to Mike Artis, Samuel Brittan, David Donald, Wim Driehuis, Mark Franklin, Bruno Frey, Graham Gudgin, Douglas Hibbs, Christopher Pissarides, Franz Schneider and Frans van Winden for their constructive comments on our work. Needless to say, we alone are responsible for any remaining errors.

We wish to thank Bobbie Coe for the preparation of our data, Ann Newton for sub-editing the book and Christine Hudson for typing successive drafts in a splendid manner. We appreciate the excellent facilities provided by the Department of Applied Economics, Cambridge University during the course of our research. The second author also wishes to acknowledge the Foundation for Economic Research (Stichting voor Economisch Onderzoek) at the University of Amsterdam for providing the appropriate environment for preparing Chapters 7, 8 and 9.

We are also grateful to the American Political Science Association for permission to reproduce Table 1 from the article by Douglas Hibbs in Vol. 76 No. 2 of the *American Political Science Review*; to the Scottish Economic Society for permission to reproduce parts of an article by us in the June 1982 issue of *The Scottish Journal of Political Economy*; to the editors of *The Manchester School* for permission to reproduce parts of an article by us in their March 1982 issue; and to Macmillan, London and Basingstoke, and St Martin's Press, New York, for permission to reproduce three diagrams from *Political Change in Britain* by David Butler and Donald Stokes.

Finally, we should like to dedicate this book to Gautam, Vidya and Carol.

Cambridge VANI K. BOROOAH
March 1983 FREDERICK VAN DER PLOEG

1

Introduction

This is a book about political economy. The term political economy is used in its most literal sense to express the complex interaction between political and economic behaviour and as such the book is concerned with two broad but interrelated themes.

The first theme to be considered is that of voter behaviour. It is a truism that in societies characterised by democratic political systems, governments have periodically to submit themselves to the judgements of the electorate. The frequency with which elections are held, the rules under which they are conducted, the criteria adopted for ushering one party into office and possibly another out of office, the scope for inter-party coalitions, all these details of course vary between different democracies. However, the one single feature of submitting to electoral judgement, no matter how misguided or irrational this judgement may appear, remains inescapable. It would appear therefore that political parties which participate in the electoral process might have an interest, first in identifying the factors that are significant influences on the electorate's judgement and second, in manipulating these factors in a manner calculated to win favour with the electors.

The first part of this book is devoted to investigating the proposition that economic factors play a major role in determining political popularity. Such an investigation may perhaps require some justification. Given that the institutional setting of most of the empirical work in this book is Great Britain over the past twenty-five years, we shall, in providing our justification, preserve the same setting.

In the General Election of 1959, in which the Conservatives under Macmillan were re-elected, voters perceived the twin problems of international affairs and of armaments and defence as constituting the major problems facing Britain. In a poll conducted by Gallup over the period 18–23 December 1959, 40 per cent of the 1000 respondents regarded these issues as 'the most important problem facing the country today'. Economic affairs were so regarded by 18 per cent of the respondents, with pensions and services for old people gaining top priority with 11 per cent of the respondents. On all three issues – international, economic and defence affairs – there was overwhelming agreement that the government's handling was superior to the opposition's.

Towards the end of 1963 there was a dramatic shift in the electorate's perception of the relative importance of the various issues. Thus in September 1963, 26 per cent of the Gallup respondents assigned the highest priority to economic affairs and only 18 per cent to the combined issues of international affairs and defence. By December 1964, slightly less than three-quarters of the respondents thought the economic situation was very serious or serious and 44 per cent of the respondents were prepared to suffer temporary hardship provided it meant a brighter future. This emphasis on economic affairs continued through the life of the first Wilson government. In March 1966, prior to the General Election, 48 per cent of respondents put economic affairs as the most urgent problem facing Britain.

The effect of a particular economic issue in focusing the electorate's attention on economic affairs was provided by the devaluation of sterling in 1967, when 40 per cent of Gallup respondents felt that the government should resign if Britain had to devalue her currency. Economic affairs continued to dominate the political debate of the late 1960s, and in June 1970, when Labour was defeated at the General Election, Gallup samples showed that a failure to keep prices down, a failure to stop strikes and a failure to prevent the rise in unemployment were regarded as the biggest failures of the Wilson government. In fact a post-election survey indicated that 25 per cent of the respondents felt that cost of living rises were the main reason for the Conservative victory.

The predominance of economic affairs in the minds of the electorate continued to increase over the seventies, showing both in a concern with general issues like unemployment and standards of living and in an anxiety with more specific matters like the miners' strike of 1974 and the 'winter of discontent' of 1979. In February 1974, at the time of the General Election which ousted the Heath government, labour relations and cost of living increases were overwhelmingly regarded as the most urgent problems facing Britain, with over 70 per cent of respondents in a Gallup survey giving them top priority. At the same time 52 per cent of respondents sympathised with the miners in their pay dispute and 51 per cent regarded the three-day week as unnecessary. By October 1977, unemployment had been added to the list of voter anxieties and 70 per cent of respondents felt that unemployment, inflation and labour relations were problems of the greatest urgency.

The evidence from the later seventies and early eighties only confirms the earlier pattern for the sixties and middle seventies, with the British public consistently regarding economic affairs as being the most important problem facing the country. There would thus appear to be a strong case for investigating closely the relationship between changes in the economic environment and the reactions of the electorate. As we stated earlier, this investigation forms the first part of the book and occupies the next five chapters.

We are very conscious of the fact that our work, if it has achieved anything of value, has done so only because it has built on the works of others. The recognition of this enormous intellectual debt is more formally acknowledged in the next chapter, which surveys some of the literature on this subject. It should be acknowledged immediately that the survey is not quite complete. A major reason is that much of the empirical work on voting behaviour is country specific and, given the wide disparity of institutional structure and electoral practice between countries, we felt that a diversification of our survey over a wide range of countries would lead to a proliferation of results that might only serve to confuse rather than instruct. Accordingly this survey focuses on two countries with a broad similarity of culture – the United Kingdom and the United States of America. We acknowledge that a vast number of studies of voter behaviour exist for other countries, particularly for the countries of Western Europe, and the interested reader is referred to Paldam and Schneider (1980), Whiteley (1980) and Hibbs and Fassbender (1981) for details of such studies.

Apart from a survey of the empirical results, Chapter 2 also includes details about the important theories of voter behaviour. One main conclusion that emerges is that most of the empirical work in this field is not rigorously grounded in a theory of the way voters behave and in particular that it is difficult to achieve such a theoretical underpinning in the context of a multi-party political system. An attempt to rectify this is the subject of Chapter 3 where we derive a theoretical model of qualitative political choice that can be applied to a multi-party framework. This model employs the technique of logit analysis which has been applied fruitfully to situations where agents have to make discrete choices rather than choices over a continuous spectrum.

A first attempt to estimate such a system of equations for Britain is reported in Chapter 4. Existing studies of voter reactions to economic performance (a notable exception being Hibbs, 1982b) make two fundamental assumptions which are repeated in Chapter 4. These assumptions are, first, that the reactions of voters do not change over time in response to changes in the economic and political climate and, second, that all voters are alike in the sense of having identical reactions to changes in the economic environment.

The first assumption is relaxed in Chapter 5 where the intertemporal stability of our qualitative choice model is considered. The investigation of stability is carried out in the context of the Butler and Stokes (1974) hypothesis according to which the criteria whereby voters evaluate a government's economic performance can and do change over time. This change could occur for a variety of reasons. Voters' perceptions of the relative importance of different economic issues could alter because of changes in their economic circumstances or because of changes in the economic debate between the rival political parties. Our study finds much evidence to support this hypothesis.

The second assumption (that of identical voters) is relaxed in Chapter 6. In this we consider the proposition that different occupational classes may have different economic interests and may therefore react differently to a given change in the economic scene. After extending our qualitative choice model to take into account different voter interests, we carry out an empirical analysis based on cross-section data for the British General Election of 1966. This concludes the first part of the book.

In the second part of the book we turn to the issue of economic policy and examine the influences that might bear upon the formulation of such policies. The economics profession has a long tradition of interest in the general principles that ought to underlie the making of policies and in this tradition the work of Tinbergen (1952) is probably seminal. In the Tinbergen approach the government was viewed as a benevolent dictator acting in the best interests of the governed. In operational terms, these interests could be encapsulated by a social welfare indicator which in turn depended upon certain pre-selected economic variables. The task of the policy maker was then to select the levels of the policy 'instruments' – government expenditure, tax rates etc. – which would yield values for the 'target' variables – unemployment, inflation etc. – consistent with society enjoying the highest possible level of welfare. It was recognized that the ability of the policy maker to manipulate his instruments would be constrained by the structure of the economy, so that the design of policy would depend greatly upon the economic environment in which it was being made.

Although this approach to economic policy making has been extended in several directions and refined in several respects, the philosophy underlying the approach – that of regarding government as acting for the 'greatest good' of the governed – has remained unchanged. Thus, for example, Theil (1964) has considered the implications for policy of alternative representations of the social welfare function; Phelps (1967) has considered the implications of social welfare maximisation constrained by the existence of an inflation–unemployment trade-off. In every extension and refinement however the concern is with what the government ought to do if it is to maintain the role of benevolent dictator.

Parallel to the interest shown by economists in the design of policy is the indifference displayed by governments to advice proffered by economists. Part of the reason for this disregard may be the fact that governments cannot play the role which is assigned to them by economists. The view of the government as a monolithic, impersonal entity executing policy for the greatest good ignores the fact that governments have objectives of their own quite apart from that of the general welfare of the governed. Some of these objectives may be ideological – a government is committed to doing certain things. These ideological commitments may in turn be entwined with class interests – a government may feel it is more committed to a particular social class with a particular set of economic interests than to another social class with a different set of economic interests. Then there is the overriding interest of governments in democratic societies in avoiding electoral defeats. This may lead them to follow policies which though socially sub-optimal are nevertheless electorally safe. Finally, compounding all this, 'government' is really an amalgam of a heterogeneous collection of organs with possibly conflicting objectives. Thus policy may be made in one department and thwarted in its execution by another.

Our view of the role of government in a modern economy, itself embedded in a democratic political structure, is illustrated in Fig. 1.1. The links between the economy, the electorate, their voting patterns in elections and the disbursements of these votes in determining who should govern and who should oppose are discussed in Chapters 2 to 6. Chapters 7 and 10 then consider the implications for policy of taking into account these factors.

The relationship between variations in economic popularity and the nature of the economic policies pursued is the theme of Chapter 7. The general argument underlying the possible existence of a 'feedback' from popularity to policies is that incumbent parties are in a position, through the use of appropriate policies, to influence the behaviour of the economy. At the same time the government of the day is aware that the economic outcomes consequent upon such policies influence its popularity with the electorate. Given this knowledge, a government interested in re-election might attempt to manipulate the economy in a manner calculated to ensure that periods of economic strength occurred immediately prior to elections and periods of economic weakness occurred when political popularity was not electorally vital. Such politically-motivated policies would then generate that cycle of booms and slumps termed the 'political business cycle'.

Fig. 1.1 *Political–economic structure*

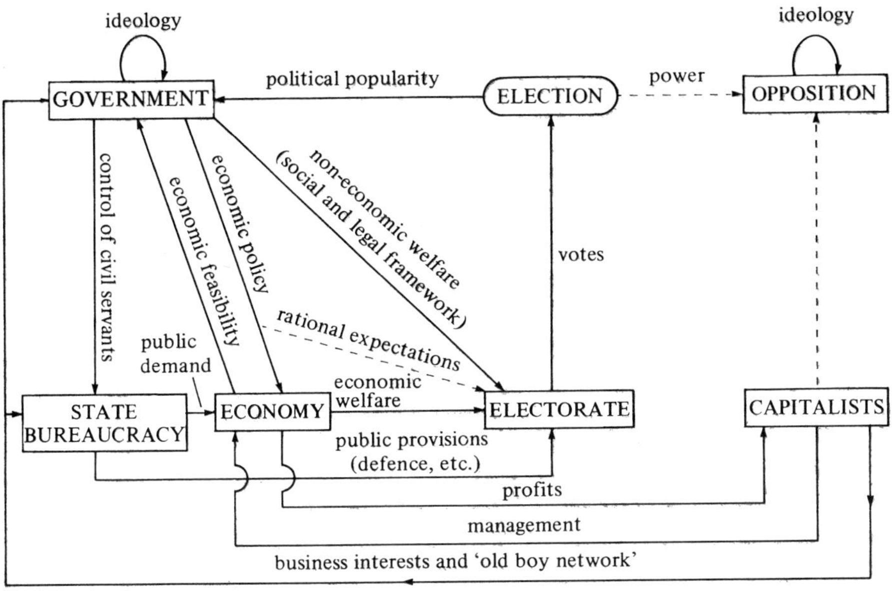

A survey of the different approaches to explaining political business cycles is also contained in Chapter 7. These can be distinguished as the optimising and the satisficing approaches. The optimising approach concentrates on the optimal behaviour of government given certain political objectives. These objectives may be many and various. Thus, for example, a government may wish to maximise its votes at the next election or it may take victory at the next election for granted and wish to concentrate on the election after next, and so on. The major conclusion that emerges from this approach is that the optimal policies that a government ought to pursue will differ significantly depending upon the nature of its political objectives.

The satisficing approach, on the other hand, seeks to explain how a government attains satisfactory levels of different objectives rather than optimising on any one. Consequently, this approach has a strong empirical bias and Chapter 7 also reviews the international evidence on the existence or otherwise of the political business cycle. It should be emphasised that the literature on the political aspects of economic policy formulation provides many insights into the behaviour of governments. In particular, the conventional view of governments acting so as to implement socially-optimal policies turns out to be invalid since a government's policies are constrained both by its ideology and by its desire to secure re-election.

Yet another set of constraints that act upon a government's policies are the relationships that exist between the different economic variables. A proper understanding of the formulation of economic policies is not possible without an understanding of the economic environment within the context of which policies are formulated. Our view of the manner in which a modern economy operates, and of the nature of the relationships embodied in such an economy, is contained in Chapter 8.

Chapter 9 examines the political aspects of policy making, taking into account a variety of constraints that impinge on a government's actions. The first of these constraints is the economy (described in detail in Chapter 8). Taking into account the constraint of the entire economy is more realistic than considering the formulation of policy in the context of the inflation–unemployment trade-off. The second constraint considered is that the nation may consist of several interest groups and the government may feel more closely allied to one than to another. The third constraint is that government is not a homogeneous entity but indeed contains a part – the civil service – which is not dependent on elections for survival. This leads to the possibility of conflict between these component parts of government. The formulation of a government's economic policy in the face of these constraints is the subject of this chapter. Within this general framework the implications of vote maximisation, promotion of ideology subject to a balance of payments and re-election constraint, and satisficing behaviour are discussed.

The final chapter uses the ideas developed in the book to examine the political aspects of economic policy making in Britain over the past twenty years. After reviewing some of the existing empirical work on endogenous government behaviour in Britain, this chapter argues for an approach which looks more closely at the institutional setting in which policy is made and which also examines, in greater detail than hitherto, the nature of the policy options available. The remainder of the chapter then follows this approach, first by setting out briefly the manner in which policy is organised in Britain and the economic context in which British economic policy, over the past two decades, has been made, and then by examining in detail three instruments of economic policy, *viz.* policies to control government expenditures and revenues, and to restrain inflation.

It is pertinent, in conclusion, briefly to compare this book with three other works on a similar theme. Hibbs and Fassbender (1981) and Whiteley (1980) are both collections of papers by different authors on the general theme of political economy. Consequently, our book represents a more coherent and consistent and, by virtue of coming later, a more up to date treatment of political economy. Our book is also grounded strongly in empirical work and this distinguishes it from van Winden (1983) who raises, in a purely theoretical context, some of the issues discussed by us in terms of both theory and data.

Part I: Economic performance, social class and voting behaviour

2

The economy as a political issue

2.1 Introduction

In March 1968, Harold Wilson declared '. . . All political history shows that the standing of a Government and its ability to hold the confidence of the electorate at a General Election depends upon the success of its economic policy . . .' (*Financial Times*, 9th March 1968).

The hypothesis embodied in this statement – that there is a causal relationship between a government's economic performance and its political popularity – forms the theme of the first part of this book. The concern of this chapter is to survey the manner in which this relationship has been articulated both in the economics and the political science literature.

Two aspects of this relationship deserve attention. The first aspect is that of the logic of the voter. Why do (or do not) voters respond to economic issues? Do voters respond to certain economic issues but not to others? Do different voters respond differently to particular economic issues and, if so, why? These are some of the questions to which the theory of voting addresses itself.

The second aspect is empirical. What, if any, are the economic issues that voters regard as important? Is it inflation, unemployment, incomes? Are they concerned with all these issues all the time, or some of these issues some of the time? What is the relative strength of their concern with these issues and are there any other issues that could be identified empirically as being of concern to voters? Do voters discount past successes and failures and, if so, what is the rate of discount?

The first part of this survey is concerned with the theory of voting. It begins by considering the classic Downsian theory of the rational voter (Section 2.2). There is then a discussion of the 'median' voter and an application of the theory of spatial competition to political parties vying for the favours of the median voter (Section 2.3). The next section, Section 2.4, is devoted to studies which rely on voters viewing the economy as a 'valence' issue, i.e. an issue on which there is essentially one body of opinion. In contrast, there are 'position' models of voting behaviour in which voters are viewed as holding different positions on particular issues. Such models are the concern of Section 2.5.

The studies of voter behaviour discussed in Sections 2.4 and 2.5 are discussed in terms of their theoretical content and the view they take of voter behaviour. Such studies, however, also usually include empirical applications of the underlying theory and the second part of this survey is concerned with the results of such applications. Several points, connected with the presentation of the empirical results, should be made at the very outset.

Typically, such applications concentrate on the econometric estimation of the electorate's reaction to movements in various economic variables. Such a reaction might be a direct reaction, measured in terms of votes cast for or against the contending parties at various elections, or it might be an indirect one, measured by the popularity rating of the various parties or political leaders as evidenced by answers to political questions by a sample of the electorate. Estimation of the direct reaction is referred to as the estimation of a 'vote function' and estimation of the indirect reaction is referred to as the estimation of a 'popularity function', it being understood that votes or popularity are a function of (i.e. depend upon) economic and other factors.

Empirical work in this field tends also to be country and institution specific. Thus for the United States one researcher might work on votes cast in congressional elections while another might concentrate on presidential popularity ratings. Therefore, to achieve depth of focus, this survey concentrates on empirical findings for vote and popularity functions for two countries, the United States and the United Kingdom. The results for the United Kingdom are presented in Subsection 2.6.1 and those for the United States in Subsection 2.6.2. Section 2.7 then concludes the chapter.

2.2 The logic of the voter: the Downsian model

The theory of voting behaviour that accords most closely with standard economic theory originated with Downs (1957). In a Downsian world of two parties (though the analysis could be modified for a multi-party system) a voter is rational in the sense that he casts his votes for the party he believes will provide him with more benefits than any other. These benefits, which may be many and various, are reduced to a common denominator, which Downs refers to as the *utility income* of government activity. To discover which party he would vote for, the voter compares the utility incomes he would receive over the coming election period from each of the parties and votes for the party from which he expects the highest utility income. The analysis recognises that, since no party can do – or will wish to do – everything it promises, party manifestoes are a poor basis for forming expectations about future utilities. Instead the voter must form some judgement about what the parties would actually do should they come to power. For the incumbent party, its performance in the current period, assuming its policies have some continuity, offers a reliable guide to its future deeds; for the party in opposition, however, no such guide exists. The model then assumes that the rational voter constructs in his mind such a hypothetical guide i.e. how the opposition party would have performed had it been in power in the current period, and then uses the present utility incomes, the one actual and the other hypothetical, to form expectations about the post-election period.

It is recognised however that collecting information for an evaluation of the different utility income streams is a costly process and for this reason no voter would attempt a comprehensive evaluation. Instead each voter will base his evaluation upon those areas where the differences between parties are sufficient to impress him. Thus the voter remains indifferent as to which party is in power until the difference in utility flows is large enough i.e. until his party differential threshold has been crossed.

2.3 The median voter and competition between parties

'Parties formulate policies in order to win elections, rather than win elections to formulate policies' (Downs, 1957, p. 28). From this assertion follows the Downsian theory of party competition (this theory in turn has antecedents in Hotelling (1929) and Smithies (1941)) and the influence of the median voter.

In the Downsian model political opinion is depicted as lying along a single left–right dimension. Every voter is assumed to have a single most-preferred position along this spectrum so that the further a party is from a voter's optimum position, the less desirable its election will be to that voter. Under these assumptions, if the frequency distribution of most-preferred positions is unimodal and symmetric and if every voter voted for the party closest to his preferred position then competition between parties would drive them to the position favoured by the median voter.

This is illustrated in Fig. 2.1(a) in which *M* represents the preferred position of the median voter, *L* and *R* the respective positions of the two parties and *X* the mid point of the line segment *LR*. Under these conditions, the party whose position is at *L* receives all the votes to the left of *X*, thus conceding an easy victory to the party at *R* which receives all the votes to the right of *X*. The party at *L* could – as could the party at *R* – increase its vote by moving towards the median-voter position, *M*, and indeed could win more votes if it was closer to *M* than the other party. A desire to win would therefore push both parties to the position favoured by the median voter.

The possibility of abstentions caused either by indifference (party positions being too close to make voting worthwhile) or alienation (party positions being too far removed from one's preferred position to make voting attractive) does not upset the above proposition so long as the frequency distribution of preferred positions remains symmetric and unimodal. If the probability that a voter abstains is an increasing function of the closeness of the parties' positions, then symmetry implies that vote losses will be equal for the two parties as they move towards the centre. If the probability that a voter abstains increases with the distance of a party away from him, then the parties are pulled towards the mode. However, if the distribution is symmetric and unimodal the mode and median coincide. Thus neither indifference nor alienation affects the median voter result (Davis, Hinich and Ordeshook, 1970).

However, either asymmetry or multimodality in the frequency distribution of voter preferences could upset the median voter result. If the distribution is asymmetric but unimodal, the optimal position for each party is the mode which now does not coincide with the median (Comanor, 1976). This is illustrated in Fig. 2.1(b). If both parties are initially at the median position, *M*, then a move of one to *X* loses him the voters in the shaded area to the right of *M* but gains him the voters in the shaded area to the left of *X*, the latter exceeding the former.

Fig. 2.1(c) illustrates the case for a bi-modal symmetric distribution. The position of the median voter at *M* may not be the optimal party position because alienation could lose it a substantial number of votes. The presence of alienation could lead both parties away from the median towards the two modes (Downs, 1957, pp. 118–122). However, if alienation is weak then the median outcome may remain unchanged (Davis, Hinich and Ordeshook, 1970).

Fig. 2.1 (a) *Symmetric and unimodal distribution of votes.* (b) *Unimodal but asymmetric distribution of votes.* (c) *Bimodal but symmetric distribution of votes*

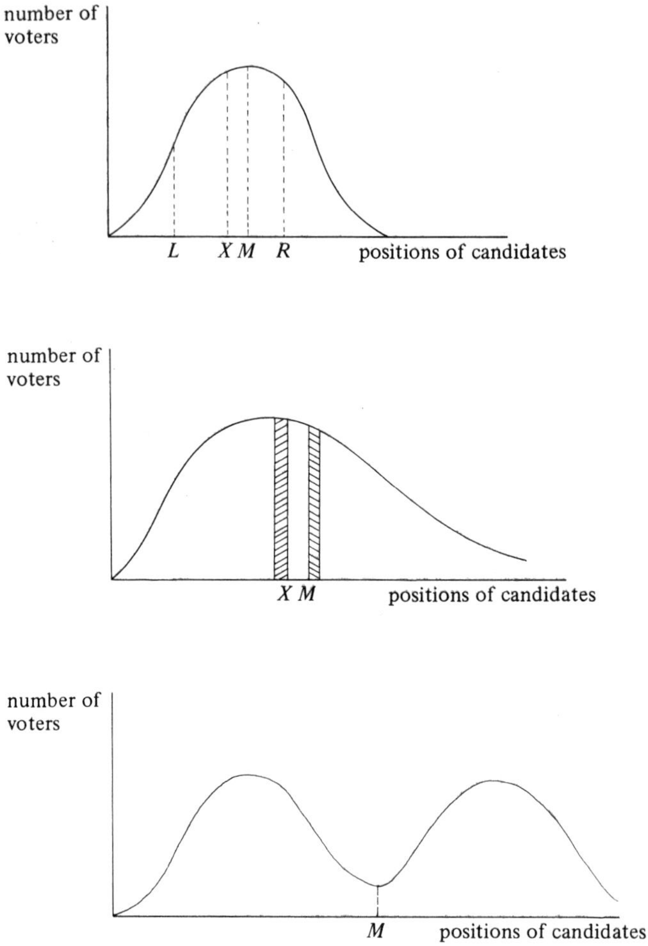

Thus the median voter result depends upon a set of very restrictive assumptions, namely, one issue dimension, unimodal and symmetric preference distributions, and two parties only. Relaxing these assumptions, as has been shown, might lead to the median-voter result being overturned.

2.4 Valence models of voting behaviour

Butler and Stokes (1974) distinguish between 'valence' issues on which there is essentially one body of opinion and 'position' issues on which there may be rival bodies of opinion. Thus, for example, a government's views on labour relations or nationalisation might be regarded as 'position' issues. On the other hand a reduction in unemployment levels or growth in real incomes might be regarded as 'valence' issues since there is a virtual consensus on the electorate's part of their desirability. The view of voter behaviour in which voters reward or punish governments for the attainment or non-attainment of certain universally-desired economic goals is a view that regards economic issues as valence issues.

Kramer (1971) takes up Downs' point on the costs of acquiring and processing information and its implications for the impossibility of attempting an exhaustive comparison between political parties. In this context the relevant decision rule for voters – even rational well-informed voters – would be based on readily available information. Thus Kramer's model assumes the following operational rule:

> if the performance of the incumbent party is 'satisfactory' according to some standard, the voter votes to retain the incumbent party in office to enable it to continue its present policies; while if the incumbent's performance is not 'satisfactory', the voter votes against the incumbent, to give the opposition party a chance to govern. (Kramer, 1971, p. 134)

Stigler (1973), on the other hand, puts forward a case for the unimportance of general economic conditions in national elections. This argument appears to be based upon Downs' point (referred to above) that a voter will concentrate his evaluation upon those areas where the differences between parties are sufficient to impress him. In Stigler's view there may be no difference in the commitment (or in the ability to fulfil these commitments) of the major parties to the goals of high employment and high and steady growth rates of real income. Thus, if, for example, per capita income falls for a year or two, the rational voter may, quite correctly, ascribe this to exogenous events outside the government's sphere of influence or to the sort of policy errors to which all governments – and not just the incumbent government – are prey. Thus he may regard it as premature to punish or abandon the party in power simply because of recent reverses in performance.

For the rational voter the process of expectations formation 'should have two properties: 1. The forecast should reflect accumulated past experience. 2. The forecast should attach more weight to recent than to remote periods' (Stigler, 1973, p. 165). Using these two properties of expectations of future performance Stigler considers real per capita income and concludes that, for the USA, 'voters disregard average income performance in deciding between parties' (Stigler, 1973, p. 166). At the same time there are several questions on which the parties may be divided. Stigler identifies these as being essentially distributional questions and suggests that it is in the area of income redistribution, rather than in the broader area of macro performance, that the economic basis for party affiliation must be sought.

Fair (1978) begins by noting that 'there is no single theory of voting to which everyone subscribes' and takes as one of his purposes to 'present a model of voting behaviour that is general enough to incorporate what appear to be most of the theories of voting behaviour in the recent literature . . . '. The model is essentially a Downsian one in which the voter evaluates his expected utility stream under each of two parties. This utility is a function of the voter's basic political bias and some measure of the performance, when in power, of the party being evaluated. This performance is suitably discounted to satisfy Stigler's twin criteria for evaluating future performance quoted above. At the same time, by choosing a discount rate of infinity (so that only the performance of the ruling party is evaluated) and by constraining the model so the two parties are evaluated by voters using the same coefficient weight for performance, Kramer's (1971) model emerges as a special case. As we shall show later, Fair's model – which assumes, for empirical applications, that the difference in inter-party bias is distributed uniformly across voters – loses its convenience for empirical purposes when more than two parties are considered. Instead, in the next chapter, we propose an alternative theory of voting behaviour which can conveniently be applied to a multi-party framework. More relevantly, from the point of view of this discussion, Fair's model is not really a general theory since he ignores some theories of voting behaviour, particularly those to be found in the political science literature. Before turning to these we consider Fiorina's (1981) model of voter behaviour, which is also based on rational choice and which also claims to be a general model encompassing other theories.

Fiorina suggests that the voter, in deciding to vote for one party or the other, would be influenced by the following factors:

(i) The changes promised in his personal welfare by the opposing parties between this election and the next; i.e. an evaluation based on party platforms.

(ii) Whether, in the present period he has prospered or not under the incumbent government. This constitutes an *a priori* bias in the mind of the voter and determines his disposition towards the incumbent political party.

(iii) The voter might conduct an exercise similar to (ii) for the opposition party. However, since this would necessarily be hypothetical it would be suitably discounted by an appropriate uncertainty rate.

(iv) Finally, the voter would take into account the totality of his experience with the two parties.

Fiorina's voter thus looks at the sort of things Fair's voter is interested in, except that in addition he also considers party platforms.

2.5 Position models of voting behaviour

The view that holds that economic issues are 'valence' issues can be distinguished from another view in which parties are seen as holding different positions regarding economic policy, with voters choosing the party whose position accords most clearly with their own view of what is desirable.

One such position model, that of Converse (1958), who begins by noting that the view that different status groups in society have different interests and that these different interests are expressed in differential voting behaviour, is fairly widely accepted. Thus, for example, 'over the last 25 years, high status persons in the United States have favoured the Republican party while the less fortunately placed have subscribed instead to the Democratic party' (Converse, 1958, p. 388). The status-vote relationship is termed 'status polarisation' and Converse takes as his purpose to study the factors that may account for variations over time in status polarisation. The hypothesis put forward is that 'polarisation would increase in terms of depression and decrease in periods of prosperity' (p. 396). Thus on this view the consequence of hard times is not a general reduction in the support for the ruling party but an increase of support for each party in the class whose interests it represents and a decline in the support for each party in the class whose interests it does not represent.

Hibbs (1982a and 1982b) develops the idea of a 'critical threshold of popularity'. He argues that political popularity is based upon two comparisons:

(i) the comparison of the performance of the political party in power with the past performance of the main opposition party or parties and
(ii) a comparison of the performance of the current administration's performance with the past performance of all previous administrations regardless of partisan comparisons.

In making these comparisons voters discount the past, so recent performances contribute more to current political judgements than do past performances.

From these comparisons springs what Hibbs terms 'the honeymoon effect'. When a new party government or administration assumes office its initial support depends considerably upon the performance of past administrations or party governments. The worse (better) this performance the higher (lower) this support. In time the new government or administration acquires a record of its own, upon which it is judged, and its support falls from earlier 'honeymoon levels' when that support was due to others' 'misdeeds'.

The outcome of these comparisons is a level of support on the part of the individual voter towards the incumbent party. This level of support, which is in principle unobservable, is a matter of degree, and in quantitative terms can take any value on the minus to plus infinity scale. What is observable (through opinion poll surveys) is a binary choice made at discrete time intervals. In other words the respondent reveals to the questioner at weekly, monthly or quarterly intervals whether he supports or does not support the ruling party. Consequently some artifact is needed to translate the continuously valued, unobserved levels of support into the binary choices that are actually observed. The device employed is the 'critical threshold of popularity', so that a respondent will support the ruling party if the value of his support function (this value being determined by the comparisons discussed above and a random error term) exceeds some critical level and will not support the ruling party if the value falls short of this critical level. This model may be extended to take account of the fact that voters are not identical by assuming that different interest groups e.g. different occupational classes, have different critical thresholds for the different political parties.

In his paper Hibbs (1982a) drew a distinction between inter-party and inter-administration performance. In other words, a voter in evaluating an incumbent's performance compared the cumulated, discounted performance of the present incumbent party with the cumulated discounted prior performance of the present opposition party. Apart from this inter-party comparison, the voter also made an inter-administration comparison in which he compared the cumulated, discounted performance of the current administration with the cumulated, discounted performance of all previous administrations (regardless of party composition). The overall evaluation of an incumbent's performance was then postulated to be a weighted average of an inter-party and inter-administration performance. This enabled an answer to two questions:

(i) the differential weights voters used in evaluating inter-party, as opposed to inter-administration, performance and
(ii) the rate at which the public discounted past performances in making current political judgements.

Kernell and Hibbs (1981) developed a 'position' model in terms of a 'critical threshold of popularity'. The question to which they addressed themselves was how different partisan subgroups would differ in judging a government's performance: in particular, how Democrats and Republicans would differ in their judgement of presidential performance. One possible hypothesis, the 'party *qua* class hypothesis', was that Democrats and Republicans would differ in the intensity of their concern for different economic indicators; plausibly Democrats might be relatively more concerned with unemployment and Republicans with inflation. An alternative hypothesis was that differences between party groups were purely partisan. If this hypothesis were true opposition party supporters would be more critical and negative in their evaluation of the president's performance than the presidential party supporters. If so, the relationship between economic conditions and popularity would be stronger among the opposition party supporters. A third hypothesis is that partisanship was not a relevant factor in determining the economy–popularity relationship. This hypothesis assumes that because both political parties were composed largely of middle-class constituents there would be no significant difference in Democratic and Republican evaluation of presidential performance.

Another 'position' hypothesis, made by Butler and Stokes (1974), is that voters might view one party as expansionist and the other not. Thus the consequences of an economic downturn might increase rather than decrease the popularity of the government if it was formed by the expansionist party. As a historical example they quote the American experience during the 1930s when economic distress did not diminish support for the Democrats who, under Roosevelt, were seen as more expansionary than the Republicans under Hoover. Stigler (1973), in stressing the importance of distributional issues as opposed to general macro-economic performance, is of course also articulating a 'position' model.

Alt (1979), however, points out that a hard and fast distinction between position and valence issues may be slightly artificial. Consensus on ends does not imply consensus on means. Thus, for example, while there may be consensus on the desirability of prosperity – an archetypal valence issue – there may be no such agreement on the appropriate means to attain prosperity. Similarly Robertson (1975) points out that underlying the consensual issue of corruption lies a continuum of how far one is prepared to go to fight it. More generally, on every issue there may be a consensus or disagreement on either the ends or the means to the ends. Furthermore, whether or not there is consensus on an issue is an empirical matter and to regard issues as though they were intrinsically position or valence issues is to confound an empirical matter with an *a priori* classification.

2.6 Empirical results on voting behaviour

It is a commonplace of political folk-lore that fluctuations in economic performance have repercussions on a government's political popularity. The question is: is this piece of received wisdom really a fact? In this section we assess the evidence for such a belief with reference to two countries: the United Kingdom, and the United States of America.

2.6.1 The United Kingdom

The earliest study for the UK investigating the link between economic performance and political popularity was that of Goodhart and Bhansali (1970). Using Gallup poll data the first question that they asked was whether political popularity was affected significantly by economic developments, when the level of unemployment and the rate of inflation were chosen as the variables of greatest concern to the electorate.

The strongest relation between unemployment and government popularity was found between popularity and the lagged level of unemployment and the most successful lag structure was a simple six-months lag. The inflation rate also had a significant immediate effect on popularity. The results also suggested that the response of the electorate to economic events was more marked and volatile in the years since 1959 than in earlier years. At the same time there was statistical evidence for certain regular movements in the popularity of the government of the day between elections. These suggested that immediately after an election there was a sizeable increase in the support for a newly-elected government. Then there followed a period of slow but steady decline in popularity but this unpopularity was reversed in the final few months preceding the next elections. The significance, strength and regularity of such movements ('the electoral cycle') were measured using dummy variables.

The Goodhart and Bhansali (1970) conclusions were questioned by two sets of investigators. Frey and Garbers (1971) argued that the existence of correlation between popularity and unemployment did not indicate the direction of causation. In particular unemployment may force the government to reduce unemployment. At the same time, in their view, the popularity series could be represented adequately by a first order autoregressive process and perhaps, therefore, did not require an economic explanation.

Miller and Mackie (1973) took as their first objective a re-examination of the economic influence model of Goodhart and Bhansali (1970). To this end they used four measures of popularity: the percentage of respondents who support the government, the percentage who support the main opposition party and the difference and sum of these two percentages. The main conclusion that emerged from this re-examination was that there was a basic asymmetry between government and opposition shares of the poll. Thus the relatively strong power of unemployment applied only to the government share of the poll, not to the opposition share. The best predictor of the opposition share of the poll was the bank rate. At the same time the economic variables by themselves never explained more than 50 per cent of the variation of any of the popularity indicators.

Their next objective was to test the economic influence model against an electoral cycle model i.e. a model which explained variations in popularity purely in terms of cycle variables. Three cycle variables were chosen: the number of months to the nearest election, past or future; the square of the number of months to the nearest election and the number of months since the last election. The result that emerged was that the economic influence model was out-performed in terms of explanatory power by the electoral cycle model in respect of three out of four popularity indicators, with only variations in the opposition's share of the poll being better explained by economic developments. Again the basic asymmetry of government and opposition shares of the poll was confirmed by the electoral cycle model: governments suffer from mid-term unpopularity but the opposition does not receive a corresponding rise in support.

Two major conclusions emerged from the Miller and Mackie study. First, the link between economic performance and popularity was not so strong as had been thought. The cyclical pattern of government popularity continued over the sample period although it was not always accompanied by a similar cyclical movement in the economic variables. An alternative explanation suggested for the observed cycles in government popularity was that the nature of the response altered as time passed. When a general election was near, the nature of the response was likely to involve comparisons between the government and the opposition parties. On the other hand, away from a general election, the response was likely to be non-comparative and hence, as a consequence, the incumbent party would emerge more unpopular in mid term than nearer elections.

The second conclusion was that, even if economic affairs did exert an influence, the relevant determinants of popularity that should be used are the voters' perceptions of economic performance. Yet most studies employed as explanatory variable time series published by the government statistical service. Thus a major area for research was the link between objective events and their reporting by the media and between this and the electorate's perceptions and thence its evaluation of the government.

One study which was based on individual perceptions was that of Butler and Stokes (1974). Their major conclusion, based on survey data, was that the influence of the economy on the electorate's mood had two channels. First, there was the link between perceptions of direct changes in individual well-being and changes in party support and, second, there was the link between perceptions, derived from the media, of the general state of the economy and party support, irrespective of whether such a state impinged directly on the well-being of the individual.

An examination of perceptions of individual well-being revealed unmistakably that 'reactions to changes of economic condition followed the lines of a 'valence' model, with the Government of the day, whichever party was in power, being rewarded for good times and disapproved of for bad times' (Butler and Stokes, 1974, p. 384).

As regards perceptions of the state of the economy, the link between such perceptions and party support depended on the extent to which the electorate held the different parties responsible for current economic conditions. Here the ability of the government of the day to unload responsibility for the current economic state onto its predecessor could be important in determining the electorate's attitude. Also the particular features of the economy that were of current electoral importance depended on the economic debate between the parties and such features were therefore capable of change over time.

The Butler and Stokes (1974) study based on individual perceptions represented a departure from the mainstream tradition of econometric work based on data from officially published sources. This tradition was continued by Frey and Schneider (1978a). They concluded, on the basis of econometric evidence, that the government's lead over the opposition was determined by both the state of the economy and the election cycle. A percentage point increase in the rate of inflation and unemployment reduced government popularity by 0.6 per cent and 6.0 per cent respectively, and a rise in the real growth rate of 1.0 per cent increased the government's lead by about 0.8 per cent.

Pissarides (1980) re-examined the relation between voting intentions and economic performance with a view to investigating the extent to which 'it is possible to model the relation between voting intentions and a few macroeconomic indicators in a stable and systematic fashion' (Pissarides, 1980, p. 569). Pissarides argued that if a government's popularity was indeed stable and systematically affected by its economic performance then popularity functions would contain useful information on how to manage the economy to ensure re-election. On the other hand if a stable, systematic relationship did not exist then such functions would not influence the policy-making process.

To investigate the relationship, Pissarides employed as his explanatory variables the percentage growth in consumption, the change in the rate of inflation, the percentage rate of unemployment, the change in the exchange rate and the ratio of GDP taken in by the government in direct and indirect taxes. In addition modified versions of the Miller and Mackie (1973) type of electoral variables were used in conjunction with the lagged value of the dependent variable which was the lead of the government over the main opposition party in the voting intentions figures.

The main conclusion of the study was that, though there was evidence of a systematic relation between economic performance and government popularity over the sample period 1955–1977, taking account of this relation in making out-of-sample forecasts reduced forecasting errors only marginally. Thus an excessive preoccupation by a government about the effect of its policies on its popularity would not appear to be justified. At the same time the popularity function estimated appeared to be stable on conventional statistical criteria. Economic conditions that favoured a faster growth in consumption, a 'stronger' pound, lower inflation and lower unemployment, all had a favourable effect on lead, though quantitatively inflation and unemployment appeared to be the least important of the economic influences.

Hibbs (1982a) employed his 'critical threshold' model (discussed earlier) for the USA, Britain and Germany to address three questions:

(i) the differential weights voters use in evaluating inter-party as opposed to inter-administration performance
(ii) the rate at which voters discount past performance in making current political judgements and
(iii) whether voters penalised the government of the day for events which clearly lay outside the government's control.

The performance vector – i.e. the economic variables on the basis of which voter evaluation was made – included, for each country, the rate of unemployment, the rate of inflation and the rate of growth of real per capita disposable income. For Britain, an additional term, the change in the exchange rate, was included to reflect the preoccupation of British governments with the international role of sterling.

The results indicated that, for Britain, political judgements were based entirely on a comparison of inter-party performance. On the assumption that voter evaluation of past performances was based on a geometrically declining lag structure (in other words if the unemployment rate in the current period, U_t, made a contribution of bU_t to popularity, the unemployment rates in the previous periods, $U_{t-1}, U_{t-2}, U_{t-3} \ldots$ would contribute respectively $bgU_{t-1}, bg^2U_{t-2}, bg^3U_{t-3} \ldots$ to popularity) the rate of decay parameter, g, was estimated at 0.89, implying that past performance weighed rather heavily with the British electorate. (Note that $g = 1$ implies that past performances are not at all discounted.)

The variables of concern to the British public appeared to be the unemployment rate, the change in this rate, the change in the inflation rate, the change in the exchange rate and the rate of growth of real per capita disposable incomes. This last variable was adjusted to take account of the decline in the growth of real incomes caused directly by the OPEC oil supply shock, which was a factor outside the control of the British government. Since the equation with the unadjusted growth rate did not have as good an explanatory power as the equation with the adjusted growth rate, this was interpreted to mean that the British public did not hold its government to blame for adverse economic conditions resulting from events clearly outside its sphere of influence. The rate of inflation – as opposed to a change in the rate – was never a significant factor, suggesting that, net of exchange rate movements, the political costs associated with any stationary rate of inflation were negligible.

2.6.2 The United States

The first satisfactory statistical analysis for the USA of the relationship between economic conditions and voting behaviour was provided by Kramer (1971). (See Section 2.4 of this chapter for a discussion of the theoretical structure underlying the Kramer model.) As discussed earlier, in the Kramer model a voter voted against the incumbent party if its performance failed to reach some 'satisfactory' standard and voted to retain the incumbent party otherwise. In operational terms the first problem was to define a 'satisfactory' standard. In Kramer's analysis expectations about the current year were formed on the basis of the previous year's experience; these expectations then defined the 'satisfactory' standard for the current year and the voter evaluated the incumbent party on the basis of the deviation of the current year's outcome from its expected value.

This model was then applied to the vote for the House of Representatives over the period 1896–1964, on the grounds that 'House contests came closest to the Downsian case of relatively anonymous candidates competing as members of a common party team' (Kramer, 1971, p. 135). Before the model could be confronted with the data two special problems had to be accounted for. Firstly, there was the problem of minor parties and secondly there was the problem of 'coat-tail' effects from residential contests. The minor party vote was interpreted as part of the anti-incumbent vote and was counted along with the vote for the major opposition party. The 'coat-tail' effect was handled by estimating, for years in which there was a presidential election coinciding with congressional elections, two equations, one for the Republican share of the presidential vote and the other for the Republican share of the congressional vote. Both equations contained the same set of performance variables. However, the presidential equations contained two error terms, one to represent the effects of unmeasured factors, such as foreign policy, which affected the party as a whole and the other to represent the effects of specific candidates. It was then assumed that part of this latter effect carried over to the congressional equation with an unknown factor of proportionality, γ. This 'coat-tail' factor γ was estimated by assigning to it different values, estimating the equations conditional upon this assigned value, and then choosing the equation (and the associated γ value) which maximised the probability (likelihood) of obtaining the sample values.

The economic variables determining the share of the incumbency vote were taken as per capita personal income in current prices and constant prices, the level of the consumer cost of living index and the unemployment rate, all for the current and the preceding year. For congressional elections, real incomes appeared the most important of these variables; with real income held constant changes in unemployment or in the rate of inflation had no significant effect. The equation also contained a variable to reflect the advantages of incumbency, this variable taking the value + 1 if the incumbent president was Republican and − 1 otherwise. The coefficient of this incumbency variable was invariably small and insignificant; this was interpreted to mean that the advantages of incumbency were more or less offset by high income expectations on the part of the electorate. The 'coat-tail' effect deriving from a presidential election was important, with as much as 30 per cent of the extra votes being attracted by a strong presidential candidate. By contrast, the presidential vote was not very sensitive to economic conditions, with less than a fifth of the variation in this vote being explained by economic factors. As Fair (1978) notes, this might be the consequence of constraining the coefficients of the equation explaining the presidential vote to be the same as the coefficients of the equation explaining the congressional vote. Indeed Lepper's (1974) results contradict the hypothesis that the coefficients are the same in both equations.

Stigler (1973) re-examined Kramer's conclusions but using a different process whereby expectations of economic variables were generated. Stigler's argument (as discussed earlier in this chapter) was that the forecasting behaviour of voters should both reflect accumulated experience and also attach more weight to recent than to remote periods. To apply this argument to the data the sample period was divided into two sub-periods: 1900–1932 when the Republicans dominated the national elections and 1934–1970 when the Democrats were similarly dominant. In each period a measure of average past performance was constructed from a weighted average of biennial changes in real per capita income, the weights decreasing with earlier experiences. Then the share of the vote received in congressional elections by the dominant political party of each period was regressed on the average income experience of voters. For no case was there a statistically significant relation between average income performance and the share of votes received by the dominant party.

Arcelus and Meltzer (1975) continued the debate on the effect of economic performance on congressional elections. Their starting point was the observation that earlier models assumed that the rational voter would choose between rival parties or candidates and not abstain from voting i.e. participate in the voting process. Given the fact that changes in the participation rate were often greater than shifts between the major parties this assumption was highly suspect. The purpose of the Arcelus and Meltzer study was therefore to develop a model which would explain both whether a member of the electorate voted and, if so, also why he voted as he did.

As regards the decision to participate or not in the voting process, a member of the electorate would vote if his perceived benefits from voting exceeded the costs to him of voting, the principal costs being those of acquiring information about parties, candidates and issues. This 'net benefit' – which would determine his decision to vote or to abstain – would depend upon several circumstances. Firstly, if the voter was fully committed to a political party i.e. if he was a 'strict partisan', his net benefits would always be positive and he would never abstain. Secondly, voter participation in congressional elections would be higher if they coincided with a presidential election, largely because the media would be more active in disseminating political information in a presidential election year. Finally a voter would be more inclined to vote if the election involved an issue about which he felt strongly, and the issue on which the Arcelus and Meltzer study focussed was the behaviour of aggregate economic variables. Three economic variables were singled out for attention – the inflation rate, the rate of change in the unemployment rate and the average real wage per man-hour. Three ways were suggested in which these variables (or any other factors) might induce voters to vote:

(i) because they perceived a difference between parties on a particular issue,
(ii) they wished to protest against a particular outcome or
(iii) they wished to reward a party for a policy or outcome.

It follows from the above discussion that the percentage of eligible voters participating in a congressional election in year t, VP_t, would be the sum of the percentage of partisan voters in the electorate, H_t, the percentage of voters in the electorate induced to vote by a coincidental presidential election, N_t, and the percentage of voters in the electorate for whom the net benefit of voting is a function of economic factors, M_t. The percentage of partisan voters, H_t, was assumed constant over the sample period 1896–1970, except for a step change in 1920 (when women were granted the vote) and 1932 (when there was a major realignment of political loyalties). N_t was entirely a function of a dummy variable which took the value unity when a presidential election coincided with a congressional election and took the value zero otherwise and M_t was a linear function of the three economic variables.

Turning next to the question of how the electorate voted, Arcelus and Meltzer adopted an identical device to explain the share of votes accruing to the Republican and Democratic parties (VR_t and VD_t). In other words VR_t and VD_t were explained by a constant, dummy variables to reflect changes in partisanship caused by the events of 1920 and 1932, a presidential election dummy and the three economic variables. Separate equations were then estimated for VP_t, VR_t and VD_t over the period 1896–1970.

Three major conclusions emerged from the empirical results. Firstly, in non-presidential years 42.6% of eligible voters were partisans. Of these, 23% voted for the Democratic candidate and 19% for the Republican candidate, the remainder being third-party partisans. Secondly, a presidential election increased overall participation by 11.8% if the incumbent was a Democrat and 12.5% if he was Republican, with the split of votes favouring the party with the incumbent president. Finally, it was only the inflation rate that had a significant effect on voting patterns. An increase in the inflation rate lowered the overall participation rate (but not significantly), significantly reduced the Democratic share of the vote but left the Republican share unaffected.

Both Bloom and Price (1975) and Goodman and Kramer (1975) presented further discussion on the Arcelus and Meltzer paper. Bloom and Price argued that changes in real income should not be treated symmetrically, that is to say prosperity might have an effect on voting behaviour quite different from that of a recession. To test this hypothesis they estimated an equation over 1896–1970 in which the Republican share of the two-party vote in the House of Representatives was explained by two variables: the long-term influence of party identification (proxied by a weighted moving average of past values of the dependent variable) and changes in real income. The sample was then divided into two sub-periods, one in which elections were preceded by declining real incomes and the other in which they were preceded by rising real incomes, and the equation was estimated separately over the two sub-periods. The results – in which the coefficient estimate on the real income variables was significant for downturns but not for upturns – appeared to support the hypothesis that real income changes had an asymmetric effect on voter behaviour. Political parties were penalised by voters in a recessionary period but not accordingly rewarded for prosperity.

The Goodman and Kramer (1975) paper presented a criticism of several aspects of the Arcelus and Meltzer paper. They began by observing that the Arcelus and Meltzer estimates of long-term partisanship were inconsistent with survey findings. This was essentially attributable to the mistaken assumption of the original paper that (except for a step change in 1920 and 1932) the percentage of partisan voters was constant over time. Indeed, an inspection of the actual participation series demonstrated that changes had been more in the nature of gradual trends than abrupt shifts.

As regards the effect of economic variables, Goodman and Kramer pointed out that the three ways in which Arcelus and Meltzer suggested economic variables might influence voting behaviour would not lead to any clear predictions. Thus for example if the inflation rate rose, those who voted on the basis of perceived differences between parties and those who voted as a protest against current outcomes would be induced to increase their participation but those who voted to reward a party would be induced to decrease their participation. In the absence of any hypothesis of the relative strengths of these three groups the net effect of a rise in the inflation rate on voter participation would be unpredictable.

A third set of criticisms related to the definitions of the variables and the estimation techniques employed. The use of the real wage per man-hour variable, for example, ignored the unemployed. Thus in a recession if low wage workers were the first to be laid off then real wages per man-hour would rise even though average prosperity in the economy declined. A more appropriate variable would be real per capita income. The estimation techniques ignored in particular the fact that the equations for the Democratic and Republican share of the vote represented a system of equations related through the constraint that their coefficients should – on the assumption that the third party vote was very small – sum to unity. Re-estimating the equations subject to the appropriate constraints, having redefined the variables appropriately, Goodman and Kramer found that many of the original results were overturned. In general all three economic variables – inflation, unemployment and real incomes – had an influence on congressional elections and the Arcelus and Meltzer lack of results on income and unemployment could be ascribed to their data and methods.

Fair's (1978) model which was discussed earlier in the context of its theoretical structure was applied to US presidential elections over the period 1892–1976. The justification for this was 'that most empirical studies in this area have concentrated on US congressional elections' and that although it has been argued that presidential elections may be more affected by personality factors and other non-economic events than are congressional elections 'this is far from obvious' (Fair, 1978, p. 165).

The basic equation employed by Fair is one in which the Democratic share of the two party vote, V, is regressed on a performance variable, M. In evaluating performance, the voter looks at the current record of the incumbent party and compares this to the past record of both the incumbent party and the main opposition party, these past records being discounted at a rate, ρ. Performance in the model is evaluated on the basis of three economic variables, the unemployment rate, real per capita GNP and the GNP deflator.

Two special problems arose in estimating the model. First, there was the possibility that an incumbent president running for re-election might have advantages (over and above his administrative performance) over a non-incumbent candidate. Second, there was the possibility that a candidate might also have been a candidate in an earlier presidential election and therefore might possess a known vote-catching ability (or 'personality factor') independent of the performance variables. This personality factor would need to be accounted for explicitly in the equation. Both problems were handled by an appropriate modification of the error term. The error term, v_t, was defined as consisting of two (additive) parts; the first part was a dummy variable which took the value unity (minus unity) if there was a Democratic (Republican) incumbent and he was running for president and zero otherwise.

The second part of the error term, v_t, was a term μ_t which incorporated all the factors that affected the vote other than performance and incumbency. In turn, μ_t was separated into three additive parts, μ_{1t}, μ_{2t} and μ_{3t}. The Democratic and Republican candidates' vote-getting ability was measured respectively by μ_{1t} and μ_{2t}, and μ_{3t} represented a 'pure' error term with mean zero and variance σ_3^2. It was then assumed that

(a) an individual's vote-catching ability was the same in all elections in which he was a candidate and that
(b) for different individuals μ_{1t} and μ_{2t} were independently distributed with zero means and common variance σ_1^2.

These assumptions resulted in a covariance matrix for σ_t of a special form: the diagonal elements of this matrix were unity and the off-diagonal elements were either zero (when two elections had no individuals in common), λ (when two elections had only one individual in common) or 2λ (when two elections had two individuals in common) where $\lambda = \sigma_1^2/\sigma^2$. (Note that σ^2, the variance of μ_t, is equal to $2\sigma_1^2 + \sigma_3^2$.) Thus λ represented an additional parameter to be estimated.

Given the relative paucity of data (16 observations for 11 parameters) a fairly systematic estimation procedure was followed. The equations were estimated with only one performance variable being considered in turn. The assumptions that voters evaluated Republican and Democratic performances identically and also that voters did not look at performances beyond the last time a party was in power were then progressively relaxed. The basic conclusions of this procedure were as follows: the best measure of performance (in terms of fit) was the growth rate of real per capita GNP in the year of the election, followed by the change in the unemployment rate. Voters appeared to have a very high discount rate, implying that they did not consider the past performance of the non-incumbent party and that with respect to the incumbent party they considered only events within the year of the election. These last conclusions would appear to support Kramer's model in which only the incumbent's record was evaluated. In evaluating performance, voters appeared not to treat differentially Republican and Democratic administrations. Finally, the variance of the two personality terms, μ_1 and μ_2, was about one-fourth of the total variance of the error term, μ. There 'thus appears to be some information contained in past error terms that is of use in explaining the current election when either or both the candidates in the current election have run before' (Fair, 1978, p. 167).

Frey and Schneider (1978b) considered the effects of economic events on presidential popularity (rather than presidential voting). The model employed, in which a respondent supported or did not support the President according to whether he was satisfied or not satisfied with the President's performance, was akin to Kramer's (1971) hypothesis for congressional elections. Presidential popularity was postulated to depend upon the behaviour of three economic variables, the inflation rate lagged one quarter, the unemployment rate and the rate of growth of consumers' expenditure. In addition there were three other variables, one to measure the popularity level of each president and two dummy variables, the first to measure the popularity depreciation of each president and the second to measure the electorate's dramatic decline in confidence in Nixon after Watergate. The dependent variable was a quarterly average of the monthly percentage 'approving or disapproving the way Mr. . . . handles his job as president'.

On estimating the equation on quarterly data over the period 1953–1975 the following conclusions emerged.

(i) The absolute level of each president's popularity had a significant effect on the course of his popularity during his term in office. Thus Kennedy always had the highest level of popularity and Nixon the lowest. However only Kennedy and Johnson suffered a decline in popularity – a reflection no doubt of the war in Vietnam. Watergate, however, had a very clear effect on Nixon's popularity during his second term.

(ii) The quantitative effects of the economic variables on presidential popularity were sizeable. A one percentage point increase in the rate of inflation decreased presidential popularity by between half to one percentage point; a decrease in the unemployment rate of one percentage point decreased popularity by more than four percentage points; and a one percentage point increase in the growth rate of nominal consumption increased presidential popularity by about 0.7 percentage points.

The 'critical threshold model' of Hibbs (1982a) has been discussed earlier with respect to its structure (Section 2.5) and with respect to its results for Britain (Subsection 2.6.1). This model addressed itself to three empirical questions:

(i) the differential weights voters used in evaluating inter-party as opposed to inter-administration performance
(ii) the rate at which voters discounted past performance in making current political judgements and
(iii) whether voters penalised the government of the day for events which clearly lay outside its control.

The performance vector – i.e. the economic variables on the basis of which voter evaluation was made – included the rate of unemployment, the rate of inflation and the rate of growth of real per capita disposable income. Three other variables, to reflect conditions peculiar to the United States, were also included. These were a term for the number of Americans killed in Vietnam, a term to capture Nixon's extraordinary decline in popularity following Watergate (this variable was formed by summing the number of 'Watergate' events in each quarter and weighting them on a scale 1–3 depending on how strongly the president was personally implicated) and finally a 'rally around the flag' variable which was the number, in each quarter, of international events involving the president directly (which typically boosted his popularity). The dependent variable was the proportion of the public responding 'approve' to the question 'Do you approve or disapprove of the way Mr. . . . is handling his job as president?' and the equation was estimated on quarterly data over the period 1961–1980.

The results indicated that about three-quarters of political support was based on inter-party rather than inter-administration performance evaluations, in contrast to Britain where all evaluations were on the basis of inter-party comparisons. The estimate of the rate of decay parameter (the lag structure was assumed to decline geometrically) was 0.84, which was considered lower than for Britain and implied that the experiences of many past periods influenced current political judgements.

All the economic variables, the unemployment rate, the inflation rate and the rate of growth of real income, were of concern to the US public, though interestingly, given the unemployment rate and the inflation rate, changes in these variables did not produce significant changes in popularity. At the same time the public did not discount youth unemployment in evaluating the president's performance as regards employment but they did discount price and income changes caused directly by the deterioration in the terms of trade caused by the OPEC oil price shock and did not hold the incumbent president responsible for such exogenous events.

The 'critical threshold' model was also applied by Kernell and Hibbs (1981) to studying whether Republicans and Democrats differed in their assessment of presidential performance. As noted earlier, at least three possible hypotheses were available to explain this differential evaluation. First, Democrats and Republicans might differ in the intensity of their concern with different economic indicators; plausibly Democrats might be relatively more concerned with unemployment and Republicans with inflation. Second, the evaluation might be purely partisan, with the opposition party identifiers more critical and negative in their assessment of presidential performance. Under this hypothesis, the relationship between performance and popularity would be stronger among the opposition party identifiers. Finally, because both political parties were composed largely of middle class constituents, a third hypothesis might be that there was no significant difference in Democratic and Republican evaluation of presidential performance.

These three hypotheses were tested by regressing the monthly index of presidential popularity among the three subgroups, the president's party identifiers, the opposition party identifiers and independents (the percentage of the population of the subgroups expressing support of the president in response to the question, 'Do you approve or disapprove of the way the President is handling his job?'), on the percentage change in consumer prices and the percentage change in the unemployment rate, both over the preceding six months. The equation was estimated on monthly data (over the period covering the Eisenhower to the Johnson administrations) along with other dummy variables which reflected conditions peculiar to American political life.

The most striking pattern to emerge from the results was not in the differences among partisan subgroups but in the overall stronger relationships for each subgroup during the Democratic administrations. As the authors pointed out, it was unclear whether this represented a structural shift of the 1960s or whether it represented the public's response to the willingness of Democratic administrations to intervene more actively in the economy. Of the three hypotheses relating to partisanship and evaluation of presidential performance, the evidence appeared to support the hypothesis that evaluation of performance follows purely party lines. The unemployment coefficients were stronger among opposition party identifiers for both administrations although for the inflation rate there did not appear any significant difference in the coefficient estimates among the president's party identifiers and the opposition party identifiers. The relationships for the political variables – Watergate, the number of US bombing missions over North Vietnam and the number of US servicemen killed in Vietnam – were also consistently stronger for opposition party identifiers.

2.7 Conclusions

This chapter has attempted to provide a broad survey of theories of voter behaviour and also of studies which applied such theories to assessing voter reactions to changes in the economic environment. The general consensus from these studies would appear to support the proposition that there was a close association between a government's economic performance and its electoral popularity. This conclusion would be valid, even though the relevant measure of economic performance differed between the various studies. At the same time, to support the proposition that economic performance and popularity are related is not to deny the importance of non-economic factors in moulding the electorate's view. Indeed it is a characteristic of studies of voter behaviour in the United States to include (where relevant) features such as those relating to the Vietnam war in their econometric relations.

In this book we hope to extend the work we have surveyed in several respects. Firstly, we shall attempt to develop a theory of voter behaviour which can conveniently be applied to multi-party systems. Secondly, we shall try to present a more coherent account of the inter-temporal stability of popularity functions. Finally we shall attempt to draw out more precisely the complexity of the relation between economic performance and class interests. Our hope is that by taking these factors into account we shall – in the words of Butler and Stokes – 'hear more clearly one of the drums to which the electorate marches'.

3

A theory of qualitative choice

3.1 Introduction

A fundamental concern of the social sciences – and particularly of economics – is to understand the processes whereby people make choices. In practice this often requires an explanation of individual decisions. Traditional economic analysis typically assumes that choices are made over a continuum of possibilities. Examples of such choices are, how much to spend of one's income, how much to buy of different commodities, how much to work, etc. However, in many other situations choices are made from a limited number of possibilities or alternatives; in other words, the possible alternatives are 'discrete' or 'qualitative'. Examples of these kinds of choice are whether or not to work, where to work, where to live, mode of transportation, size of family etc.

The theory of qualitative choice, using as its tools logit and probit analysis, provides a widely-used method (see McFadden, 1973; Hausman and Wise, 1978; and Daganzo, 1980) for estimating the relationship between choices, on the one hand, and the attributes of the alternatives and the individual decision makers, on the other, when the number of alternatives is limited. Applications of this theory have been extensive – to college choice, occupational choice, plant location, to name but a few (see Amemya, 1981). In this chapter we show how this theory can also be applied to voter behaviour, where the problem of the voter is to choose one out of a finite number of political parties.

3.2 A model of voting behaviour under the uniform probability distribution

Consider a system that is characterised by N political parties ($k = 1 \ldots N$) and a large electorate. The problem before an individual voter in the electorate is to decide on the party for which he is going to vote.

Suppose that the election is to be held at time t and let U_{it}^k be the utility that voter i anticipates, at time t, that he will enjoy under party k. The voter then chooses the party under which he anticipates the largest level of utility. In other words, voter i, at time t, votes for party s, if and only if

$$U_{it}^s > U_{it}^k \quad \text{for all} \quad k \neq s \tag{3.2.1}$$

In evaluating his anticipated utility under the different parties, it is hypothesised that the voter will be guided by two considerations. Firstly, there will be his individual 'loyalty' for or prejudice against the various political parties. This concept is akin to that of party identification in the political science literature and we denote by b_i^k the loyalty of voter i for (or prejudice against) party k. (Note that this loyalty/prejudice is assumed to be time invariant.)

In addition to his inherent political loyalties, the voter may also consider the past and present 'performances' of the various parties. This evaluation of performance will of course involve an assessment of successes and failures in a variety of fields (social, political, legal, economic etc.). For the moment it is assumed that the 'performance' of party k at time t is represented by a variable, M_t^k, on the understanding that M_t^k can be further decomposed into a catalogue of achievements (or failures) by party k in different areas of electoral concern. Following from this we assume that

$$U_{it}^k = b_i^k + M_t^k \tag{3.2.2}$$

For the theory to be operational, it is necessary to proceed from hypotheses about individual behaviour to propositions about the behaviour of human aggregates. This is so because the data – on which the theory is to be tested – are typically in the form of information about aggregate rather than individual choices. One possible way of making this transition is to make some assumption about the manner in which the 'bias' terms of voters for party k over party s, that is $b^{ks} = b^k - b^s$, are distributed over voters. Suppose, following Fair (1978), that one assumed that the bias is uniformly distributed across voters. This means that the probability density function of b^{ks} is described by

$$f(b^{ks}) = \begin{cases} \dfrac{1}{q^{ks} - r^{ks}} & \text{for} \quad r^{ks} < b^{ks} < q^{ks} \\ 0 & \text{elsewhere} \end{cases} \tag{3.2.3}$$

where q^{ks} and r^{ks} denote the bounds of the uniform distribution (see Fig. 3.1). It is further assumed that the different bias terms are distributed independently of one another.

From (3.2.1) and (3.2.2) an individual voter i will vote for party s if and only if

$$b_i^{ks} < M_t^s - M_t^k, \quad \text{for all} \quad k \neq s \tag{3.2.4}$$

Since, by assumption, the terms b^{ks} are uniformly distributed across voters, the proportion of votes cast for party s at time t, say p_t^s, is given by

$$\begin{aligned} p_t^s &= \text{prob}\,(b^{ks} < M_t^s - M_t^k), \\ &= \prod_{k \neq s} \left(\frac{M_t^s - M_t^k - r^{ks}}{q^{ks} - r^{ks}} \right), \\ r^{ks} &< M_t^s - M_t^k < q^{ks} \quad \text{for} \quad k \neq s \\ p_t^s &= 1, \; M_t^s - M_t^k > q^{ks} \quad \text{and} \quad p_t^s = 0, \; M_t^s - M_t^k < r^{ks}. \end{aligned} \tag{3.2.5}$$

The intuition behind equation (3.2.5) is as follows: the proportion of votes going to party s is equal to the probability that the performance of party s (relative to all other parties) will exceed the bias against party s (relative to all other parties). Since the bias terms are assumed to be independently and uniformly distributed across voters, this probability takes the specific form shown by the last term of

Fig. 3.1 *Uniform distribution of political biases*

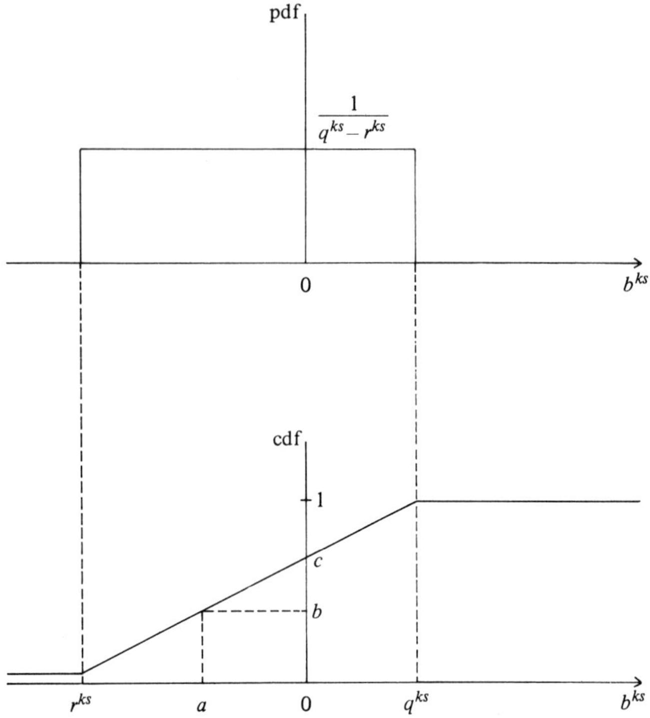

equation (3.2.5). It follows that one can find the proportion of votes cast in favour of party s from Fig. 3.1 by simply reading off the function value corresponding to the performance differential, say $M_t^s - M_t^k = a$, which gives 100b%. The figure shows that 100c% is the neutral proportion of votes cast in favour of party s, i.e. when both parties offer the same performance. It is also clear that when the performance differential exceeds (falls below) a certain value, party s will capture all (none) of the votes. This latter feature is particular to the uniform distribution, but in practice one usually assumes the performance differentials remain within the bounds of the uniform distribution.

Now if there are only two political parties, party 1 (the incumbent party) and party 2 (the opposition party), it follows from equation (3.2.5) above that the arithmetic lead at time t of the incumbent party over the opposition party, say L_t, is given by

$$L_t = p_t^1 - p_t^2 = \alpha + \beta(M_t^1 - M_t^2) \tag{3.2.6}$$

where $\beta = 2(q^{21} - r^{21})^{-1}$, $\alpha = -(r^{21}\beta + 1)$.

Thus when there are only two parties competing for the voters' favours, the assumption that the bias terms are distributed uniformly across voters results in an equation in which the lead of one party over another is linearly related to the difference in their respective 'performances'. The assumption of an uniform distribution for the bias terms however loses its convenience when more than two parties are involved, for then the equation for the lead term, L_t, becomes a complicated non-linear function of the performance variables, M_t^s.

In any event, the assumption that the bias terms are uniformly distributed has very little to recommend itself on grounds of realism. Firstly, it implies that extreme political views are as likely to prevail among the electorate as are more moderate views. Secondly, there is no constraint built into the model to prevent it from giving nonsensical predictions. Thus, for example, there is nothing to prevent a prediction for the lead, $L_t = p_t^1 - p_t^2$, from exceeding unity in out-of-sample simulations.

3.3 Models of voting behaviour under bell-shaped probability distributions

One solution to the above problems would be to assume a bell-shaped distribution for the bias terms so that extreme views are found in the tails of the distribution and more moderate views are located in the middle (see Fig. 3.2). The bell-shaped distribution assumes that extreme views are less likely to occur than moderate views and has the advantage that neither party ever captures all of the votes or gets none of the votes. An obvious candidate is the normal distribution. In this case equation (3.2.5) becomes

$$p_t^s = \prod_{k \neq s} F^N(M_t^s - M_t^k;\ \mu, \sigma^2) \qquad (3.3.1)$$

where $F^N(\,.\,)$ is the cumulative density function of the normal distribution with mean μ and variance σ^2.

In other words, the proportion of votes cast for party s is the probability that all the bias terms, b^{ks} $(k = 1 \ldots N, k \neq s)$, which are independently and normally distributed with mean and variance σ^2, take values less than $\mu_t^s - \mu_t^k$ $(k = 1 \ldots N, k \neq s)$. For the two-party case, this results in the binary probit model, familiar from the literature on biological assay, and is easily estimated (Finney, 1971). The political analogue of the biological applications is as follows. A political party prescribes a dose of (economic and social) medicine to the patient (voter) and the probit model determines the proportion of patients being cured (by voting for the particular political party). Estimation of (3.3.1) for the multi-party case is however extremely difficult to estimate due to the fact that no explicit solution for $F^N(\,.\,)$ is available.

A more convenient solution is to assume that the bias terms, b^k $(k = 1 \ldots N)$, are independently identically distributed with the Weibull (Gnedenko, extreme value) distribution

$$\text{prob}(b^k \leq \epsilon) = \exp\{-\exp(-\epsilon)\} \qquad (3.3.2)$$

This distribution, which is also called a logistic distribution, differs from the normal distribution mainly in the tails of the distribution. Under the logistic distribution for the bias terms it can be shown (McFadden, 1973) that the proportion of votes going to party s at time t, p_t^s, is

$$p_t^s = \frac{\exp\{M_t^s + \mathrm{E}(b^s)\}}{\sum_k \exp\{M_t^k + \mathrm{E}(b^k)\}}, \quad s = 1 \ldots N \qquad (3.3.3)$$

where E(.) is the expectations operator.

Fig. 3.2 *Bell-shaped distribution of political biases*

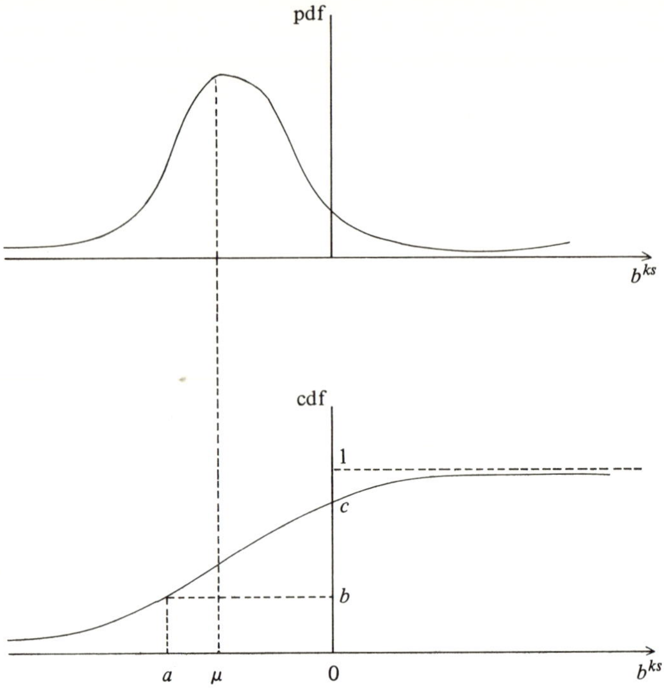

The logit formula of (3.3.3) satisfies the property of 'independence of irrelevant alternatives', which states that the relative probability of one alternative being chosen over another should be independent of the presence or absence of unchosen third alternatives. This can be seen from (3.3.3) since

$$\frac{p_t^s}{p_t^k} = \frac{\exp\{M_t^s + \mathrm{E}(b^s)\}}{\exp\{M_t^k + \mathrm{E}(b^k)\}} \qquad (3.3.4)$$

Although this property is a limitation of the model, the estimation of models which allow for dependence of irrelevant alternatives poses complicated and as yet unresolved problems when applied to multi-choice situations (Finney, 1971; Hausman and Wise, 1978; Daganzo, 1980). However, the axioms underlying the logit model have received considerable psychological support (see Luce, 1959).

Leaving aside this problem, the logit model implies a simple equation for the (logarithmic) lead, l_t^{sk}, of party s over party k, of the form

$$l_t^{sk} = \log(p_t^s) - \log(p_t^k) = M_t^s - M_t^k - \mathrm{E}(b^{ks}) \qquad (3.3.5)$$

and is therefore one of the few models that is computationally tractable while at the same time having a plausible stochastic specification.

3.4 Party performance and the memory of voters

In the preceding sections the past and present performance of party k ($k = 1 \ldots N$) was encapsulated into a single variable, M_t^k. In this section we attempt to disentangle this variable. It is reasonable to suppose that past performances that are relatively recent are weighted more heavily. This section formalises this concept of 'loss of memory' by voters and incorporates it into the world of voter behaviour set out in the preceding two sections.

Let the integral measure of performance by party k at time t be given by

$$M_t^k = \sum_{j=0}^{\infty} w_j m_{t-j}^k \tag{3.4.1}$$

where m_{t-j}^k ($j = 0, 1, 2, \ldots$) is the performance of party k in period $t-j$, i.e. j periods removed from the present, and w_j denotes the weight attached by the electorate to m_{t-j}^k. Obviously, the weights must add up to unity, i.e. $\Sigma_{j=0}^{\infty} w_j = 1$, and the weight must be zero, i.e. $w_j = 0$, when the government was not in power j periods ago. Using a geometric lag distribution, we obtain

$$M_t^k = c_t^k \sum_{j=0}^{\infty} \lambda^k (m_{t-j}^j \delta_{t-j}) \tag{3.4.2}$$

where λ is the geometric weight, $\delta_{t-j} = 1$ (0) if the government was in office (opposition) j periods ago, and c_t^k is a scaling constant defined as

$$c_t^k = \left(\sum_{j=0}^{\infty} \lambda^j \delta_{t-j} \right)^{-1}$$

Because c_t^k depends nonlinearly and in a time-variant manner on λ, this is a rather awkward formulation. Hence, some authors prefer to use instead

$$M_t^k \cong (1-\lambda) \sum_{j=0}^{\infty} \lambda^j m_{t-j}^k \tag{3.4.3}$$

by employing the approximation that the government has been in power for a long time. The best solution is to use (3.4.2), but (3.4.3) may be used when the observations immediately after a change of government are omitted. Provided λ is less than unity, past performances contribute less to the overall evaluation, M_t^k, than relatively recent performances. If λ is equal to unity the past and present are evaluated equally; λ equal to zero implies that the past is discounted completely. It is assumed that λ (and hence the discount rate $\rho = (1-\lambda)/\lambda$) is the same for all parties. The scale factor, $(1-\lambda)$, in equation (3.4.3) should ensure that M_t^k represents an average of present and past performances. In fact $(1-\lambda)$ slightly underestimates the correct scaling factor immediately after a change in government.

Now suppose that the achievements of party k at time t, m_t^k, are a linear combination of a vector $\mathbf{x}_t^k$ of variables relevant, from the voters' point of view, for party k. This yields

$$m_t^k = \boldsymbol{\gamma}_t^{k\prime} \mathbf{x}_t^k \tag{3.4.4}$$

where $\boldsymbol{\gamma}_t^k$ is a vector of parameters used for evaluating party k at time t and the $'$ indicates a transpose.

The vector $\mathbf{x}_t^k$ may contain any variables that voters consider relevant for assessing party k. (Needless to say, for empirical purposes, it is essential that they be quantifiable.) Substituting (3.4.4) and (3.4.3) into (3.3.5) yields

$$l_t^{sk} = (1-\lambda)[\gamma_t^{s'} x_t^s - \gamma_t^{k'} x_t^k - E(b^{ks})] + \lambda l_{t-1}^{sk} \tag{3.4.5}$$

with parameters γ_t^s, γ_t^k, λ and $E(b^{ks})$.

Only $(N-1)$ independent equations based on (3.4.5) need to be estimated since the Nth equation follows from the fact that the proportions of all voters voting for the N parties sum to unity. Examples of estimating this type of model are given in Chapters 4 and 5.

3.5 Conclusions

The theory proposed is essentially based on strategic voting, that is any individual votes for the party which offers the highest utility. In terms of the theories of voter behaviour surveyed in the previous chapter it is a Downsian model in which the economy is regarded as a valence issue. Voters have anticipated utilities under the different parties. These anticipated utilities depend upon an evaluation by voters of the performance of the various parties when they were last in power with relatively recent performances being weighted more highly in this evaluation. In other words voter expectations are formed by an autoregressive process. At the same time there is consensus among voters, with respect to all the performance variables, that movements in one direction are 'good' and in the opposite direction are 'bad' (for example a fall or rise in the rate of unemployment). One may wonder why a political party which has never held office, such as the Liberal party in post-war Britain, should according to our theory attract any votes at all. The reason is that political bias terms are distributed according to some bell-shaped distribution across voters, so that there will always be some individuals with a very high loyalty to this (Liberal) party who will therefore vote for this party. According to this model the average utility of a government which becomes an opposition party settles down to within s per cent of the loyalty term in at most $\log(100s/\lambda)$ periods.

Other authors (e.g. Kirchgässner, 1979; Paldam and Schneider, 1980) have examined the popularity of a variety $(K > 2)$ of political parties by relating the popularity of each party (p_t^k) to a vector of economic variables $(\mathbf{x}_t)$, regardless of whether the party holds office or not, and to a loyalty term (b^k), say $p_t^k = \gamma_k' \mathbf{x}_t + b^k$. Unfortunately these studies ignore certain cross-equation constraints, such as $\Sigma b^k = 1$ and $\Sigma \gamma_k = 0$, which must hold to ensure that all proportions add up to unity. Furthermore it is not clear if this approach is consistent with the framework of qualitative choice, except for the two-party uniform model (3.2.5), and their work may therefore contain specification errors.

In developing our theoretical model, one assumption that we made was that the party choice of an individual voter was based upon his inherent bias and upon party performance but not upon his own individual characteristics. In other words we assumed that voters behaved homogeneously in evaluating performance and that this evaluation was independent of the class, occupational or educational background of the voter. This assumption, which is unduly restrictive, was made in order to facilitate the clarity of exposition. It can readily be relaxed and indeed in a later chapter we consider a generalised form of the model in which voter choice is dependent on voter attributes.

One final comment relates to the desirability of publishing the results of opinion polls just before the onset of an election. The problem is that an individual who marginally prefers party 1 to party 2 and substantially dislikes party 3 may, when the opinion polls suggest that either party 2 or part 3 will win and party 1 will lose, vote *tactically* in favour of party 2. In terms of our theory the individual utility, U_{it}^k, is no longer given by (3.2.2) and will depend upon the *expected actions of the other voters*. A proper account of this phenomenon of tactical voting probably requires our theory to be cast in a game-theoretic framework. In practice some people are prompted to argue against publishing the results of opinion polls just before an election to avoid individuals not revealing their preferences correctly. The applications reported in Chapters 4, 5 and 6 are mainly concerned with general elections, where opinion polls and therefore tactical voting are relatively unimportant. An analysis of voting patterns at bye-elections (witness the recent 1983 Bermondsey bye-election), however, must incorporate a theory of tactical voting, but will not be further considered in this book.

4

British government popularity and economic performance

4.1 Introduction

A knowledge of the determinants of electoral popularity is obviously very important both to parties in office and to parties aspiring to office. A major theme of this book is that an important (though by no means the only) factor in moulding the electorate's dispositions is the state of the economy. The literature on political economy abounds with evidence (some of it anecdotal) about the electoral importance of the economy. Thus Mr Wilson lost the 1970 elections because of a bad run of balance of payments figures, Mr Heath lost the 1974 election through a confrontation with the miners and Mr Callaghan lost the 1979 election through an ill-judged pay policy. A significant feature of such causal associations is that they afflict all parties; voters as a group are very demanding and their demands fall equally on all the major parties.

The time has now come to test some of these propositions and in particular the overriding proposition that voters react to changes in the economic environment. A first attempt to do so is the theme of this chapter.

4.2 Application of the theory of qualitative choice

In Chapter 3 we developed a theoretical model of voter behaviour based on the theory of qualitative choice. The model was cast in a form suitable for empirical testing by assuming that the bias of voters for or against the various political parties obeyed a logistic distribution. When 'loss of memory' by voters – i.e. the fact that recent events counted for more than events in the relative past – was incorporated into the model, it resulted in the following equation for l_t^{sk}, the logarithmic lead of party s over party k (cf. equation (3.4.5))

$$l_t^{sk} = (1-\lambda)[\boldsymbol{\gamma}_t^{s'}\mathbf{x}_t^s - \boldsymbol{\gamma}_t^{k'}\mathbf{x}_t^k - \mathrm{E}(b^{ks})] + \lambda l_{t-1}^{sk} + \epsilon_t^{sk} \qquad (4.2.1)$$

where λ is the rate at which voters' memories decay, $\boldsymbol{\gamma}_t^s$ and $\boldsymbol{\gamma}_t^k$ are the parameter vectors voters employ, at time t, to evaluate parties s and k respectively, $\mathbf{x}_t^s$ and $\mathbf{x}_t^k$ are the vectors of variables on the basis of which voters evaluate, at time t, parties s and k respectively and ϵ_t^{sk} is a random error term.

In this chapter we make a first attempt at giving empirical content to equation (4.2.1) above by estimating it on quarterly British data over the period 1955–1977. In order to do so, however, certain simplifying assumptions are made in order to aid the estimation process. Firstly, there is the problem of defining a concept of performance for a party in a period when it was not in power. Thus, for example, in equation (4.2.1), if party k was not in power in period t it becomes difficult to give empirical meaning to the vector $\mathbf{x}_t^k$. This problem is particularly acute in a British context because, although Britain operates a three-party system, over the period in question one of the parties – the Liberals – though enjoying a significant amount of electoral support, was never in power. To handle this we assume in our empirical work that

$$\mathbf{x}_t^k = \text{constant, if party } k \text{ was not in power at time } t. \tag{4.2.2}$$

Alternatively as it is constant this term is subsumed in the bias term.

Then there is the problem that in equation (4.2.1) the parameter vector $\boldsymbol{\gamma}$ is allowed to vary both over time and between parties. Although in principle there is no reason why $\boldsymbol{\gamma}$ should not so vary, such variations complicate the estimation process enormously and therefore as a first approximation we assume

$$\boldsymbol{\gamma}_t^s = \boldsymbol{\gamma}_t^k = \boldsymbol{\gamma} \quad s, k = 1 \ldots N \tag{4.2.3}$$

Equation (4.2.3) therefore implies that voters use the same parameters in evaluating the performance of the different parties and these parameters do not change over time. It should be emphasised that these assumptions are only first approximations and in the next chapter we shall present empirical models in which they are relaxed.

4.3 Model specification

We now consider the United Kingdom in the context of its three main political parties, Conservatives (C), Labour (L) and Liberal (LIB). The assumptions embodied in (4.2.2) and (4.2.3) can be substituted into (4.2.1) to yield

$$l_t^{\mathrm{L,C}} = (1-\lambda)[\boldsymbol{\gamma}'\mathbf{x}_t^{\mathrm{L}} + \mathrm{E}(b^{\mathrm{L,C}})] + \lambda l_{t-1}^{\mathrm{L,C}} + \epsilon_t^{\mathrm{L,C}} \tag{4.3.1}$$

if Labour is the ruling party at time t and

$$l_t^{\mathrm{C,L}} = (1-\lambda)[\boldsymbol{\gamma}'\mathbf{x}_t^{\mathrm{C}} + \mathrm{E}(b^{\mathrm{C,L}})] + \lambda l_{t-1}^{\mathrm{C,L}} + \epsilon_t^{\mathrm{C,L}} \tag{4.3.2}$$

if the Conservatives are the ruling party at time t.

It is obvious that (4.3.1) and (4.3.2) can be combined into a single equation by redefining the lead as the lead of the ruling party (R) over the main opposition party (O), denoted by $l_t^{\mathrm{R,O}}$. This yields

$$l_t^{\mathrm{R,O}} = (1-\lambda)[\boldsymbol{\gamma}'\mathbf{x}_t + \delta_{1t}\mathrm{E}(b^{\mathrm{L,C}})] + \lambda l_{t-1}^{\mathrm{R,O}} + \epsilon_t^{\mathrm{R,O}} \tag{4.3.3}$$

where δ_{1t} is the dummy variable taking the value + 1 when Labour is in power and − 1 when the Conservatives are in power and $\mathbf{x}_t$ is the performance vector of the government of the day.

To complete the system we need a second equation which in our case is the (logarithmic) lead of the main opposition party over the Liberals. Again if we consider the parties separately this takes the form of two equations

$$l_t^{\mathrm{C,LIB}} = (1-\lambda)(\mathrm{E}(b^{\mathrm{C,LIB}}) + \lambda l_{t-1}^{\mathrm{C,LIB}} + \epsilon_t^{\mathrm{C,LIB}} \tag{4.3.4}$$

when the Conservatives are the main opposition party and

$$l_t^{\mathrm{L,LIB}} = (1-\lambda)(\mathrm{E}(b^{\mathrm{L,LIB}}) + \lambda l_{t-1}^{\mathrm{L,LIB}} + \epsilon_t^{\mathrm{L,LIB}} \tag{4.3.5}$$

when Labour is the main opposition party.

Denoting by $l_t^{O,LIB}$ the logarithmic lead of the main opposition party over the Liberals, equations (4.3.4) and (4.3.5) can be combined to yield

$$l_t^{O,LIB} = \delta_{2t}E(b^{C,LIB}) + (1-\delta_{2t})E(b^{L,LIB}) + \lambda l_{t-1}^{O,LIB} + \epsilon_t^{O,LIB} \qquad (4.3.6)$$

where δ_{2t} is a dummy variable taking the value + 1 when Labour is in power and the Conservatives are the main opposition party and 0 when the Conservatives are in power and Labour is the main opposition party. Note that in deriving (4.3.3) from (4.3.1) and (3.4.2) and (4.3.6) from (4.3.4) and (4.3.5) we have appealed to the relationships, $l_t^{R,O} = l_t^{L,C}\delta_{1t}$ and $l_t^{O,LIB} = l_t^{L,C}(1-\delta_{2t}) + l_t^{C,LIB}$.

Equations (4.3.3) and (4.3.6) can then be estimated subject to the cross-equation constraint:

$$E(b^{L,C}) + E(b^{C,LIB}) - E(b^{L,LIB}) = 0 \qquad (4.3.7)$$

Before the system can be estimated however, the variables that enter the system must be specified and in this, as a first approximation, we follow Pissarides (1980). A hypothesis that has been put forward as an independent explanation of the behaviour of government popularity is the 'electoral cycle hypothesis' (see the discussion of Goodhart and Bhansali (1970) and Miller and Mackie (1973) in Chapter 2 of this book) whereby the government's lead over the main opposition party declines just after an election but picks up again just before the next election. To incorporate this hypothesis into our equations we used two dummy variables. The first dummy variable, denoted *E*1, attempted to capture the 'fear of change effect' whereby the reluctance of voters to vote the incumbent party out of power grew, as a general election approached. This variable, *E*1, took the value 6 one quarter before a general election, 5 two quarters before the election and so on down to zero or the next general election whichever came first. The other dummy variable, *E*2, attempted to capture the 'new government' effect whereby a new government came into power with a stock of electoral goodwill which it then, through inevitable political and administrative errors, proceeded to dissipate. This variable took the value 8 in the quarter of a general election, 7 in the following quarter, and so on down to 0, or to the next general election whichever came first. Three other dummy variables *CP*64, *CP*70 and *CP*74 were used. These took the value 1 in the three quarters in which there was a general election resulting in a change of ruling party (1964:4, 1970:3 and 1974:1).

The other variables that entered the equations were those relating to the government's economic performance. (Note that these variables only entered equation (4.3.3).) These were the percentage growth in consumption, *GRC*, the change in the rate of price inflation, ΔIR, the percentage of the working population unemployed, *UR*, the change in the dollar/sterling exchange rate, ΔE, and finally, *TAX*, which was the ratio of gross domestic product taken in by the government in income and expenditure taxes. All the variables were seasonally unadjusted and changes were quarter to quarter changes. *A priori*, one would expect increases in consumption growth and in the exchange rate to increase government popularity and increases in inflation, unemployment and the tax ratio to decrease it. Lastly, the one-quarter lagged value of the dependent variable entered both equations of the system.

The dependent variables, $l_t^{R,O}$ and $l_t^{O,LIB}$, were obtained from Gallup Poll reports from answers to the question 'if there were a general election tomorrow which party would you support?' The observations were end-of-quarter observations.[1]

4.4 Estimation results

The results of estimating equations (4.3.3) and (4.3.6) subject to the constraint (4.3.7) are reproduced below[2] (with t ratios in parentheses).

$$l^{R,O} = \underset{(0.91)}{0.013\delta_1} + \underset{(1.92)}{0.232\,CP64} + \underset{(0.01)}{0.001\,CP70} + \underset{(2.50)}{0.324\,CP74}$$

$$+ \underset{(3.61)}{0.023E1} + \underset{(1.41)}{0.008E2} + \underset{(2.98)}{0.006GRC} - \underset{(2.89)}{0.016\Delta IR}$$

$$+ \underset{(1.21)}{0.080(1/UR)_{-2}} + \underset{(3.38)}{0.690\Delta E} - \underset{(3.10)}{0.377TAX} + \underset{(12.57)}{0.675 l^{R,O}_{-1}}$$

$$\bar{R}^2 = 0.646 \quad DW = 2.39 \quad s = 0.116$$

Estimation period: 1955:3–1977:4.

$$l^{O,LIB} = \underset{(5.49)}{0.388\delta_2} + \underset{(5.66)}{0.401(1-\delta_2)} + \underset{(12.57)}{0.675 l^{O,LIB}_{-1}}$$

$$\bar{R}^2 = 0.581 \quad DW = 2.08 \quad s = 0.222$$

Estimation period: 1955:3–1977:4.

Statistically the regressions are satisfactory, given that the Gallup Poll is calculated from a small number of questionnaires and so is subject to statistical error, and the $\bar{R}^2$ and the standard error estimate indicate a good fit. The null hypothesis that restriction (4.3.7) was validly imposed was not rejected at the 5 per cent significance level with an $F(1, 166)$ value of 0.153.

All the economic variables, except unemployment, performed better without a lag. Unemployment however performed best non-linearly and with a lag of two quarters. This difference in the lag structure is as expected, because unemployment is reported with a lag and most voters are not able to observe it directly, before it is reported. All the other economic variables are either reported by the mass media, or observed by the electorate, without a lag.

The long-run equilibrium of the system corresponds to no growth in consumption, no changes in the inflation rate, the exchange rate and the level of taxation, and to a constant stock of goodwill for the incumbent party. The corresponding steady-state proportions of popularity (evaluated at the sample means) for the Labour, Conservative and Liberal parties are 38.0 per cent, 47.6 per cent and 14.4 per cent respectively when Labour is in office and 49.2 per cent, 36.4 per cent and 14.4 per cent when the Conservatives are in office. These figures suggest that the sample means of the economic variables are such as to make the ruling party more unpopular than the main opposition party and perhaps indicate that electoral dummies are not essential for the explanation of the electoral cycle. When one only considers party loyalty (the terms δ_1 and δ_2) one arrives at 44.4 per cent, 42.7 per cent and 12.9 per cent for the votes cast in favour of the Labour, Conservative and Liberal parties respectively. Hence a slight bias exists in favour of the Labour party. The Pissarides (1980) specification gives rise to a long-run arithmetic lead in favour of the main opposition party of similar magnitude (10.0 per cent) but does not predict party loyalty or the long-run proportion of votes going to the political parties in Britain.

4.5 Stability of econometric estimates

In order to test for the temporal stability of the estimated relationship the sample period, 1955:3–1977:4, was divided into seven overlapping sub-periods, each starting in 1955:3 and ending in 1970:4, 1971:4 . . . 1976:4. Thus each successive sub-period extended the previous sub-period by a full year. For each sub-period we estimated the system embodied in equations (4.3.3) and (4.3.6) subject to the constraint in (4.3.7). (The estimation results for this constrained estimation, over the entire sample period, have been presented earlier in this section.) The estimated regressions were then used to test for significant changes in the values of the estimated coefficients and to forecast the government's lead in the four quarters immediately after the end of the estimation period.

The first set of tests (reported in columns 1–4 in Table 4.1) is a Chow test of parameter constancy and compares the estimates obtained from each sub-period to those obtained when the equations were estimated over the entire period. Let SS be the residual sum of squares when all observations are used, SS_1 be the residual sum of squares when m observations are excluded and n the degrees of freedom of the latter regression. Then the statistic:

$$\frac{(SS - SS_1)/m}{SS_1/n}$$

has an F-distribution with m and n degrees of freedom. If the computed F-statistic exceeds its critical value for any specification then there is evidence of a statistically significant change in the estimated parameters (or alternatively that the additional m observations do not come from the same population as the set that excludes them). The computed statistics show that no evidence of significant parameter changes exists.

However, low computed statistics here may simply indicate large standard errors of the estimated coefficients, in which case the chances of statistically significant changes in the estimates are reduced. The forecasting analysis (reported in columns 5 and 6 of Table 4.1) is designed to test further the equation's performance by testing for the numerical constancy of the estimates. The government's lead is forecast in the four quarters following the end of the sub-period over which the regression is estimated. For each forecast two statistics are reported. First, a χ^2 test on the constancy of the estimated coefficients, defined by

$$\frac{\sum_{1}^{4} e_i^2}{SS/n} \sim \chi^2(4)$$

where e_i is the forecasting error for quarter i, SS is the residual sum of squares for the regression and n its degrees of freedom. Thus this statistic tests whether the point estimates obtained remain sufficiently close to their values when new

Table 4.1 *Tests of constancy of estimated coefficients and forecasting analysis, 1971–76*

Period	m	n	F_n^m	$\chi^2(4)$	RMSE
1955–70	28	51	1.14	10.50	0.179
1955–71	24	55	0.95	1.68	0.074
1955–72	20	59	1.15	4.69	0.122
1955–73	16	63	1.25	5.73	0.210
1955–74	12	66	1.16	8.89	0.170
1955–75	8	70	0.96	7.51	0.159
1955–76	4	74	0.44	2.63	0.088

Notes:

m is the number of observations excluded

n is the degrees of freedom

F_n^m is the F-statistic from a Chow test of parameter constancy

$\chi^2(4)$ is a χ^2 statistic with 4 degrees of freedom based on 4 quarters ahead forecasting errors.

The forecasts for 1974 omit the first quarter, when there was a change of party in power, so that for that year the χ^2 test has 3 degrees of freedom.

observations are added, so as to be capable of predicting the value of the dependent variable outside the sample without statistically significant errors.

The second statistic reported is the square root of the mean squared forecast error, defined by

$$RMSE = (\Sigma e_i^2/4)^{1/2}$$

This gives an indication of the absolute average error that one is likely to encounter from forecasts using the estimated regression.

The forecasts provide evidence of a significant break in the estimated coefficients in only one year, 1971. The explanation for this perhaps lies in the fact that the Heath government elected in the third quarter of 1970 became unpopular relatively quickly, compared with other new governments in the sample. If 1971 is excluded the specification seems to forecast well. There is no evidence of forecasting errors, indicating that over this period the point estimates of the parameters did not change significantly.

4.6 Conclusions

In this chapter we have applied the model of qualitative political choice, developed in the previous chapter, to examining the relationship between British government popularity and economic performance. This exercise, which is seen as a first approximation towards explaining this relationship, used the equation specification adopted by Pissarides (1980). However, our model, which is estimated as a system subject to cross-equation constraints, is explicitly based on choice-theoretic arguments and can be readily applied to multi-party political systems. As we showed in the previous chapter, under such a derivation, equations which postulate a linear relation between the arithmetic lead (of the ruling party over the main opposition party) and governmental performance, explain voting intentions only for a two-party system.

An important feature of British politics is, however, that it operates within an essentially three-party system. By this it is meant that British voters exercise a genuine choice between the three main parties – Conservative, Labour and Liberal. The size of the Liberal vote is not inconsiderable. In the February 1974 election the Liberals won 19.3 per cent of the vote and in the 1979 general election they won 13.8 per cent of the vote, far more than the Free Democrats in West Germany, who under a different electoral system have a considerable share in the government. Thus it would be wrong to infer from the Liberals' lack of Parliamentary representation – brought about by the first-past-the-post system – that they lack electoral support.

It has been emphasized that the results of this chapter are only a first approximation. In the next two chapters we shall extend this model to show, first, how voters react differently at different points in time to economic stimuli and, second, how at one point in time, voters with different backgrounds react differently to economic events.

Although we have demonstrated in Section 4.5 of this chapter that the parameters remain stable over time, i.e. the popularity functions do not significantly change when we omit a few of the latter observations, there is no reason why they should be stable for all subdivisions of history. More precisely, the popularity functions (defining the criteria of political-economic success) may be different for each administration. From the political point of view this is a more interesting issue than the conventional econometric testing procedure for stability adopted in Section 4.5, since it implies that governments are to a certain extent able to mould the criteria by which their own success is measured. This is the theme of the next chapter.

Appendix: Data

$l^{\mathrm{R,O}}$ logarithmic lead of ruling over main opposition party

$l^{\mathrm{O,LIB}}$ logarithmic lead of main opposition party over the Liberal party

CP64, CP70, CP74 three dummy variables taking the value 1 in, respectively, 1964:4, 1970:3 and 1974:1, and the value 0 at other points in time

*E*1 a dummy variable taking the value 6 one quarter before a general election, 5 two quarters before the election and so on down to 0, or to the previous general election whichever comes first

*E*2 a dummy variable taking the value 8 in the quarter of a general election, 7 in the following quarter and so on down to 0, or to the next general election whichever comes first

GRC rate of growth in real consumption, C_t, equals

$$((C_t - C_{t-1})/C_t) \times 100$$

IR percentage growth in GDP deflator, P_t, equals

$$((P_t - P_{t-1})/P_t) \times 100$$

ΔIR	$= IR_t - IR_{t-1}$
UR	percentage of labour force unemployed
E	spot \$ exchange rate
ΔE	$E_t - E_{t-1}$
TAX	ratio of the sum of direct taxes and expenditure taxes to gross domestic product

Source: We are grateful to Dr Christopher Pissarides for making available the data used in this chapter. Data sources are as in Pissarides (1980).

5

The changing criteria of economic success

5.1 Introduction

In the preceding chapter we applied the theory of qualitative political choice, based on the logistic distribution, to estimating the relationship between economic performance and government popularity for Britain, over the period 1955–1977. In doing so we emphasised that, for several reasons, our empirical results were only a first approximation to the underlying reality. One of these reasons was our assumption that the parameter vector that voters used to evaluate government performance remained constant over time. In economic terms this assumption implied that, over the sample period, the economic factors with which voters were concerned did not change and further that the intensity with which they were concerned with these economic factors also did not change. To take a concrete example, the estimation results presented in Section 4.4 of the previous chapter implied that voters were, over the period 1955–1977, always concerned with movements in the inflation rate (the variable ΔIR) and the intensity of their concern with inflation rate movements – measured by a coefficient estimate of -0.016 – did not vary over time.

The equation therefore excluded the possibility that in certain periods voters might not be concerned with the inflation rate and that, even in periods when they were so concerned, the degree of their concern might vary. If this possibility were a real one then such an equation may contain serious mis-specification errors. This mis-specification may be of two kinds. First, variables may be omitted from the analysis because, estimated over the sample period as a whole, they had insignificant coefficient estimates. This, however, still leaves open the possibility that they exerted a significant influence over part, though not the whole, of the estimation period. Second, variables included in the equation are postulated to exert a uniform influence over the period, though in fact their influence may have been changing.

The purpose of this chapter is to estimate, within the framework of the theory of qualitative choice, a model that will take account of these difficulties and indicate the possible extent of the mis-specification when these problems are not considered. In doing so we hope to show that the criteria by which voters evaluate governmental performance has, in the context of British politics, changed over the past 25 years, with a shifting pattern for the economic variables that are given prominence in the minds of voters.

Fig. 5.1 *Economic perceptions over the 1966 Parliament*

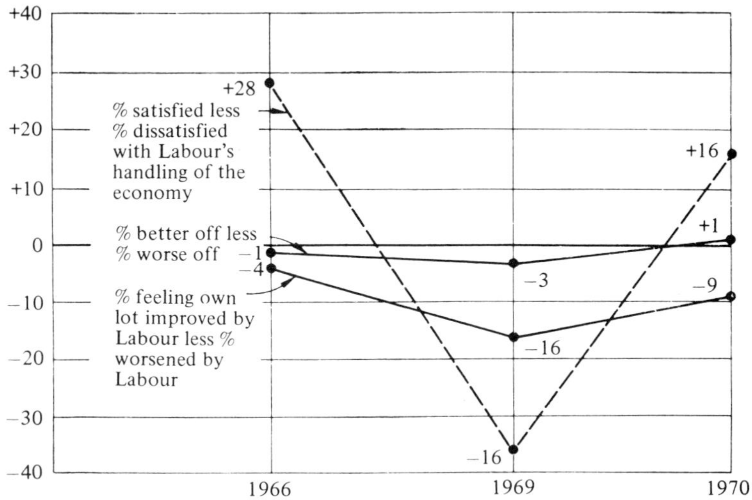

Source: Political Change in Britain, 2nd edition, by David Butler and Donald Stokes. © 1976 by Macmillan, London and Basingstoke, and St Martin's Press, New York. Reprinted by permission.

5.2 Political interpretation of the economic scene

Butler and Stokes (1974) argued that 'what the economy means as a national issue depends on the economic debate between parties and is capable of changing over time' (p. 391). We refer to the hypothesis embodied in this statement, namely that the criteria for evaluating economic success could alter over time, as the Butler and Stokes hypothesis, and one of the purposes of this chapter is to test, within the context of the British political and economic scene of the 1960s and 1970s, the validity of this proposition.

The authors began by noting that the electoral effect of a government's handling of the economy was not simply confined to those in the electorate who perceived themselves advantaged or disadvantaged by such handling but instead evoked reactions even from those voters who did not feel personally affected by the government's performance. Surveys carried out over the life of the 1966 Parliament showed that the balance between respondents who were satisfied and those who were dissatisfied with Labour's stewardship of the economy varied greatly between 1969 and 1970: there was a heavy balance of satisfaction with Labour's economic performance in 1966, a greater balance of dissatisfaction in 1969 and a moderate balance of satisfaction in 1970. Relative to this fluctuation in judgements on Labour's handling of the economy, there was little fluctuation in the perception of respondents of changes in their individual well-being. These contrasts are shown in Fig. 5.1. Two of the curves in the figure relate to individual well-being and are remarkably flat. The third curve, which relates to the balance of satisfaction with Labour's economic performance, fluctuates considerably.

Given that the management of the economy had consequences which extended over the electorate at large, Butler and Stokes then observed a strong association

Fig. 5.2 *Labour's lead over the Conservatives and approval of parties' handling of the economy, December 1959 to August 1964*

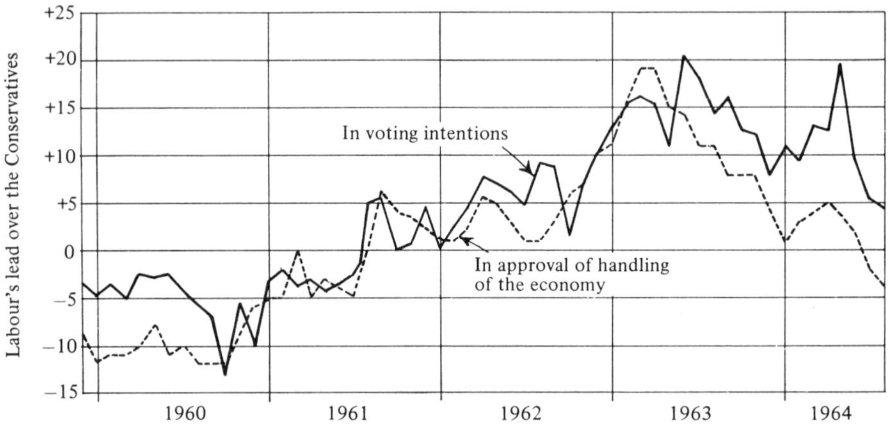

Source: Political Change in Britain, 2nd edition, by David Butler and Donald Stokes. © 1976 by Macmillan, London and Basingstoke, and St Martin's Press, New York. Reprinted by permission.

between polling results for voting intentions and for the parties' perceived ability to deal with economic affairs. This is illustrated in Fig. 5.2 by superimposing two series calculated from the Gallup Poll over the period 1959–1964. The first of these is the positive or negative lead that Labour enjoyed over the Conservatives in voting intentions as recorded by Gallup's monthly index.[1] The second is the positive or negative lead of Labour over the Conservatives in terms of the proportions in successive Gallup samples that said they approved or disapproved of each party's handling of economic affairs.[2]

Although, over the period, the two series fit remarkably well, it should be emphasised that this fact in no way denies the importance of non-economic factors in determining the divisions of party strength. The relationship between voting intentions and economic performance is further highlighted if one matches perceptions of the government's economic performance with movements in party strength (see Fig. 5.3). A casual inspection indicates that this fit is closer and is therefore some evidence that it is the government's economic performance (rather than the relative performance of the two parties) that is of greater relevance to the electorate.

Turning to the specific components of economic performance, Figs 5.4 and 5.5 plot the relationships between voting intentions and the unemployment rate and the inflation rate respectively. Again, although there is a correspondence in shifts in party support and movements in each of these economic variables, the extent of the correspondence is different at different times.

Thus Fig. 5.4, for example, shows that for certain periods a very clear inverse relationship existed between unemployment rates and popularity. This is particularly marked in the middle fifties and again in the seventies. For the inflation rate, a less clear relationship emerges from Fig. 5.5. Although years can be identified in which peaks in popularity can be related to troughs in the rate of inflation,

Fig. 5.3 *Gallup's monthly series on approval of handling of economic affairs by Conservative Government and Labour Opposition, December 1959 to August 1964*

Source: Political Change in Britain, 2nd edition, by David Butler and Donald Stokes. © 1976 by Macmillan, London and Basingstoke, and St Martin's Press, New York. Reprinted by permission.

a sustained relationship like the one between unemployment and popularity does not emerge. The sharp fall in popularity over the middle sixties must be ascribed to a third factor, the balance of payments. What emerges therefore is a situation where the relationship between economic variables (illustrated in Figs 5.4 and 5.5 by unemployment and inflation rates) and political popularity is a fluid one. At times the variables under consideration have little effect on popularity and appeal must be made to other variables; at other times they have an effect on popularity but the strength of this effect varies.

Two competing hypotheses might be put forward to explain these phenomena. The first hypothesis is that of Miller and Mackie (1973),[3] whereby there is a natural cycle of electoral support, broadly independent of economic events, through which a government's support reaches a low in the middle of its term in office, but then rises as a new election approaches. Other proponents of this view include King (1968) and Lawson (1968), who use this hypothesis to explain why governments might be expected to fare better in a general election than in bye-elections. One explanation for the existence of such a cycle lies in the observation that questions about voting intentions might mean different things to voters depending on how far off a general election is. Thus, in a poll conducted in the middle of a parliament, a voter could disapprove of a government without any thought of bringing it down but closer to an election the same question about voting intentions might elicit a more cautious response based on a comparison of the competing parties.

An alternative explanation for the shifting impact of economic factors on political popularity is the Butler and Stokes hypothesis (referred to above) whereby it is speculated that 'the electorate's judgement of the Government's economic performance has continued to shape the movements of party support, but the test of

Fig. 5.4 *Government lead over opposition and unemployment, 1955–1980*

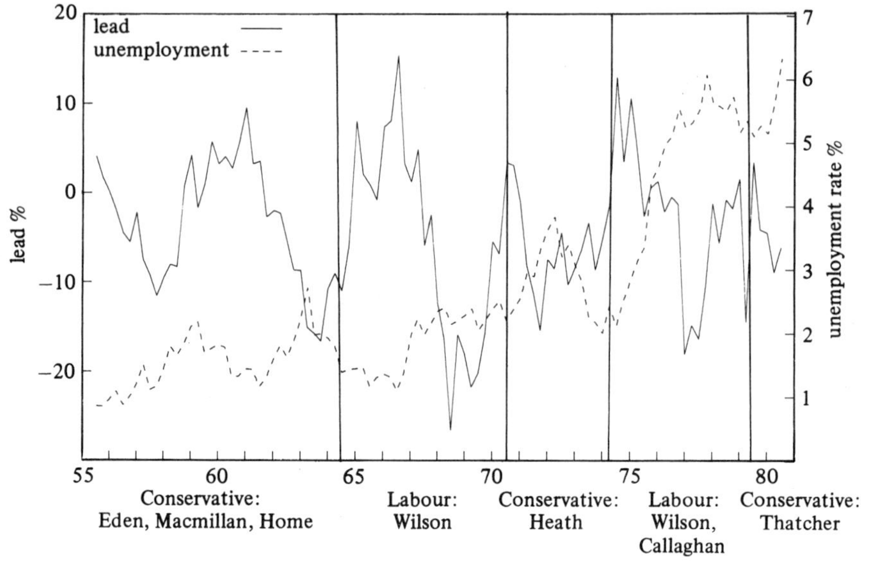

Fig. 5.5 *Government lead over opposition and the inflation rate, 1955–1980*

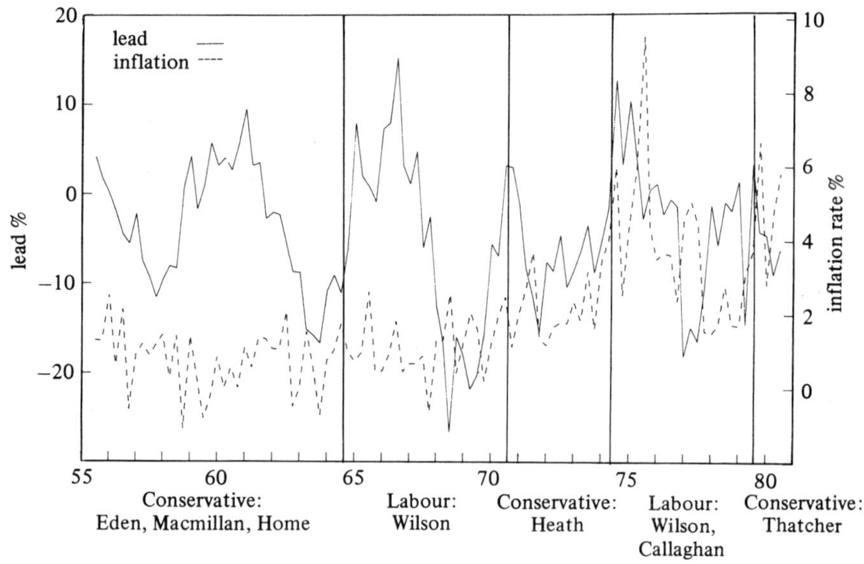

economic success can change' (p. 399). In arguing this thesis Butler and Stokes began by noting that the political popularity (as evidenced by figures for voting intentions) that obtained in the early and middle sixties no longer held in the late sixties. Thus there was some evidence that the influence of unemployment as a factor determining electoral popularity had declined over the period 1960–1970. Several explanations could be offered to explain the declining influence of unemployment: predominant among these are that memories of the 1930s were growing dimmer and that the adoption of more generous unemployment benefits made the prospect of unemployment less fearsome.

Continuing this theme Butler and Stokes then argued that the circumstances in which Labour came to power in 1964 (and the political debate that ensued from these circumstances) caused the balance of payments to occupy a more central position in the electorate's judgement of government performance – a position which it earlier did not enjoy. Thus, on winning the 1964 election, Harold Wilson consistently reminded the electorate of the large balance of payments deficit that Labour had inherited from the Conservatives. After the devaluation of 1966, following its own problems with the balance of payments, Labour virtually invited the electorate to judge it on its ability to cope with Britain's external trade problems. The Conservatives, believing that Labour could not so cope, agreed to this test and thus, given the form of the inter-party economic debate, the balance of payments became an important criterion in the electorate's evaluation of the Labour government's performance.

In the early seventies, Butler and Stokes argued that the substance of the economic debate altered, with rising prices and ways of combating wage inflation being the central preoccupations of the economy. Accordingly, in the February 1974 election, neither unemployment nor the balance of payments featured prominently in the electoral campaigns even though there was speculation about an impending slump and even though the country was experiencing a record trade deficit. Butler and Stokes concede that this alternative account is no more than a hypothesis but argue 'that it can explain much of the gross variation of party strength without jettisoning the view that the electorate will judge a Government partly in economic terms' (p. 401).

In the context of the above discussion, the purpose of this chapter is to provide a systematic test for these alternative views on the variable impact of economic factors on a government's political popularity. In doing so we continue to use as our framework the theory of qualitative political choice detailed in an earlier chapter. However, in contrast to the previous chapter, we no longer regard the equation coefficients as being constant over the estimation period. Instead, we sub-divide the estimation period (1955–1979) into sub-periods, each one corresponding to the rule of a particular government, and attempt to test the stability of the popularity functions across these sub-periods. The manner in which this division is carried out and the results of the test procedure are the subjects of the next section.

5.3 The stability of popularity functions for successive governments

The starting point in our analysis of the stability of popularity functions are equations (4.3.3) and (4.3.6) of the preceding chapter which, for ease of reference, are reproduced below:

$$l_t^{R,O} = (1-\lambda)[\gamma' x_t + \delta_{1t} E(b^{L,C})] + \lambda l_{t-1}^{R,O} + \epsilon_t^{R,O} \qquad (5.3.1)$$

$$l_t^{O,LIB} = \delta_{2t} E(b^{C,LIB}) + (1-\delta_{2t}) E(b^{L,LIB}) + \lambda l_{t-1}^{O,LIB} + \epsilon_t^{O,LIB} \qquad (5.3.2)$$

where the superscripts R, O and LIB denote the ruling, main and opposition and Liberal parties respectively; $l_t^{R,O}$ and $l_t^{O,LIB}$ are the logarithmic leads of the ruling over the main opposition party and of the main opposition party over the Liberal party respectively; $\mathbf{x}_t$ is the performance vector of the government of the day and δ_{1t} and δ_{2t} are dummy variables taking the values + 1 when Labour is in power and − 1 and 0 respectively when the Conservatives are in power.

These equations are subjected to the cross-equation constraint

$$E(b^{L,C}) + E(b^{C,LIB}) - E(b^{L,LIB}) = 0 \tag{5.3.3}$$

where this constraint follows from the fact that the proportions of voters favouring the three parties (ignoring minor parties) must sum to unity.

The first problem in estimating equations (5.3.1) and (5.3.2) subject to the constraint (5.3.3) lay in the specification of $\mathbf{x}_t$, the performance vector. In the preceding chapter we had adopted the specification of Pissarides (1980). However, this specification, in our view, did not fully reflect the substance of the Butler and Stokes hypothesis and consequently the Pissarides formulation was modified to make it more consistent with our needs. In making these modifications we followed Kaldor (1971) who argued that the objectives of price stability, full employment, external stability and real growth were the four major objectives of post-war British economic policy. Kaldor further observed that there was general consensus in post-war Britain that the government could and should assume responsibility for the management of the economy and that successful management comprised the simultaneous attainment of at least these four major objectives.

In line with this argument, our performance vector had four components: the rate of inflation, *IR*, measured by the percentage change in the retail price index; the unemployment rate, *UR*, measured by the percentage of the working population unemployed;[4] the change in foreign reserves, *BP*, measured by the deficit (−) or surplus (+) in the balance of payments, and finally the percentage rate of growth in real per capita personal disposable income, *GR*. The possibility that governmental performance might be assessed both in terms of the levels and in terms of changes in the levels of the relevant variables was allowed for by including initially all variables in levels and first differences. The only exception to this procedure was the balance of payments surplus or deficit, since that itself represented a change in foreign reserves.

The second problem was the appropriate choice of sub-periods for testing the hypothesis that, although a government's economic performance was a significant determinant of its popularity, the British public's criteria for measuring economic success had changed over time. We chose to sub-divide the estimation period 1955 to 1979 into three sub-periods: 1955 :3–1964 :3; 1964 :4–1970 :2; and 1970 :3–1979 :1.

Period I was a period of Conservative rule under Eden, Macmillan and Home; Period II of Labour rule under Wilson and Period III of both Conservative rule under Heath (up to 1974: Q1) and Labour rule under Wilson and Callaghan. This particular choice of sub-periods was initially suggested by Butler and Stokes (1974), though later in this paper an *ex post* justification for the choice is provided. On the Butler and Stokes hypothesis there was, between these broad periods, a change in the relative importance of different economic issues. Thus, in their view, unemployment was the relatively important economic issue till 1964. The circumstances surrounding Labour's accession to power in 1964 (they inherited a large balance of payments deficit from the Conservatives) and the substance of the economic debate between the parties in the 1966 parliament promoted Britain's balance of payments to a more central role in the electorate's assessment of the government's economic performance (see Brittan, 1964). Finally they suggested that in the post 1970 period inflation began to preoccupy the electorate's mind.

An alternative interpretation of our choice of sub-periods is that each sub-period corresponds to a regime of a different kind. In Period I there was a Conservative government, in Period II there was a Labour government and in Period III there was a broadly Keynesian Conservative administration followed by a broadly monetarist Labour government. Some would argue that the Heath regime and the Callaghan/Healey regime (constrained by IMF intervention, etc.) were indistinguishable from many points of view and therefore the chosen sub-periods reflect the evaluation of different types of administrations. Changes in the criteria of economic success are according to this interpretation partly due to the re-appraisal and moulding of the criteria of success by each new government.

To test the hypothesis that movements in governmental popularity were due to the existence of an 'electoral cycle' which had little to do with economic events, two electoral variables were included in the equation. The first variable $E1$ took the value 6 in the quarter preceding a general election, 5 two quarters before an election and so on down to 0 or to the previous election. This variable was designed to capture, with the onset of a general election, the electorate's increasing reluctance to change the party in power. The second electoral variable, $E2$, took the value 8 in the quarter after a general election, 7 two quarters after a general election and so on down to zero or to the next general election, whichever came first.[5] This variable was designed to capture the gradual dissipation of a new government's stock of goodwill with the electorate through errors of policy and administration. The inclusion of these two electoral variables allows one to test the strength of the 'electoral cycle' (cf. King, 1968; Lawson, 1968; Miller and Mackie, 1973). Their influence may also reflect the fact that the nation is less inhibited and more critical of the government when questioned by representatives of the Gallup Poll in between elections, but becomes less critical as an election approaches.

Defining the dummy variables D^{I}, D^{II} and D^{III} as taking the value unity in Periods I, II and III respectively and zero elsewhere, one obtains the general model with 29 parameters defined by the system

$$l_t^{\mathrm{R,O}} = \sum_{i=\mathrm{I}}^{\mathrm{III}} [\alpha_1^i IR_t + \alpha_2^i \Delta IR_t + \alpha_3^i UR_{t-2} + \alpha_4^i \Delta UR_{t-2} + \alpha_5^i BP_t + \alpha_6^i GR_t + \alpha_7^i \Delta GR_t + \alpha_8^i l_{t-1}^{\mathrm{R,O}}] D^i + \alpha_9 E1_t + \alpha_{10} E2_t + b^{\mathrm{L,C}} \delta_{1t} + \epsilon_t^{\mathrm{R,O}} \tag{5.3.4}$$

$$l_t^{\mathrm{O,LIB}} = \sum_{i=\mathrm{I}}^{\mathrm{III}} [\alpha_8^i l_{t-1}^{\mathrm{O,LIB}}] D^i + b^{\mathrm{C,LIB}} \delta_{2t} + b^{\mathrm{L,LIB}} (1-\delta_{2t}) + \epsilon_t^{\mathrm{O,LIB}} \tag{5.3.5}$$

Table 5.1 *Results of sequential hypothesis testing on estimating equations (5.3.4) and (5.3.5) subject to constraint (5.3.6)*

	Null hypothesis	Alternative hypothesis	Result	Test statistic
H1	$\alpha_8^{I} = \alpha_8^{II} = \alpha_8^{III}$	most general case	not rejected	$\chi^2(2) = 1.08$
H2	$\alpha_4^{I} = \alpha_4^{III}$ and H1	H1	not rejected	$\chi^2(1) = 0.02$
H3	$\alpha_4^{I} = \alpha_4^{II} = \alpha_4^{III}$ and H1	H1	rejected	$\chi^2(1) = 6.04$
H4	$\alpha_7^{II} = \alpha_7^{III}$ and H2	H2	rejected	$\chi^2(1) = 12.20$
H5	$\alpha_6^{II} = \alpha_6^{III}$ and H2	H2	not rejected	$\chi^2(1) = 3.60$
H6	$\alpha_1^{II} = \alpha_1^{III} = \alpha_2^{I} = \alpha_2^{III}$ $= \alpha_3^{I} = \alpha_3^{III} = \alpha_5^{I} = \alpha_5^{III}$ $= \alpha_6^{I} = \alpha_7^{I} = \alpha_9 = 0$ and H5	H5	not rejected	$\chi^2(11) = 5.32$

subject to the cross-equation constraint for transitivity

$$E(b^{L,C}) + E(b^{C,LIB}) = E(b^{L,LIB}) \qquad (5.3.6)$$

where $l_t^{O,LIB}$ denotes the logarithmic lead of the main opposition party over the Liberal party and $\delta_1(\delta_2)$ a dummy taking on the value $+1(+1)$ when Labour is in office and $-1(0)$ when the Conservatives are in office. The economic data were obtained from *Economic Trends* and the data on voting intentions were derived from the Gallup Poll (see Appendix to this chapter).

5.4 Estimation results for different administrations

This system was estimated[6] and subjected to sequential testing procedure, whereby at each stage a null hypothesis was tested against an alternative hypothesis. If the null was not rejected it was taken at the next test as an alternative with it and a further hypothesis being adopted as the null. The procedure was halted when all further null hypotheses were rejected, and the restrictions implied by the last level of non-rejection were incorporated into the final equation. The procedure is similar to the methodology of Davidson *et al.* (1978). The sequence of tests was as follows. The first set of restrictions that were imposed and tested were equality restrictions whereby coefficients on the different variables were constrained to be the same over the periods. After the appropriate equality restrictions had been imposed, variables, with whose coefficient estimates were associated low *t* values (in general less than unity), were eliminated from the equations. The zero restrictions were imposed after the equality restrictions to ensure that in testing for equality the equations had the same specification in the different time periods. The details of the testing procedure are shown in Table 5.1.[7]

As noted above, the explanatory variables that were chosen were regarded as representing the four major objectives of post-war economic policy. At this stage, other variables were also experimented with and the only variable whose coefficient estimate was significantly different from zero was the tax burden, *TAX*,

Table 5.2 *Government lead over main opposition party* ($l_t^{R,O}$)

	Period I 1955:3–1964:3	Period II 1964:4–1970:2	Period III 1970:3–1979:1
IR	-0.0352 (2.20)		
ΔIR		-0.0588 (3.10)	
UR		-0.0197 (1.32)	
ΔUR	-0.123 (3.66)	-0.319 (3.55)	-0.123 (3.66)
BP		0.000183 (3.54)	
GR		0.0198 (2.21)	0.0198 (2.21)
ΔGR		0.0227 (2.66)	0.0085 (1.16)
TAX			-0.0950 (1.93)
$\ell_{t-1}^{R,0}$	0.780 (18.02)	0.780 (18.02)	0.780 (18.02)
$E2$	0.0057 (1.80)	0.0057 (1.80)	0.0057 (1.80)
δ_1	0.0147 (1.11)	0.0147 (1.11)	0.0147 (1.11)

$\bar{R}^2 = 0.74$ $SE = 0.09$ $DW = 2.1$ $RHO = -0.06$ $N = 94$

Table 5.3 *Lead of the main opposition party over Liberals* ($l_t^{O,LIB}$)

	Period I 1955:3–1964:3	Period II 1964:4–1970:2	Period III 1970:3–1979:1
$\ell_{t-1}^{0,LIB}$	0.780 (18.02)	0.780 (18.02)	0.780 (18.02)
δ_2	0.299 (4.80)	0.299 (4.80)	0.299 (4.80)
$(1-\delta_2)$	0.314 (4.75)	0.314 (4.75)	0.314 (4.75)

$\bar{R}^2 = 0.98$ $SE = 0.19$ $DW = 1.85$ $RHO = 0.05$ $N = 94$

(defined as the ratio of total taxes to gross domestic product) and furthermore it was significant only in the third period. This seems reasonable, since in the third period the UK experienced problems with the public sector deficit. The final estimation results are shown in Tables 5.2 and 5.3.[8] The final system corresponds to the equations (5.3.4)–(5.3.5) subject to the constraints (5.3.6) and H6 and has 14 independent parameters. Both equations are well determined and characterised by an absence of serial correlation. Also, all the coefficient estimates are correctly signed and mostly significantly different from zero.

A consistent feature of the estimates was that changes in the unemployment rate were primary sources of concern to the public. The inflation rate (and changes in this rate) had relatively little effect. This is not surprising given that the rate of growth in real disposable income exerted a significant influence in Periods II and III. Thus, voters appeared indifferent to inflation so long as nominal incomes kept ahead of prices. In fact, the only period in which the inflation rate exerted a significant effect (Period I) was a period in which growth in real incomes was not a significant influence. For reasons discussed earlier, the balance of payments was an important and contentious issue in the political debate of Period II and this was the only period when external surpluses or deficits significantly altered the government's popularity with the electorate.

There was no evidence of increasing popularity of the ruling party as an election approaches, but there was some support for the proposition that the government loses goodwill as soon as it enters office. This may contribute to rapid changes in government, since the electorate holds the party in office responsible for the errors of bureaucracy and voters do not hesitate to remove an unpopular government. This suggests there is only evidence for the upward components of the electoral cycle pointed out by King (1968), Lawson (1968) and Miller and Mackie (1973). The high discount rate (28.2 per cent) tends to accentuate the electoral cycle, since individuals evaluate performance by looking only at recent records of the incumbent party. This agrees with Butler and Stokes (1974, p. 395) and may be due to a rapid loss of memory or to the high costs of information on past economic records.

The most important message that the equations convey is that the influence of the economic variables has *varied over time*. Indeed the extent of the mis-specification, consequent upon assuming that they do not so vary, can be judged by estimating (5.3.4)–(5.3.6) and restricting the coefficients to be the same across time. These results (not shown in this book) indicated that the system was very poorly determined. The equation for $l^{R,O}$ had only one significant economic effect which was on the change in the unemployment rate. As noted earlier, this was the only economic variable which exerted a significant influence over all the time periods. Other variables which exerted significant influences over only certain sub-periods did not show up significantly in this equation. Indeed a $\chi^2(18)$ value of 34.7 rejected the null hypothesis of time-invariant coefficients.

Finally, as an *ex post* justification for their choice, a test was carried out on the stability of the adopted sub-periods. To do this the final system shown in Tables 5.2 and 5.3 was estimated separately over the sub-periods with and without the last four observations in each sub-period. A Chow-test was then carried out on each sub-period and in all three cases the null hypothesis of parameter stability was not rejected at the 5 per cent significance level. This was further confirmed by a χ^2 test on the sum of squares of forecasting errors. Table 5.4 presents the details.

5.5 Simulation properties of the popularity model

The long-run equilibrium of the estimated system corresponds to no changes in the levels of inflation, rate of unemployment, economic growth and foreign reserves and to a constant stock of goodwill for the incumbent party.

Table 5.4 *Stability tests on the sub-periods*

Period I	Period II	Period III
37 observations 5 variables	23 observations 9 variables	34 observations 7 variables
$F(4,28) = 1.03$	$F(4,10) = 0.91$	$F(4,23) = 0.5$
$\chi^2(4) = 4.41$	$\chi^2(4) = 8.8$	$\chi^2(4) = 2.35$

Table 5.5 *Elasticities at the mean*

	IR^{I}	UR^{II}	BP^{II}	GR^{II}	GR^{III}	TAX^{III}	$E2$
Sample mean[a]	0.7473	1.9065	-75.392	0.4762	0.6633	0.4480	2.745
Standard deviation[a]	1.0278	1.7273	390.860	1.8126	2.2472	0.3613	3.286
Coefficient	-0.0352	-0.0197	0.000183	0.0198	0.0198	-0.0950	0.0057
β-coefficient	-0.1922	-0.1811	0.3806	0.1906	0.2363	-0.1823	0.0996
Short-run elasticity	-0.0263	-0.0376	-0.0138	0.0094	0.0131	-0.0426	0.0156
Long-run elasticity	-0.1196	-0.1707	-0.0627	0.0429	0.0597	-0.1935	0.0711

[a] The sample mean and standard deviation apply to the relevant sub-period.

The long-run equilibrium distribution of votes evaluated at the sample means may be calculated from the long-run elasticities presented in Table 5.5. For example in Period II the steady-state proportion of votes going to the Labour, Conservative and Liberal Party would be 43 per cent, 45 per cent and 12 per cent respectively when Labour is in office, but would be 48 per cent, 40 per cent and 12 per cent when the Conservatives were in office. These figures suggest that the sample means are such as to make the ruling party more unpopular than the main opposition party and perhaps suggest that electoral dummies were not essential to the explanatory power of the model. When one only takes account of the loyalty terms (δ_1 and δ_2) the long-run proportion of votes going to the Labour, Conservative and Liberal party are 46 per cent, 43 per cent and 11 per cent (irrespective of which party is in office). It is clear that, after removing the effects of economic performance on government popularity, there is a bias against the Conservatives. The elasticities and standardised β-coefficients given in Table 5.5 illustrate that the economic variables contribute rather more to the explanation of the (logarithmic) lead than the electoral dummy variables, so that economic factors play a major role in the determination of political popularity. It is also clear how important the balance of payments issue was in the late sixties and how growth in real personal disposable income has taken over from the traditional factors, inflation and unemployment.

Fig. 5.6 *Actual and predicted arithmetic lead of the ruling over the main opposition party and of the main opposition over the Liberal party*

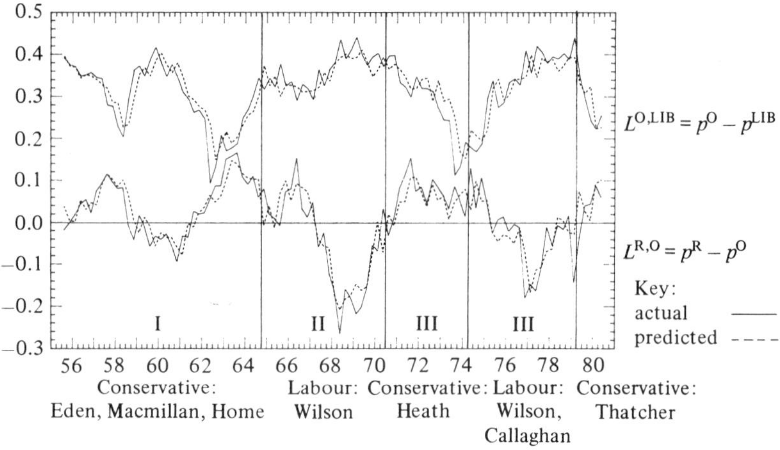

The results of simulating the estimated model (5.3.4)–(5.3.5) subject to (5.3.6) and H6 have been unscrambled to produce arithmetic, rather than logarithmic, leads and are presented in Fig. 5.6. The system performs surprisingly well within the sample period (1955:3–1979:1), although predictions beyond the sample period (1979:2–1980:3) deteriorate a little. There is a tendency to over-predict the lead of the ruling over the opposition party, when the lead of the opposition party over the Liberals is under-predicted. The extremities seem to be predicted reasonably well, even though not much use of electoral dummies has been made. Forecasts derived from Tables 5.2 and 5.3 may need modification, since it is likely that parameters have changed as monetary aggregates have been emphasised by the current Conservative administration and now feature in the political debate.

5.6 Conclusions

In this chapter the theoretical model of qualitative political choice developed in Chapter 3 was estimated on quarterly British data over the period 1955–1979. In doing so, the equations (as demanded by the analysis) were treated as an interdependent system and estimated using appropriate systems estimation techniques. The hypothesis that the British electorate's criteria for evaluating the success or failure of its government's economic performance had changed over time (and depended on the type of administration) was then systematically tested, by dividing the sample period into 3 sub-periods. This hypothesis, if true, would have powerful implications for electoral behaviour and the results, based upon equations which were remarkably well determined, lent it considerable support. The nature of these changing criteria was two-fold. First, the behaviour of certain variables (e.g. the unemployment rate) was a consistent source of concern to the electorate. However, the intensity of this concern varied across the sub-periods. Second, the behaviour of some variables was a source of concern to the electorate in certain periods but not in other periods. The outstanding example of this is Britain's balance of payments performance which significantly affected the government's electoral popularity in the 1964–1970 period, but did not exercise such influence either before or after this period. The consequence of ignoring such changes must be serious mis-specification errors and an attempt was made to evaluate the extent of this mis-specification.

The evidence for changes in the criteria of economic success provided in this paper provides some insight into the apparent instability of empirical voting and popularity functions found previously in the literature (see Stigler, 1973; Arcelus and Meltzer, 1975). The results suggest that voting and popularity functions may be improved by allowing for changes in perception over time and for different criteria for each type of administration.

This paradox of stability of popularity functions *within* a period relating to a particular government and of instability *between* different governments is not really surprising. The economic problems that are highlighted – and by implication the problems that are underplayed – differ between governments. This may be partly due to genuine differences in ideology and partly to a desire to take advantage of existing economic conditions (witness Mr Wilson on the balance of payments). To some extent this alters voters' perceptions of what is important; to another extent voters judge governments by the criteria the governments themselves set. Both these factors combine to produce what we term the 'changing criteria of economic success'.

However once a set of criteria has been established for a particular government, it remains unaltered until a change of government leads to a change in the tone of the political debate, and hence to a change in the criteria. To take an example: it is not difficult to imagine a Labour government, elected on a platform of ensuring near-full employment, paying a heavy electoral price for three million unemployed. However we think that Mrs Thatcher will not have to pay such a price.

Most obviously, Mrs Thatcher has altered the nature of the economic debate by downgrading high employment and upgrading low inflation rates as objectives of economic policy. In terms of her own criteria, the falling rate of inflation would indicate that she is succeeding, and her strong position in the recent polls bears witness to this. Our findings show that it is not so much the level of unemployment but changes in these levels that worry the electorate. Unemployment becomes an election-losing issue – particularly when it has already been downgraded to a price one has to pay for a better future – only through the insecurity that high and rising levels of unemployment communicate to those already in employment. Remove the 'rising' part of unemployment and you remove a large part of the insecurity.

The electorate, according to our findings, shows a marked predilection for growing levels of real per capita income. Thus rising living standards might well see the return of Mrs Thatcher at the next general election, in spite of high, but stable, levels of unemployment.

Appendix: Data

Exogenous variables

IR — rate of change in the retail price index, RPI, $= ((RPI_t - RPI_{t-1})/RPI_{t-1}) \times 100$ (seasonally unadjusted)

ΔIR — $= IR_t - IR_{t-1}$

UR	unemployment rate = total unemployed (including school leavers) as a proportion of total working population × 100 (seasonally unadjusted)
ΔUR	$= UR - UR_{t-1}$
BP	Balance for Official Finance (seasonally unadjusted)
GR	rate of growth in per capita personal disposable income, *PDI*, $= ((PDI_t - PDI_{t-1})/PDI_{t-1}) \times 100$
ΔGR	$GR_t - GR_{t-1}$
TAX	ratio of the sum of direct taxes and expenditure taxes to gross domestic product (seasonally unadjusted)
t	quarterly time subscript

Source: *Economic Trends, Annual Supplement 1981*, published by the CSO.

Endogenous variables

In response to the question, 'If there were a general election tomorrow, which party would you support?', let P_{La}, P_C, P_{Lib} be the proportions supporting Labour, Conservative, Liberal respectively after excluding the don't knows and supporters of the minor parties. Thus the dependent variables are:

$l_t^{R,O}$	logarithmic lead of ruling over main opposition party
$l_t^{O,LIB}$	logarithmic lead of main opposition party over the Liberal party.

The quarterly figures for voting intentions were obtained by averaging monthly figures.

Source: *The Gallup Political Barometer* published by Social Surveys (Gallup Poll) Ltd.

6

Economic conditions and class interests

6.1 Introduction

In Chapter 3 of this book we developed a theory of qualitative political choice and in Chapter 4 we applied this theory to estimating a model, for the United Kingdom, of voter reactions to changes in the economic environment. In implementing the theoretical structure we made, in Chapter 4, two fundamental assumptions. First, we assumed that voter reactions did not vary over time so that voters reacted with the same intensity to a particular change in economic circumstances regardless of the historical period in which this change occurred. The implications of relaxing this assumption were the subject matter of Chapter 5 in which the intertemporal stability of voter reactions to changes in governmental economic performance was investigated.

The second fundamental assumption was that voters could be regarded as a homogeneous group so that changes in economic indicators would elicit identical responses from all voters. This chapter investigates the implications of dropping this assumption and instead regards voters as comprising a heterogeneous collection of sub-groups with each sub-group having perceived economic interests that may differ markedly from those of other sub-groups.

In this chapter, given our purpose of studying voter behaviour, we consider a division of the British electorate along class lines. The next section argues, on the basis of existing studies, that class remains the most important factor in explaining party allegiances in Britain in spite of evidence that the extent of class voting has declined in recent years. One of the arguments put forward for the pre-eminence of class in explaining voter behaviour is the existence of class interests and the links between these interests and their representation by political parties. In Section 6.3 we argue that a given change in the economic environment may have different effects on the different classes and that therefore it may be quite natural for class interests to develop. Section 6.4 extends our theory of qualitative political choice to take into account the fact that voters might react differently to a particular economic change. This last proposition is tested in Section 6.5 where the model is estimated on data for the British General Election of 1966. Sections 6.6 and 6.7 modify the theory to take account of voting patterns within occupational classes and re-estimate the model. Section 6.8 presents the results of a time-series analysis of the same problem and Section 6.9 concludes the chapter.

6.2 The class basis of voting

It is generally acknowledged that class is the most important factor in explaining party allegiance in British politics. In fact, in a comparative study of four Anglo-American democracies, Alford (1963) showed that the order of class voting was highest in Great Britain, followed by Australia, the United States and Canada. The regional cultures of Scotland and Wales and religious differences modified, but did not erase, the fundamental class basis of the Conservative and Labour parties.

A general association between social class and voting behaviour, regardless of the country in question, is not surprising, given 'the existence of class interests, the representation of these interests by political parties, the regular association of certain parties with certain interests and the tendency of voters to choose the party historically associated with social groups to which they belong' (Alford, 1963, p. 37). One of the reasons put forward for the greater incidence of class-based voting in Britain (relative to the other countries cited above) is the nature of the Labour party in Britain which 'was founded by the trade unions to secure Labour representation in Parliament and to support by political action the objectives sought by the trade unions in the interests of their members . . . ' (Jennings, 1961, p. 235). Thus given the historic links between trade unions and the British Labour Party, British politics contain more explicit links between class and party than do the politics of the other countries.

Before proceeding further, it is important to define the attributes that constitute the concept of class. Survey analysts use a simple definition of class: class is defined as the occupation of the head of the household of the respondent. Butler and Stokes (1974) found that the overwhelming majority of their respondents accepted or volunteered a middle or working class identification and further that occupation provided the main basis for characterising the classes with 74 per cent describing 'working class' in occupational terms and 61 per cent similarly describing the 'middle class'. Thus they concluded that 'occupational status is the best guide to whether individuals place themselves in the middle or working class'. In our empirical work we too follow the practice of defining class by occupation.

An alternative view of class is given by Rose (1974). This is the notion of ideal classes. Rose defines an ideal-type working class family by five characteristics: minimum education, trade union family, council house residence, working class identification and manual occupation. In his 1970 sample only 9 per cent were ideal-type working class. Thus the essence of this view of class is that very few people can be considered members of a class but instead are linked, more or less strongly, to each of the core classes.

Given the importance of class in explaining voting behaviour, survey data provides estimates of the relative amounts of support that the Labour and Conservative parties draw from the working and middle classes. Alford (1963) estimated that the Labour vote of the middle class rarely rose over 20 per cent; at the same time the non-Labour vote of the working class seldom dropped below 40 per cent. Thus the interdependence of party and class emerged clearly from these results; a Conservative victory depended on heavy working class support and Labour's successes depended largely on gaining more of the middle class vote. The Butler and Stokes (1974) survey, conducted in 1970, came to very similar conclusions: the Conservatives drew 45 per cent of their support from the manual occupations, while Labour drew only 20 per cent of its support from the non-manual occupations. The support that the Conservative party attracts from the working class – the phenomenon of 'working class Conservatism' – has in turn attracted the attention of political sociology and has been interpreted as the deferential response of the working class to superior elements in the social order. Thus Parkin (1967) argues that the Conservatives are the beneficiaries throughout British society of their alignment with the dominant religious, educational and economic institutions and that only where residential or occupational concentration allows the working class to build defences against a 'dominant' value pattern will it be able to assert its own 'deviant' values, including support of the working class party.

One hypothesis concerned with the movement over time of the working class Conservative vote is that of the process of 'embourgeoisement' whereby with the spread of affluence the prosperous working class might be acquiring the self-images of the middle class and hence shifting its party allegiance from Labour to Conservative. Although this view has come under sharp attack (see Goldthorpe, Lockwood, Bechhofer and Platt, 1968), Butler and Stokes (1974) argue that in respect of the change in life style associated with a change in housing tenure, this hypothesis might be valid. Indeed they demonstrate, using survey evidence, that a move from council house occupation to owner occupation might be expected to produce a corresponding change in partisanship from Labour to Conservative. We shall have occasion to return to this theme of housing in the later sections of this chapter.

Earlier in this section we suggested that party cleavages along class lines might be due to the existence of class interests and the systematic representation of these interests by the different parties. Class interests in the economic sphere might be present if the impact of economic variables was unequally distributed among the different classes and it is to this theme that we turn in the next section.

6.3 The differential impact of economic variables

The idea that different status groups in society have different interests and that these differing interests find expression in differential voting behaviour is of course well accepted in the literature. Thus Converse (1958, p. 388) argued that 'over the last 25 years, high status persons in the United States have favoured the Republican party while the less fortunately placed have subscribed instead to the Democratic party'. Again Runciman (1963, p. 94) remarked: 'There is nothing, in a sense, that needs to be explained about a South Wales miner voting Labour or an executive of General Motors voting Republican. The simplest model of rational self-interest is enough to explain these cases.' In the context of the economics literature Stigler argued that it was in the more specific areas on which parties were divided (for example income distribution) rather than in the broader area of macro performance that the economic bases for party affiliation should be sought.

These general ideas translate very readily to the specific character of the British economic scene and it is perhaps appropriate, since this book is being written at a time when the numbers out of work in Britain are unprecedentedly high, to begin with unemployment and to examine its effect on society's sub-groups.

The characteristics of individuals comprising the unemployment stock are determined by two distinct selection processes: the ease with which people lose their present job and thus join the unemployed pool and the ease with which they find a new job and thus leave the unemployed pool. Daniel (1981) using survey data demonstrated that people becoming unemployed tended to over-represent (in relation to the overall working population) the young, the less skilled and the low paid. Thus in May 1980, 40 per cent of the unemployed in Britain were unskilled or semi-skilled while only 27 per cent of the male working population in Britain worked at those levels. Even more significantly, this picture had not altered over the past decade. Thus Hibbs (1982b), using the General Household Survey of 1971 and the Department of Employment's survey of the registered unemployed in 1973, calculated that the incidence of unemployment among manual workers was nearly twice that among non-manual employees.

In terms of the ease with which new jobs could be found, a lack of skills again proved to be a major handicap. Thus Mackay and Reid (1972), while examining the unemployment experiences of male employees made redundant from twenty-three engineering plants in the West Midlands of England over the period 1966–68, discovered that the average duration of unemployment was highest for unskilled workers (20.45 weeks), next highest for semi-skilled workers (12.56 weeks) and lowest for skilled workers (9.70 weeks). Skilled workers of course have the option of resuming employment at a lower point in the occupational scale and this further aggravates the position for the unskilled job-seeker. These conclusions are reinforced by the Royal Commission on the Distribution of Income and Wealth (1978). Using data for 1975 they demonstrated that unskilled and semi-skilled workers had longer durations of unemployment than skilled workers. At the same time they confirmed earlier evidence that unskilled and low-paid workers were more likely to become unemployed than other categories of workers.

The effects of unemployment would therefore appear to fall most heavily upon certain clearly identifiable groups. The young, the unskilled, the low paid and the disabled – who collectively form the weakest and poorest sections of the community – are particularly vulnerable to unemployment. The fact of being unemployed is of course made worse by the economic, social and psychological costs of enforced joblessness. Thus the Royal Commission (1978) for a 1972 sample of the unemployed found that after taking account of all benefits and tax refunds, the average shortfall of household income for the unemployed was 25 per cent. At the same time 40 per cent of the unemployed were losing more than 30 per cent of their net income as a result of being unemployed. In addition of course the income loss would be greater the longer the duration of unemployment.

Compounding the economic costs are the social and psychological miseries of being out of work. In a survey analysed by Daniel (1974), 71 per cent of unemployed respondents said that being out of work had been a 'bad' experience. Although the chief source of hardship was economic, psychological and social costs also featured prominently. The most common complaint was 'boredom' followed by depression or apathy. Third came feelings of inadequacy and a sense of failure. Thus, given the economic and other costs of unemployment and the particular vulnerability of the weak and disadvantaged to unemployment, it follows that a rise in unemployment levels exacerbates inequality.

The differential effects of inflation on the different social sub-groups are more intangible and harder to ascertain. Hibbs (1976 and 1977b) pointed out that the real wage of British manufacturing workers had not been significantly eroded by inflation. On the contrary it was corporate profits which suffered relative declines in inflationary times. Piachaud (1978) argued that it was investment yields that did not keep pace with inflation thereby disadvantaging the relatively well-off and those dependent on unearned income (cf. Chapter 9, Section 3.1).

In terms of the perceptions of individuals of the deleterious effects of inflation the best evidence is provided by a survey of 2,364 adults analysed by Daniel (1975). The results of this survey indicated that the expression of concern about inflation as an economic problem and the feeling that it was personally harmful was common to all sections of the community irrespective of social class, employment status or sex. Thus 73 per cent of the total respondents felt that they had suffered personally from inflation and this varied from 78 per cent for respondents who were in the managerial/professional category to 70 per cent for respondents in the semi-skilled/unskilled manual category. (These figures should be used in conjunction with the fact that the lower the social grade the higher the proportion unable to make an assessment.)

A more interesting picture emerges from the survey when respondents were confronted with the proposition that higher levels of unemployment would be desirable as a means of reducing the inflation rate. Although 77 per cent of the respondents rejected the proposition, the degree of rejection differed markedly between social groups. The proposition was most vehemently rejected by the households of manual workers while among the professional and managerial groups the proportion rejecting the proposition dropped below half.

The conclusion that emerges from the above discussion is that it is the weaker sections of the community – the unskilled and the low paid – who are particularly vulnerable to unemployment and to long durations of unemployment. On the other hand, no significant differences would appear to exist between the different social groups in the perception of their vulnerability to inflation. However, the groups most at risk through rising unemployment would most strongly reject the idea of using unemployment as a means of controlling inflation.

6.4 A general model of attributes and voting behaviour

We now turn to an extension of our theory of qualitative political choice that will enable us to consider the differential impact of economic variables.

Let U_{ij}^k denote the utility of voter i in constituency j ($j = 1 \ldots H$) when party k is in power. This utility is defined as

$$U_{ij}^k = b_i^k + M_j^k \tag{6.4.1}$$

where M_j^k is a measure of constituency j's perception of the economic and electoral performance of party k and b_i^k is a term specific to voter i representing his loyalty towards party k. Voter i then votes for party k in constituency j only if

$$U_{ij}^k > U_{ij}^s \quad \text{for all } s \neq k \tag{6.4.2}$$

Suppose now that the bias of voter i for party k over party s, say b_i^{ks}, is uniformly distributed over voters, where

$$b_i^{ks} = b_i^k - b_i^s \tag{6.4.3}$$

Then it can be shown (see Chapter 3)[1] that the arithmetic lead of party k over party s in constituency j is given by

$$L_j = p_j^k - p_j^s = \alpha + \beta(M_j^k - M_j^s) \tag{6.4.4}$$

where p_j^k denotes the proportion of votes in constituency j going to party k and α and β depend on the upper and lower bounds of the uniform distribution.

Now suppose that constituency j's perception of the government's economic and electoral performance is influenced by the character of the constituency. In other words, the performance of a government which goes to the polls with, say, unemployment at x per cent and inflation at y per cent will be evaluated differently by the different constituencies depending upon their class composition, their house tenure patterns etc.

Let the character of the jth constituency be captured by the m dimensional vector of measured attributes, $\mathbf{y}_j$, and let the economic performance of the political party under consideration, say party k, be captured by the n dimensional vector, $\mathbf{x}^k$. Then the notion of constituency dependent perceptions can be formalised as follows:

$$M_j^k = \boldsymbol{\gamma}_j'\mathbf{x}^k \tag{6.4.5}$$

If perceptions were identical across constituencies, then $\boldsymbol{\gamma}_j = \boldsymbol{\gamma}_h$, for all constituencies j, h. However, perceptions are hypothesised to differ between constituencies. Suppose therefore that the perceptions in constituency j depend on its attributes as follows

$$\boldsymbol{\gamma}_j = \boldsymbol{\Gamma}\,\mathbf{y}_j \tag{6.4.6}$$

where $\boldsymbol{\Gamma}$ is an $n \times m$ matrix. Upon substitution of (6.4.6) into (6.4.5) one obtains

$$M_j^k = (\boldsymbol{\Gamma}\cdot\mathbf{y}_j)'\mathbf{x}^k \tag{6.4.7}$$

and hence from (6.4.4)

$$L_j = \alpha + \beta(\boldsymbol{\Gamma}\cdot\mathbf{y}_j)'(\mathbf{x}^k - \mathbf{x}^s) \quad j = 1 \ldots H \tag{6.4.8}$$

In this paper only cross section data[2] are used, so that the difference in performance between the parties is constant across constituencies and may therefore be subsumed in the coefficients of (6.4.8). Hence

$$L_j = \alpha + \boldsymbol{\theta}'\mathbf{y}_j \quad j = 1 \ldots H \tag{6.4.9}$$

where the m component vector of parameters, $\boldsymbol{\theta}$, is given by

$$\boldsymbol{\theta} = \beta\boldsymbol{\Gamma}'(\mathbf{x}^k - \mathbf{x}^s) \tag{6.4.10}$$

An alternative and more preferable specification assumes that the bias terms, b_i^{ks}, are distributed according to the bell-shaped Weibull distribution and leads to the logit model

$$l_j = \log(p_j^k/p_j^s) = \mathrm{E}(b_i^{ks}) + (M_j^k - M_j^s) \quad j = 1 \ldots H \tag{6.4.11}$$

and by the argument employed above this reduces to

$$l_j = \mathrm{E}(b_i^{ks}) + \boldsymbol{\varphi}'\mathbf{y}_j \quad j = 1 \ldots H \tag{6.4.12}$$

where the vector $\boldsymbol{\varphi}$ is defined as is $\boldsymbol{\theta}$ in (6.4.10). The logit model satisfies the axioms of independence of irrelevant alternatives, irrelevance of alternative sets and positivity and also ensures that p_j^k is between zero and unity (McFadden, 1973). It has the additional advantages that the distribution of the bias terms is more realistic and that the extension to the multi-party case is trivial (see Chapter 3).

The next section presents the results from estimating (6.4.9) and (6.4.12).

6.5 The empirical results for the attribute model

Before presenting our results we should say a few words about our data. Both models were estimated on data for 177 constituencies during the 1966 British General Election. The choice of the 1966 election was guided by the consideration that in 1966 over 90 per cent of voters chose Labour or Conservative. Hence it was reasonable to simplify the analysis by concentrating on the Labour versus Conservative share of the vote. The 177 constituencies chosen for analysis were all the borough constituencies in Lancashire (46), Yorkshire (34) and London (97) and they shared the characteristic of being urban constituencies in large metropolitan areas.

The basic data sources were Butler and King (1966) and a parliamentary constituency volume of the 1966 census.[3] The latter gave, for each constituency, data on class, unemployment rates, the incidence of owner occupation of dwellings and other variables relevant to party appeal. In particular, for each constituency the proportions in each of six socio-economic groups (employers and managers, professional workers, other non-manual, skilled manual, semi-skilled manual and unskilled manual) were available. Based upon this grouping the definition of 'working class' adopted in this paper is an aggregate of the latter three categories. Similarly the aggregate of the first three categories was defined as 'middle class'. This data had earlier been used by Miller (1977) to study the problem of class-based partisanship although he did not adopt the perspective of this study, which is the role of the economic environment in modifying the class bias of voters.

In the empirical application of the theory of the previous section, the dependent variable is defined as the arithmetic difference in the proportion of votes going to the Labour (ruling) and Conservative (opposition) party in constituency j for the uniform model (L) and as the logarithmic difference for the logit model (l_j).

The vector of attributes of constituency j, y_j, was postulated to have three components:

u_j the unemployment rate in constituency j,
w_j the proportion of economically active and retired males in constituency j, who are working class,
and h_j the proportion of dwellings in constituency j which are owner occupied.

The variable u_j was chosen to represent the local economic performance of the ruling party in constituency j as well as an attribute of constituency j. The choice of w_j and h_j was guided by Butler and Stokes (1974, p. 107), who observed that 'housing may rival occupation in the extent to which it expresses social self-images and economic self-interests . . . In a word, housing probably has more to do with defining the sub-cultures of social classes than all else but occupation itself'.

The estimation of the uniform model (6.4.9) yielded[4]

$$l_j = -0.506 - 4.608u_j - 0.473h_j + 1.528w_j$$
$$\quad (9.83) \quad (6.02) \quad (11.02) \quad (25.5)$$

$$s = 0.093, \quad \bar{R}^2 = 0.862$$

and the estimation of the logit model yielded

$$L_j = -1.043 - 10.178u_j - 1.074h_j + 3.271w_j$$
$$\quad (8.71) \quad (5.71) \quad (10.76) \quad (23.44)$$

$$s = 0.217, \quad \bar{R}^2 = 0.844.$$

Both equations explained over 84 per cent of the variation in the dependent variable and all parameters are well determined. The estimates suggest that constituencies with a high proportion of middle class voters or a high proportion of owner occupiers tended to vote in favour of the Conservative party. On the other hand constituencies with high unemployment rates tended to vote against the Labour party, which could plausibly be interpreted as voting against the ruling administration. There was also a party bias, independent of attributes of the constituencies, against the ruling party. The lead from estimating (6.4.9) evaluated at the mean was 16.3 per cent implying that 58.15 per cent of the votes went to Labour and 41.58 per cent of the votes went to the Conservatives.[5]

In order to avoid non-linearities in subsequent formulations, the remainder of this chapter focuses on the uniform model (6.4.9).

6.6 Voting behaviour within occupational classes

The results of the previous paragraphs indicated that the class composition of a constituency was a major determinant of its voting patterns. Indeed it explains by itself 76.5 per cent of the total variation in the lead. At the same time other attributes (like unemployment rates and the incidence of owner-occupation) also had a significant influence on the lead. Implicit in this formulation however was the assumption that the non-class attributes exerted an influence on constituency voting patterns independently of the class composition of the constituency. Thus, for example, a rise in the incidence of owner occupation would bring about the same changes in the voting lead in constituencies of differing class compositions or, to put the point differently, voters of different class backgrounds would react identically to changes in their non-class attributes. This assumption is not realistic and the purpose now is to relax it by analysing voting patterns within occupational classes.

Let the lead of Labour over Conservative in constituency j among working class voters be defined as

$$l_{j,w} = p_{j,w}^{\mathrm{L}} - p_{j,w}^{\mathrm{C}} \qquad (6.6.1)$$

where $p_{j,w}^{\mathrm{L}}$ and $p_{j,w}^{\mathrm{C}}$ are the proportions of working class voters in constituency j voting Labour and Conservative respectively.

Redefining the vector of attributes as $\mathbf{y}_j = (u_j, h_j)$ and using the argument of Section 6.4 one obtains

$$l_{j,w} = \alpha_w + \boldsymbol{\theta}_w' \mathbf{y}_j \quad j = 1 \ldots H \qquad (6.6.2)$$

where α_w and $\boldsymbol{\theta}_w$ are respectively a measure of party bias and a vector of attribute coefficients among working class voters.

Similarly, one could obtain $l_{j,m}$, the lead among middle class voters in constituency j, as

$$l_{j,m} = \alpha_m + \boldsymbol{\theta}'_m \mathbf{y}_j \quad j = 1 \ldots H \tag{6.6.3}$$

One of the aims of the next section is to test whether or not the vectors of coefficients in (6.6.2) and (6.6.3) differ significantly. Unfortunately it is not possible to estimate (6.6.2) and (6.6.3) directly as the appropriate data on voting patterns within social classes is not available. Consider therefore the accounting identities

$$p_j^{\mathrm{L}} = p_{j,w}^{\mathrm{L}} w_j + p_{j,m}^{\mathrm{L}}(1 - w_j) \tag{6.6.4}$$

$$p_j^{\mathrm{C}} = p_{j,w}^{\mathrm{C}} w_j + p_{j,m}^{\mathrm{C}}(1 - w_j) \tag{6.6.5}$$

Upon taking the difference of p_j^{L} and p_j^{C} one obtains the overall lead of Labour over Conservative in constituency j. It is given by

$$l_j = (\alpha_w - \alpha_m) w_j + (\boldsymbol{\theta}_w - \boldsymbol{\theta}_m)' \mathbf{y}_j w_j + \alpha_m + \boldsymbol{\theta}'_m \mathbf{y}_j \tag{6.6.6}$$

The complete model consists of six equations and is defined by (6.6.2), (6.6.3), (6.6.6) and the three identities $p_{j,w}^{\mathrm{L}} + p_{j,w}^{\mathrm{C}} = 1$, $p_{j,m}^{\mathrm{L}} + p_{j,m}^{\mathrm{C}} = 1$ and $p_j^{\mathrm{L}} + p_j^{\mathrm{C}} = 1$. It explains aggregate voting behaviour $\{p_j^{\mathrm{L}}, p_j^{\mathrm{C}}\}$ and voting behaviour within classes $\{p_{j,w}^{\mathrm{L}}, p_{j,w}^{\mathrm{C}}, p_{j,m}^{\mathrm{L}}, p_{j,m}^{\mathrm{C}}\}$ in each constituency. For example, $p_j^{\mathrm{L}} = 0.5 + 0.5 l_j$ and $p_j^{\mathrm{C}} = 0.5 - 0.5 l_j$. All parameters are identified and may be obtained by ordinary least squares estimation of equation (6.6.6).

6.7 Empirical results from the class model

Estimation of (6.6.6) by ordinary least squares yielded

$$\begin{aligned} l_j = {} & \underset{(6.59)}{1.855 w_j} + \underset{(0.26)}{1.744 u_j w_j} - \underset{(2.86)}{0.905 h_j w_j} - \underset{(3.50)}{0.709} \\ & - \underset{(1.20)}{6.041 u_j} + \underset{(0.43)}{0.090 h_j} \end{aligned}$$

$$s = 0.090, \quad \bar{R}^2 = 0.872$$

The result suggests there is little evidence that the proportion of house owners has a significant effect on the voting behaviour of the middle classes and there is no reason to believe that the impact or perception of the local unemployment rate on the lower and middle classes is different. Re-estimation of equation (6.6.6) with two restrictions, that is the coefficients on h_j and $u_j w_j$ set to zero, yielded

$$l_j = \underset{(32.50)}{1.841 w_j} - \underset{(12.17)}{0.769 h_j w_j} - \underset{(18.21)}{0.700} - \underset{(6.54)}{4.788 u_j}$$

$$s = 0.089, \quad \bar{R}^2 = 0.873$$

Using the likelihood-ratio test to compare the restricted equation with the unrestricted equation gave a $\chi^2(2)$ value of 0.772, so that the null hypothesis (that the two restrictions are validly imposed) could not be rejected at the 5 per cent significance level. The above equation is well determined and explains 87.3 per cent of the

Table 6.1 *Parameter estimates for explaining the lead of Labour over Conservative within classes*

Attribute	Working class	Middle class
party bias	1.141	-0.700
u_j	-4.788	-4.788
h_j	-0.769	-

variation in the lead and has the additional advantage that it may be used to analyse voting patterns within occupational classes. In fact the present equation – the restricted version of (6.6.6) – compares well with the general model (6.4.9) developed in Section 6.4.[6] Unscrambling the coefficient estimates gives rise to the parameters of equations (6.6.2) and (6.6.3) shown in Table 6.1.

Table 6.1 shows that the party bias and the voting response attributed to owner occupied dwellings differ significantly between the two occupational classes, although unemployment affects both classes in the same fashion.[7] The results of Table 6.1 lead to some interesting and plausible conclusions.

Firstly, the pro-Labour bias of the working classes is stronger than the pro-Conservative bias of the middle classes. Secondly, a rise in the level of owner occupation shifts the working class vote away from Labour but leaves the middle class vote unaffected. Presumably home ownership has little effect on middle class voters, since many of the middle class voters already own their own home. This is consistent with survey findings that 'within each of the manual and non-manual occupational groups there remained measurable differences in the party allegiance of those living in council and owner-occupied dwellings' (Butler and Stokes, 1974, p. 109). Finally, constituencies suffering from a high unemployment ratio tended to vote against the ruling (i.e. the Labour) party. This effect is the same for working and middle class voters.

This model is able to predict for each class and for every constituency the proportion of votes going to the Labour and Conservative party, which would not have been possible without the present analysis. Table 6.2 evaluates these proportions for the sample means of the explanatory variables. The results suggest that in the 1966 election for the 177 constituencies considered, on average 91.5 per cent and 8.5 per cent of the middle classes voted Conservative and Labour respectively and 15.9 per cent and 84.1 per cent of the working classes voted Conservative and Labour respectively. The post-sample predictions of the Cambridge constituency are 84.1 per cent, 9.8 per cent and 51.9 per cent of the votes going to the Labour party among working-class voters, middle-class voters and all voters in Cambridge respectively. Since the actual proportion of the votes going to Labour during the 1966 election was 51.2 per cent, the error for Cambridge is only 0.7 per cent.

6.8 A time-series analysis of class-based perceptions

In this section we present a time-series analysis of the proposition that different occupational classes react differently to economic events. This analysis

Table 6.2 *Leads and votes evaluated at the mean for the class model*

$\bar{u}_j$	$\bar{h}_j$	$\bar{w}_j$	$\bar{L}_{j,w}$	$\bar{L}_{j,m}$	$\bar{L}_j$	$\bar{p}_{j,w}^L$	$\bar{p}_{j,m}^L$	$\bar{p}_j^L$
0.02722	0.427	0.652	0.682	−0.830	0.164	0.841	0.085	0.582

and the associated results are derived from Hibbs (1982b). Hibbs considers a model in which the support for the ruling party (as evidenced by a sample of Gallup Poll respondents answering the question 'If there were a General Election tomorrow, how would you vote?') depends on its cumulative performance record with respect to certain economic variables. In assessing past performance, the electorate, it is assumed, employs a geometrically declining weighting scheme. The feature that makes the Hibbs study applicable to the problem of class-based economic perceptions is the fact that there was information on the occupational class of the respondents constituting the sample. This meant that for the three occupational classes considered by Hibbs – non-manual, skilled manual and semi-skilled, and unskilled manual – it was possible to know the proportion within each class expressing support for the ruling party.

The logarithm of the proportion of support expressed by each class divided by 1 minus this proportion was then regressed on a vector of economic variables, the components of which were the unemployment rate, the change in the unemployment rate, the growth rate in per capita real income, the change in the inflation rate and the change in the exchange rate. The equations were estimated from the third quarter of 1962 till the fourth quarter of 1978. The intercept terms of the three equations were allowed to vary over the five governments that prevailed over this period, but the coefficients on the economic variables were not allowed so to vary. The detailed results are reproduced below in Table 6.3.

If the intercept terms of the equations are interpreted as the class-based support for the various governments, independent of the economic performance of these governments, then a major conclusion that emerges from the results is that there is no evidence of a decline in class-based party allegiances.

On the economic variables, there is a considerable difference in the reactions of manual and non-manual respondents to the level of the unemployment rate, with the former group displaying a greater degree of aversion to the unemployment rate. At the same time the change in the unemployment rate exercised the minds of only the semi-skilled and unskilled respondents. The reactions to the growth in per capita real income were similar to that for the unemployment rate, while the three groups displayed an almost identical aversion to changes in the inflation rate.

6.9 Conclusions

This chapter relaxed the assumption that all voters had identical reactions to economic events and considered instead the proposition that differing economic interests among voters might lead them to adopt different views towards a given economic change. In order to do so the theory of qualitative political choice, set

Table 6.3 *Economic influences on political support among occupational groups, 1962:3–1978:4, by weighted least-squares estimates (T = 65)*

	Nonmanual employees, social grades ABC1	Skilled workers, social grade C2	Semi- and unskilled workers, state pensioners, and widows, social grades DE	Support proportion (mean)
Average sample fraction	0.38	0.32	0.30	
Constant terms (a_{jq})				
Macmillan-Home	-0.13 (0.025)[a]	-1.03 (0.035)	-1.43 (0.04)	0.32
Wilson I	-1.10 (0.019)	-0.11 (0.019)	0.078 (0.019)	0.37
Heath	0.12 (0.015)	-0.83 (0.017)	-1.10 (0.017)	0.35
Wilson II	-0.92 (0.043)	0.15 (0.042)	0.36 (0.045)	0.38
Callaghan	-0.73 (0.048)	0.39 (0.044)	0.56 (0.048)	0.36
Lag weight rate of decay (g)	0.88	0.85	0.38	
Economic terms (Z)				Variables (mean)
Unemployment rate (U)	-0.0095 (0.0015)	-0.023 (0.0015)	-0.016 (0.0014)	3.19
Change in unemployment rate $\ln(U_t/U_{t-1}) \times 400$	0.00016 (0.00014)	0.00022 (0.00016)	-0.00061 (0.00016)	6.63
Per capita real income growth rate (R)	0.0032 (0.00094)	0.0085 (0.0009)	0.0055 (0.00090)	2.64
Change in inflation rate $(P_t - P_{t-1})$	-0.016 (0.0051)	-0.017 (0.006)	-0.017 (0.0019)	0.02
Change in exchange rate $(EXR_t - EXR_{t-1})$	0.59 (0.060)	0.71 (0.060)	0.63 (0.062)	-0.03
Fit: x^2/df	7.04	8.24	7.41	
Correlation of actual and fitted proportions	0.98	0.93	0.96	

Note: Data on P'_{jt} for 1966:1 were missing. All percentage rates of change are quarter-on-quarter changes of the logs at annual rates: $\ln(Z_t/Z_{t-1}) \times 400$. Dependent variable in the regressions is the logit: $\ln[P'_{jt}/(1 - P'_{jt})]$. Inflation and real income variables are adjusted for the OPEC supply shocks.
Numbers in parentheses are asymptotic standard errors.

Source: Hibbs (1982b).

out in Chapter 3, was extended so that voting patterns in each constituency were explained in terms of the attributes of that constituency.

The attributes considered were the proportion of owner-occupiers of dwellings in that constituency, its class composition and its unemployment rate. The model was subsequently reformulated to consider the situation where the non-class attributes exerted an influence which was chiefly dependent on the constituency's class composition. The reformulated model also allowed the prediction of voting patterns for two occupational classes. When estimated on data for 177 constituencies for the British General Election of 1966 both models performed well and yielded plausible conclusions, although the model for analysing voting problems within occupational classes was preferred.

It should be emphasised that research in this area is still in its infancy and a great deal more remains to be done. In particular it would be desirable to consider a combination of cross-section and time-series data covering all constituencies over a series of General Elections. This would allow one to consider the influence of changes in national economic events on voting patterns at constituency level. This combination seems very important, because the class perspective developed in this chapter mainly explains the composition of *block* votes and the economic time-series perspective developed in Chapters 3, 4 and 5 mainly explains changes in *marginal* votes. The former has previously been the domain of political scientists, whereas the latter has been the concern of politico-econometricians. The conjunction of both approaches should pave the way for truly interdisciplinary research.

Part II: Votes, ideology and economic policy

7

Political aspects of economic policy formulation

7.1 Introduction

The time has arrived to examine the other side of the political-economic relationship and to enquire whether political considerations play a role in the formulation of a government's economic policy. Much of the literature that deals with the political aspects of economic policy formulation examines the interplay of political and economic forces that combine to generate what is termed the 'political business cycle'. The assumption underlying the presumed existence of such a cycle is that governments by adopting suitable policies are able to influence economic outcomes. Given that these economic outcomes will in turn affect its political popularity, a government interested in re-election may attempt to manipulate the economy so that periods of economic strength occur prior to elections and periods of economic weakness are confined to years when electoral popularity is not so vital.

From this follow two approaches to the theory of economic policy – the optimising and the satisficing approach. The optimising approach is concerned with the way governments behave if they are to optimise on some given political objective. Early studies using the optimising approach focused on the best way a government could exploit politically the short-run inflation-unemployment trade-off and a critical review of this literature is the subject matter of Section 7.3. A major conclusion of that section is that the nature of the exploitation will differ according as to whether it is assumed that the electorate has a memory for past outcomes (see Subsection 7.3.2).

Whether such an exploitation is at all possible depends upon the ability of the government to deceive the electorate or conversely upon the inability of the electorate to perceive the links between politics and the economy. The implications for the economy if the electorate was not naive are examined in Section 7.4.

The political motivation underlying the desire to manipulate the electorate through the economy is usually assumed to be the government's desire to win the next election. The implications of an alternative political objective, that of maximising the uninterrupted length in office, are examined in Section 7.5. It turns out that under such a formulation it is possible that the political aspects of business cycles may not exist.

Apart from formulating policies on political grounds a government may have ideological objectives that may give an independent dimension to its policies. The possibility of conflict between expedience and ideology and the manner in which this may be resolved is the subject of Section 7.6.

The satisficing approach to the formulation of economic policy is concerned with the manner in which governments react *ex post* to an economic or political crisis. A review of the literature which draws attention to the way political considerations affect governments' actual behaviour is contained in Section 7.7. This approach takes the view that governments' satisficing behaviour may be captured by political-economic reaction functions and the primary exponents of this view are the 'Zürich School', whose work is reviewed in Subsection 7.7.2.

Arguing against the possibility of the existence of the political business cycle is the rational expectations school, according to whom there is no room for vote-maximizing policies when agents are rational and possess complete information on the structure of the economy and the nature of the policy rules adopted. Their work is discussed in Section 7.8.

The international evidence on the existence of the political business cycle is reviewed in Section 7.9 and the shortcomings of the existing literature are discussed in Section 7.10. Section 7.11 then concludes the chapter.

A distinguishing feature of the approaches discussed above is that they adopt a restricted view of the political process and depend upon the existence of elections to lend a political flavour to economic policy formulation. An alternative view, derived from Marx, is political in a broader sense in that the mechanism generating business cycles is class conflict with the government aiding the capitalist class and the working class constraining the government's ability to do so. It is to a consideration of this broader view that we first turn in Section 7.2.

7.2 Marxist views on political manipulation of the working class

'The goal of macropolicy is not to eliminate the (business) cycle but to guide it in the interests of the capitalist class.' This quotation from Boddy and Crotty (1975, p. 10) summarises the modern Marxist view of the political business cycle. Marx's own view was that the conflict between labour and capital over their shares of the national income would lead to cyclical booms and slumps. In the expansionary phase of the cycle, employment would rise, the reserve army of the unemployed would diminish and workers would bargain successfully for higher shares of the rising national income. The counterpart of this would be a profits squeeze with the share of profits in national income falling. To end this decline in profits, capitalists would have to take steps to bring the expansionary phase of the cycle to a halt. This they would do by slowing down the rate of capital accumulation so that 'the movement of rise in wages receives a check. The rise of wages therefore is confined within the limits that not only leave intact the foundations of the capitalist system, but also secure its reproduction on a progressive scale' (Marx, 1967, vol. I, p. 620).

Marx's view on the nature of the business cycle did not include the view that the operation of government policy itself generated cycles. In Marx's schema the generation of cycles was entirely in the power of the capitalist class. The recognition that government policies, through a manipulation of expenditure and taxes, would influence the level of employment had to await the birth of Keynesianism. With this recognition grew the assumption among Keynesians that one of the objectives of government policy was the maintenance of full employment in the economy, an assumption, which if true and if capable of being executed, would, of course, imply an end to business cycles.

This assumption was challenged by Kalecki who argued that

> the assumption that a government will maintain full employment in a capitalist economy if it only knows how to do it is fallacious . . . the *maintenance* of full employment would cause social and political changes which would give a new impetus to the opposition of business leaders . . . the class instinct of [business leaders] tells them that lasting full employment is unsound from their point of view and that unemployment is an integral part of the normal capitalist system (Kalecki, 1943, pp. 138–139 and pp. 140–141).

Although Kalecki's views were grounded in Marx's theories of class conflict, Kalecki's reasons for the basis of the conflict were more social than economic. Thus Kalecki argued that the businessman's dislike of continued full employment was based on the fear that under such a regime the self-assurance of the working classes, who could not be fired from their jobs, would grow, with a consequent undermining of the social position of the bosses. In fact, in terms of economic (as opposed to social) self-interest businessmen had no reason to fear continued full employment, for under Kalecki's theory of monopoly pricing businesses could maintain profit margins under full-employment conditions. The implication of the above argument for business cycles was that governments would attempt to maintain full employment but would retreat from this policy whenever periods of high employment were sufficiently protracted to arouse the opposition of the capitalist class.

More recently the orthodox Marxist view of business cycles being generated through class conflict based on a clash of economic interests has been resurrected by Boddy and Crotty (1975). In their analysis, the main concern of capitalists is assumed to be the maximisation of profits and they argue on the basis of post-World War II evidence that macropolicy has served the interests of the capitalist class, that is to say, macropolicy has aided and abetted capitalists in their primary aim of profit maximisation. Organised labour, on the other hand, has merely served as a constraint to the pursuit of the economic interests of the capitalists. Business cycles, in turn, are generated by the twin phenomena of macropolicy serving capitalists and organised labour seeking to constrain this service.

This thesis is based upon the observation that profits are at their highest in the earlier part of the expansion. In the latter part of the expansion, profits come under severe pressure and indeed profits continue to decline during the contraction, thereby sowing the seeds for the destruction of the boom period. Thus, although in an ideal world capitalists would like to avoid recession, a recession is a necessary stage for attaining the high profitable first phase of the expansion and also for avoiding the sustained full-employment dangers of the second phase of the expansion. This view is illustrated in Fig. 7.1 where as the economy moves from recovery to boom (the first and second phases of the expansion) the share of wages in value added falls, reaching a minimum at the turning point. In the boom phase the share of wages rises and continues to rise through the first phase of the recession and is only made to fall when the second phase of the recession is reached. The above

Fig. 7.1 *A Marxist view of the political business cycle*

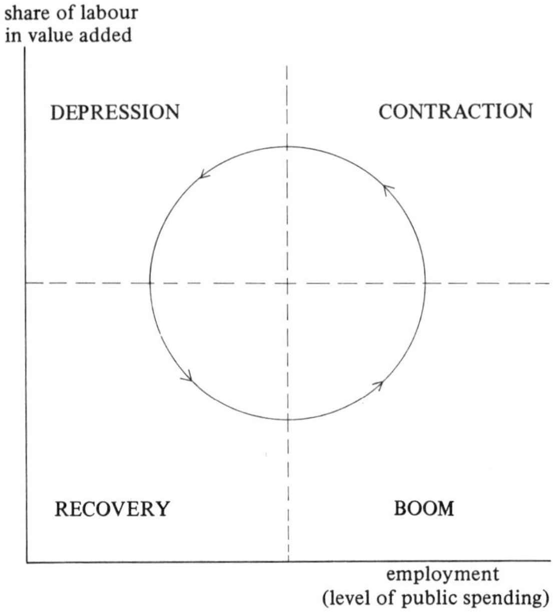

story is very similar to an alternative class struggle interpretation of the business cycle (see Goodwin, 1967; van der Ploeg, 1982e), which assumes full capacity utilisation. In this alternative framework capitalists can undermine the power of the workers by withdrawing machinery and demand for labour during a profit squeeze, but in the case of under-utilisation the capitalists need to be aided by the government to check the bargaining strength of unions (cf. Boddy and Crotty, 1975).

The Marxist view of business cycles is 'political' in a broad sense in that the mechanism generating the cycles is class conflict based on conflict over the division of economic spoils, with the government aiding the capitalist class and organised labour constraining their ability to do so. The more conventional theories of political business cycles adopt a narrower perspective on the political process and depend for the generation of cycles upon the desire of governments, in democratic societies, to be re-elected. It is to such theories that we now turn.

7.3 Political exploitation of the short-run inflation–unemployment trade-off

7.3.1 Purely myopic political welfare optimum

After Kalecki's classical contribution to understanding the political business cycle, there was a long period of neglect of the political aspects of economic policy formulation in the literature. The revival of interest in the political business cycle was due to an interesting paper by Nordhaus (1975). However, Nordhaus did not present his theory in terms of a struggle between social classes

Fig. 7.2 *Political exploitation of the inflation–unemployment trade-off when the electorate has no memory*

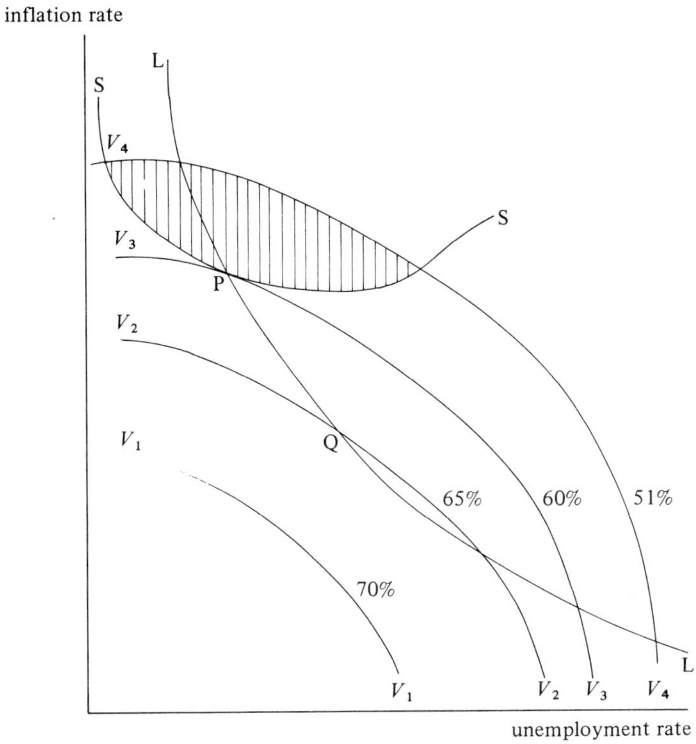

but instead focused on the short-run trade-off between inflation and unemployment. This shift in emphasis is understandable given the debate in the 1960s and early 1970s about how vertical the price-expectations augmented Phillips curve was and by how much the short-run Phillips curve can be shifted (see Subsection 8.8.2).

Nordhaus (1975) assumed that the electorate is only concerned about the level of unemployment and the inflation rate and praises/blames the government for the outcome of these two variables only. Other factors such as disposable income, taxes, balance of payments and social class structure are ignored. Fig. 7.2 shows the iso-success contours V_1V_1, V_2V_2, V_3V_3 and V_4V_4, where each one corresponds to a particular value of the current measure of political success (cf. m_t^k in Chapter 3). It is clear that, due to the convex shape of these contours, the electorate dislikes both unemployment and inflation and also is prepared to substitute some additional jobs for an increase in the inflation rate. As the contours move outwards from the origin the current measure of political success becomes worse. When the electorate does not have any memory, in the terms of Chapter 3 the discount rate is infinite (or $\lambda = 0$), the current measure of political success is a proxy for the lead of the government over the main opposition party and the iso-success contours correspond to *iso-vote contours.* This particular case is also called the case of a *purely myopic electorate* and implies that the voters judge the government's performance only by conditions in the election year.

We now make the assumption that the incumbent government wishes to maximise its lead over the main opposition party on election eve. The idea behind this assumption is that a government depends on re-election for its survival and will do its utmost to secure a victory at the forthcoming election. The government is assumed to be able to manipulate public demand, by varying the rate of taxation or implementing public works programmes, to attain any level of unemployment it desires. The unemployment rate may then be regarded as an instrument of economic policy.

However a government is constrained by the actions of the private sector agents. In our case these actions are represented by the price-expectations augmented Phillips curve, which says that the rate of wages inflation depends negatively on the unemployment rate and positively on the expected rate of price inflation (see equation (8.8.13) in Chapter 8). The rationale behind this behavioural hypothesis is that when there is a large pool of unemployed workers the power of the employed workers to press for high wage increases diminishes and that trade unions wish to maintain the *expected* real income of their members. In the long run there is a stable trade-off between inflation and unemployment, but in the short term the trade-off shifts because of changes in the expected inflation rate (see also Subsection 8.8.3). Fig. 7.2 also gives the long-run Phillips curve LL and a short-run curve SS. The long-run curve is steeper, since in the long run the trade unions anticipate inflation correctly.

When the electorate does not have any memory and judges the government only by its current performance, the incumbent political party chooses the level of the unemployment rate that secures the maximum number of votes. This is achieved when the short-run marginal rate of substitution between inflation and unemployment is the same for both the private sector *and* for the government, that is where the short-run Phillips curve is tangential to an iso-success contour. The resulting optimum P is called the *purely myopic political welfare optimum* and is attained on election eve only. When $V_3 V_3$ corresponds to at least 50 per cent of the votes (in a two-party system), the government will have secured itself another term in office. In actual fact the government usually has some scope for discretionary policy, since when $V_4 V_4$ corresponds to the political lead necessary to secure re-election (say 51 per cent of the votes) then the shaded area in Fig. 7.2 shows the combinations of inflation and unemployment that will secure re-election. The discretionary room may be used for implementing ideology (cf. Section 7.6), but it seems likely given the many uncertainties surrounding the views on economic behaviour that a government will opt for the vote-maximising policy just to be sure of survival.

7.3.2 Political welfare optimum when the electorate remembers

From the empirical work in Chapters 4 and 5, it is clear however that the electorate also judges a government by its past record (see equation (3.4.1) in Chapter 3). In this case the lead of the government on election eve is a weighted average of the current measures of political success over the preceding election period. The weights increase towards election eve, since the voters discount past

Fig. 7.3 *The optimal political business cycle*

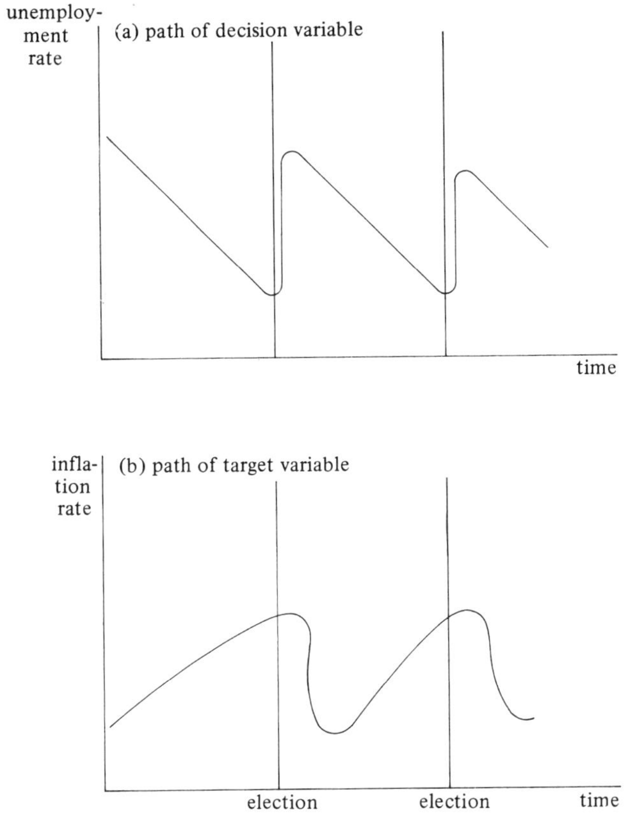

performance. This implies that the government in the beginning of its regime faces a forward-looking vote function so that the government effectively employs a forward-looking rather than a backward-looking discount rate. As before the government is assumed to maximise votes and weigh the future more heavily than the present. This 'upcounting' of the future may be likened to Pigou's defective telescopic faculty (Nordhaus, 1975).

Nordhaus shows that the optimal outcome is a political business cycle of the following form. Immediately after the election the government raises unemployment to a high level in order to fight inflation and depress inflationary expectations. The rationale for this policy is that it acts like an 'investment' by shifting the short-run Phillips curve towards the origin for the latter years of the election period. Towards election eve unemployment is gradually decreased at the expense of an increase in actual inflation. The upshot of it is that the government attempts to deceive the electorate towards election eve by having a low expected and a high actual inflation rate and thereby lumbers the next administration with the inflationary consequences of this myopic policy. On election eve the government has secured the lowest unemployment rate and the highest inflation rate. The outcome on election eve corresponds to the purely myopic political welfare optimum, because on election eve the government does not care about the future at all and is wholeheartedly devoted to winning the election. This cycle repeats itself for each election period and is illustrated in Fig. 7.3. The inflation rate rises over the election period and follows a much smoother path than the unemployment rate due to the gradual adaptation to changes in the costs of living.

The existence of a Nordhaus-type political business cycle depends on three essential assumptions. The first assumption is that the government must exploit the dynamic properties of the economic system, which in the Nordhaus model are the lags in the formation of price expectations. The second is that voters are essentially backward-looking and do not contemplate the consequences of the government's policy for periods following the election. This assumption is relaxed in the next section. The third assumption is that the government is myopic in the sense that it only cares about the number of votes at the forthcoming election. When the government is fairly sure of winning the next election it may already start 'investing' by depressing inflationary expectations even further in order to secure victory at the election after the next. The consequences of the government having a time horizon longer than the next election are discussed in Section 7.5.

7.4 Strategic behaviour of the electorate

The type of political decision making discussed in the previous section deceives the voters and therefore relies on a naive evaluation of the incumbent political party by the electorate. In other words the electorate is presumed to know what it likes, but to fail to understand (and take account of) the interactions between politics and the economy. A more strategic electorate would not only care about the track record of the various political parties, but would also penalise any undesirable actions occurring after the forthcoming election. It is interesting to investigate if when a government took account of a strategic electorate it would implement the *social* optimal policies. The purpose of this section is to examine the actions the electorate can undertake in order to eliminate the political business cycle.

One way of forcing a government to undertake a non-myopic policy is for the electorate to withdraw its support when the government attempts to implement a vote-maximising strategy. Such a strategic tactic corresponds to the electorate changing its preferences *on* election eve (see MacRae, 1977), that is increasing the importance of inflation and/or reducing the importance of unemployment in the vote function relevant on election eve. The result of this tactic is that economic cycles caused by the government are penalised, since the government is persuaded to deflate demand so as to have the same outcome on election eve as after the election. In other words the government is forced to act as if it were a benevolent dictator with an infinite time horizon. The success of such a strategic tactic requires a strategic vote decision and complete information about the political-economic game being available to both the electorate and the government. The required change in the pattern of voting could be induced by the media, which has the advantage that the government would also be informed and have the opportunity to modify any myopic actions. When the tactic succeeds the economy remains on the purely myopic political welfare optimum at all periods in time.

As far as the electorate is concerned, there is a trade-off between conventional and strategic voting. The former causes economic instability, whereas the latter puts the economy at the purely myopic welfare optimum with relatively high inflation and low unemployment. It is not clear *a priori* whether voters prefer stability or short sightedness.

The next section will show however that a government might avoid myopic decision making when the objective of vote maximisation at the forthcoming election is abandoned.

7.5 Maximising the uninterrupted length in office

It is not clear whether it is advisable for a government to maximise votes at a forthcoming election when it also aspires to win the election after a possible second term in office. When the government has some political slack at a forthcoming election, it may prefer not to create a pre-election boom, in order to avoid the inflationary consequences during a possible second term in office and thereby spoil its chances of re-election a second time round. The same argument applies when the government is confident of winning the first and the second election, since then it will neither create a pre-election boom for the first nor for the second election, in order not to spoil the chances for the third election. The above argument may be summarised by stating that a government sure of re-election has no reason to value the current election period more highly than future election periods, except for the usual 'upcounting' of the future, and should therefore take account of the current and all future election periods. An implication of this argument is that a government that is certain of winning all future elections has no incentive to maximise votes or to introduce a political business cycle and a government that is not sure of winning all future elections must take account of its *re-election chances.*

Frey and Ramser (1976) suggested that for a non-myopic government a more appropriate objective than maximising votes at the next election may be maximising the expected uninterrupted length in office. This requires the shares of votes cast in favour of the government (see Chapter 3) to be interpreted as the probability of winning an election, which requires a minor modification of the theory developed in Chapter 3.[1] When the electorate suffers from complete memory loss (cf. Subsection 7.3.1), Frey and Ramser show that the optimal outcome is to set the economy at a *social* welfare optimum with a *backward-looking discount rate equal to the probability of not being re-elected.* Thus by employing the non-myopic objective of maximising the uninterrupted length in office, a government becomes backward-looking rather than forward-looking and therefore discounts the future as in the derivation of the conventional social welfare optimum (see Phelps, 1967). In terms of Fig. 7.2 the government chooses the point Q where the marginal rate of substitution between inflation and unemployment for the electorate equals a constant somewhere in between the slope of the short-run and long-run wage equation. Hence the optimal outcome is no longer purely myopic in democratic systems and there is no recurring political business cycle any more.

The above ignored any utility derived from returning to power after a period out of office, but the government may well value a return to office after a period in opposition. Considerations of this type may alter the behaviour of an outgoing administration. For example, a government faced with the prospect of losing the next election may prefer to ruin the economy in order to leave the incoming administration worse off and thereby increase its own chances of winning the election after the next. The government may find it worthwhile to implement an expansionary demand management package in a desperate attempt to saddle the opponent with very high inflationary expectations. Obviously, a proper analysis of this phenomenon requires a careful consideration of issues of blame, as the electorate may well see through the game and penalise the outgoing administration accordingly.

7.6 Frustration of long-term ideology due to re-election efforts

The political business cycles discussed in Sections 7.3–7.5 assumed that the incumbent political party, the government, seeks to maximise the probability of winning the expected plurality at the forthcoming election or alternatively to maximise the uninterrupted length in office. This formulation is not entirely realistic, since a government may have ideological goals which are in conflict with the values revealed by the electorate in the process of voting. For example, an extreme Conservative administration may seek to minimise the intervention of the state in the private sector economy as much as possible in order to promote efficiency even when the electorate wishes otherwise. Alternatively, a Labour government may reflate the economy at the expense of an increase in inflation in an attempt to satisfy its own ideology or to serve its 'clients', the working class voters.

A more realistic model may therefore be obtained by postulating a government which maximises its own ideology, which may be interpreted as party utility, subject to a number of constraints to ensure re-election. In this formulation the electorate evaluates the government in a retrospective manner whereas the government evaluates its own ideological welfare in a prospective manner. The optimal strategy for a government maximising ideology subject to re-election constraints depends on a number of factors. A future election is called a *bottle-neck* election when the government today judges the chances of winning that election unlikely unless it engages in a strategy of 'buying votes' by implementing a popular policy. When there are no future bottle-neck elections, the government is sure of staying in office and can implement its own ideology without having to worry about political survival. This case seems unlikely for most Western democracies, but some might argue that this is the situation in certain Eastern European or Latin American countries without (or with 'no choice') elections. When the forthcoming election is neither a bottle neck nor a guaranteed success, the government realises no policy will persuade the electorate to offer it another term in office. The government may then implement its ideology, because re-election prospects are bleak anyway, or alternatively may adopt a *kamikaze* strategy of ruining the economy in order to spoil the chances for the opposition party of gaining a second term in office. Some political commentators thought during 1981 that this was the strategy of Mrs Thatcher. In some cases a government faced with a prospective political death may in a desperate attempt to gain votes appeal to the nation's pride and engage in warfare. Some would argue that this was a major motive for both Argentina and the United Kingdom during the 1982 conflict over the Falkland Islands. To the student of political economy the case of bottle-neck elections is presumably more interesting and we will now turn to a discussion of this case.

The problem for the *bottle-neck election problem* may be decomposed, for analytical purposes, into finding first the post-election and then the pre-election strategy. After the bottle-neck election votes are not considered important, hence the political weight is zero and the optimal (equilibrium) strategy is simply the ideological welfare optimum. This yields the outcome on the morning after the bottle-neck election. The derivation of the pre-election strategy yields a shadow price for the re-election constraint, which shows the increase in ideological welfare the government obtains due to a relaxation of the required share of votes at the forthcoming election. Chapter 9 will derive the pre-election strategy more formally for a specific model, but here we can say something on the general nature of the pre-election strategy. The shadow price on popularity increases with time, so that towards the bottle-neck election the importance of the re-election objective increases relative to the ideology objective. It is therefore optimal for the government to pursue a fairly ideological policy at the beginning of the election period and progressively to adjust its strategy in order to gain votes as election eve approaches (cf. Frey and Lau, 1968).

7.7 Satisficing approaches to government behaviour

7.7.1 Critique of optimal political–economic policy formulation

It may be argued that a government is unlikely to formulate the type of political–economic strategies discussed in Sections 7.3–7.6 for at least three reasons (cf. Frey, 1978a, b). Firstly, the derivation of *optimal* political–economic strategies is for most practical problems a complicated task and one cannot expect a government to be able to 'optimise the economy'. We think this argument is no longer valid since the advent of excellent digital computer technology and the availability of algorithms to perform the numerical optimisation of long-term (social or political) welfare criteria subject to large-scale nonlinear, simultaneous, dynamic econometric models and inequality constraints on economic or political target variables (see UK Treasury, 1978; Fair, 1975; van der Ploeg, 1982a, b, c). Secondly, the assumption of *ex ante* policy formulation is questionable for many governments. Instead a government is more likely to carry on with established plans until a crisis arises, so that economic policy should be seen as an *ex post* reaction to the violation of economic or political targets. This view implies that when the target variables move into undesirable zones, and not before, the authorities attempt to remedy the situation in a Pavlovian spirit. This *ex post* formulation of economic policy may also be found in the feedback engineering (or reaction function) approach to the theory of economic policy (see the classic works of Tustin, 1954, and Phillips, 1954), although these approaches typically have a normative character whereas the idea of political economics is to provide a positive explanation of government behaviour. Also, the feedback formulation usually restricts the acceptable zone of the target variables to one desirable value only because of the symmetry assumptions employed. Thirdly, the government may not possess the required information, or have conflicting evidence on the present and future behaviour of the economy and the electorate. In such a case the government may prefer to adapt its policies to changing economic and political circumstances.

Similar arguments have previously been raised against neo-classical approaches to the theory of the firm (e.g. by Simon, 1952; Cyert and March, 1963) and the optimisation of macro-economic policy (e.g. Mosley, 1976), which resulted in the *behavioural* or *satisficing* approach to the formulation of economic policy. Satisficing is based on the sequential exploration of alternatives for the alleviation of a crisis, where the definition of a crisis is flexible and relaxed when aspiration levels have not been met in the past.

The remainder of this section discusses the implications of the behavioural approach to political economics.

7.7.2 The Zürich School

The primary objective of a government is to promote its own ideology. However, a government must also take actions to remain in office, since in opposition it cannot implement its own ideology. A crisis is then defined as a situation where re-election is judged unlikely. A government pursues its own ideology in periods of satisfactory popularity, but when popularity is judged to be too low the government implements policies that please the electorate. The aspiration levels for popularity might be flexible, since just after an election low popularity is considered less serious than on election eve. In practice a government's ideology may also be frustrated by legal constraints, conflict with the state bureaucracy (civil servants) and efforts to maintain the feasibility of key economic target variables (such as the balance of payments or the public sector borrowing requirement).

In the light of these comments, it has been suggested that a government may adjust its policy instruments (taxes, subsidies, public spending, *etcetera*) according to a three-tier political–economic reaction function (e.g. Frey, 1978a, b, or Frey and Schneider, 1978a). The first component is only active when there is a popularity deficit and usually involves reflationary measures such as cutting taxes or implementing public works. The implicit assumption underlying such a strategy is that the popularity deficit is caused by too high unemployment or a too low growth in disposable income rather than a balance of payments crisis or too much inflation, since the latter two factors would require deflationary measures. In other words such a simple vote-satisficing strategy typically fails to take account of the cause of the popularity crisis. The second component of the political–economic reaction function is active when there is scope for discretionary policy, that is when there is a popularity surplus. A Conservative administration may cut public spending and taxes, whereas a Labour government may take the opportunity to increase taxes to finance an expansion of the state. The third component of the political–economic policy rule is active regardless of the government's popularity, since it captures purely economic factors. For example, the unemployment benefit component of public spending may rise when the unemployment level or, assuming that the benefit rate is related to the private sector wage rate, average earnings rise. The other components of public spending may rise when unemployment escalates, in order to reflate the economy and create more jobs. These two causes of public spending increases represent respectively cost factors and stabilisation factors. It may be argued that when unemployment becomes a problem this will manifest itself in a popularity crisis, as a loss of jobs immediately affects the welfare of the electorate, so that a government only reflates the economy in order to secure more jobs when there is a political crisis. Perhaps a better example of stabilisation is a government deflating the economy when there is a balance of payments crisis, since the level of foreign reserves does not directly influence the welfare of voters. Even here there is an indirect effect upon economic policy, since in Chapter 5 we found that the electorate sometimes does consider the balance of payments in judging the government's performance.

7.8 Rational expectations *versus* the political business cycle

The foregoing sections rely on a naive evaluation of the government's record by the electorate. However it has been pointed out that there is no scope for such vote-maximising policies when agents are rational and possess complete information about the structure of the economy and the policy rule adopted:

> Incumbent governments cannot, even if they so desire, regularly manufacture booms during the latter portion of their elected terms. Prices may be bid up and inventories drawn down, but output and employment will be unaffected. The argument assumes (i) that departures of the unemployment rate from its natural level are initiated by expectational errors and (ii) that expectations are formed rationally in the sense of Muth. Under these conditions, Phillips-type relations may exist but will not be exploitable by monetary and fiscal authorities: regular attempts by the authorities to manufacture election-time prosperity will be anticipated by private consumers and firms, and the real effects negated. (McCallum, 1978, p. 504)

The idea is that manipulation of votes will be fully anticipated and exactly offset, except for an unbiased and uncorrelated forecast error, by changes in the actions of the private sector. This argument holds whether voters are backward-looking or not.

It should be said that under the twin assumptions of the New Classical School, the natural rate and the rational expectations hypothesis, *any* type of policy rule is ineffective. The New Classical School argues on the basis of an uninhibited belief in the self-regulating market economy that it is *impossible* for any policy systematically to alter the outcome of real variables and that the effect of *any* demand management package is likely to lead to accelerating inflation and interest rates. However, when the private sector agents do not have complete information, when markets do not clear instantaneously, when models are nonlinear or when economic policy affects the natural rates, the government does have an impact on real outcomes and vote-maximising (and other) strategies become feasible again. This breakdown of the policy neutrality proposition is further explored in Section 9.7 of Chapter 9.

7.9 International empirical evidence

A glance at the development of the world economy during the years 1979–1982 suggests casual evidence for the Marxian view of the political business cycle. During the late sixties and seventies most of the capitalist economies experienced a wages explosion, the strength of trade unions increased considerably and the share of profits was squeezed. This led to rampant inflation and large public sector budget deficits, which provided an ideal argument of persuasion for the big corporations. Even in France under the socialist government led by Mitterrand and in West Germany under Schmidt the government decided to deflate the economy in order to control a 'wage explosion'. The United Kingdom under Mrs Thatcher and the USA under Reagan adopted similar strategies. Since most capitalist economies acted in the interests of the capitalists, in certain cases even at the expense of political popularity, the experience of the last three years provides some evidence for the Marxian views. More detailed evidence is provided by Feiwel (1974) and Boddy and Crotty (1975).

Both Nordhaus (1975) and Frey (1978a, Chapter 10) provide some casual observations on the optimal political business cycle discussed in Section 7.3, by checking whether the optimal partisan policy will lead to a political business cycle, with unemployment and deflation in early periods followed by an inflationary boom as elections approach (Nordhaus, 1975, p. 185). Nordhaus checks whether inflation and employment rise (fall) in the latter (early) part of an election period on annual data for the period 1947–1972 for nine countries. He finds there is no evidence for a political cycle in Australia, Canada, Japan and the UK, modest evidence for France and Sweden and marked evidence for Germany, New Zealand and the USA. He notes that the concern with the balance of payments in the UK may have swamped the political cycle. Frey (1978a, Chapter 10) finds that in twenty-one out of twenty-seven democracies over the period 1960–1972 the growth rate in real disposable income was higher in election years than in non-election years. The clearest evidence was for Israel. These results suggest the importance of examining the vote-winning impact of cutting taxes (cf. Chapter 9).

MacRae (1977) provides more rigorous evidence for the USA by casting the Nordhaus (1975) model in a discrete-time framework and explicitly estimating the parameters of the price-expectations augmented Phillips curve in conjunction with the parameters of the vote functions. MacRae (1977) finds that during the Kennedy–Johnson and Johnson election periods there is evidence for the myopic version of the optimal political business cycle (see Section 7.3) and during the Eisenhower and Nixon election periods there is evidence for a strategic electorate (see Section 7.4). Chrystal and Alt (1979b) repeat MacRae's exercise for the UK during the years 1951–1974 and reject the myopic version of the optimal political business in favour of a strategic electorate or a naive hypothesis regarding government policy. This disappointing evidence does not rule out however the possibility of a different version of the optimal political cycle. For example, real disposable income or the balance of payments may be important in deciding on the optimal political–economic policy (see Chapter 9) or the price-expectations augmented Phillips curve may be inappropriate.

The problem with the empirical literature discussed so far is that it is impossible to distinguish between purely economic and political–economic strategies, since data on popularity or votes cast in favour of the government are not employed. Thus it is not clear in the exercises of Nordhaus (1975), MacRae (1977), McCallum (1978) or Chrystal and Alt (1979b) whether they are simply revealing the purely economic preferences of the government or whether they have found evidence for political effects upon economic policy.

This problem does not arise in the work on political–economic reaction functions (see Section 7.7), since here one considers directly the effects of a popularity crisis on the *instruments* rather than on the *targets* of economic policy. Furthermore, the reaction function approaches distinguish between ideology and re-election. Frey and Schneider (1978a, b; 1981) provide empirical evidence for the USA and UK of political–economic reaction functions. In particular they find that changes in taxes and different components of public expenditure are significantly affected by ideology considerations (size of the state), re-election motives (measured by the popularity deficit), attempts to stabilise the economy (for controlling the balance of payments) and cost considerations (wage bill of civil servants and unemployed). Wright (1974) provides similar evidence for the USA. Frey and Schneider (1981) extend the political–economic reaction function approach to central bank behaviour and Gärtner (1981) to political incomes policies. Chrystal and Alt (1979a, b; 1981a, b) criticise the influence of political factors on economic policy and claim to have found evidence for a simple 'permanent income' model of government expenditures.

McCallum (1978) examines an unemployment time series for the US for the period 1948–1974 and finds that the series fits a third-order autoregressive process. He then shows that the inclusion of dummy variables representing the electoral cycle does not improve the explanatory power significantly, which provides some support for the rational expectations hypothesis. However Minford and Peel (1982) argue that future expectations in supply functions and asset effects in demand functions interact to give the authorities leverage on (the natural levels of) output and provide some evidence for the non-neutrality of economic policy under the rational expectations hypothesis in the UK, 1959–1975. They find that popularity depends on the expected levels and variances of inflation and disposable income and that these economic variables feed back into economic policy. Both these studies are open to the observational equivalence critique,[2] since political popularity does not feature *explicitly* in the reaction functions and purely economic rules cannot therefore be distinguished from political–economic rules.

7.10 Shortcomings of the previous literature

The literature and ideas on political aspects of economic policy formulation discussed so far in this chapter provide many valuable insights into the behaviour of governments. In particular the orthodox view of a government as a benevolent dictator implementing socially-optimal policies turns out to be invalid, since a government's strategy is very much constrained by its ideology and its attempts to secure re-election. Perhaps the major lesson to be drawn from the existing literature on political economics is that we should abandon the idea of a normative theory of economic policy and replace it by more positive explanations of government behaviour. Instead of asking what a government *ought* to do, we are interested in how a government *actually* behaves.

Nevertheless we feel that the existing theory of political economics is only in its infancy and still requires much further development. The remainder of this section therefore evaluates the useful insights and the shortcomings of the previous literature and indicates promising areas for further research.

The argument underlying the Marxian view of the political business cycle is that when there has been a sustained boom period, the bargaining power of workers increases at the expense of the influence of firms, profits are squeezed and big businesses persuade the government, by pointing at the disastrous consequences of rampant inflation, to deflate the economy in order to teach the trade unions a lesson. Eventually profits recover, investment and employment increase and the next boom period commences (see Section 7.2). There are only a few papers on this type of Marxian conflict between workers and capitalists. The analysis seems to rely on a 'coalition' between big business and government, which is essential because of the small number of capitalists represented at the polls. The two main lessons to be drawn from these studies are firstly that the agents in an economy may well have competing interests and secondly that a government does not necessarily represent the various interest groups in an economy equally. In the Marxian view of the political process capitalists and workers have conflicting interests, that is they are both interested in a certain share of the cake, whilst the cake may be too small to satisfy both groups, and the government represents the interests of firms relatively more than the interests of workers. However, other examples of non-proportional representation of conflicting interests exist.

For example, the interests of private sector workers and state sector workers may be contradictory, since the latter group might prefer an expansion of state projects to improve job security or higher wages whereas the first group might not be prepared to pay the corresponding increase in taxes. A similar argument might hold for people dependent on the state for their income (pensioners, unemployed, *et cetera*). The above ideas have led van Winden (1983) to develop the interest function approach to political economics. This approach says essentially that a government takes a weighted average of the preferences of the different interest groups[3] in an economy, where the preferences of each interest group depend on the disposable income, state spending and employment enjoyed by a particular group. Minford and Peel (1982) implicitly also adopt the interest function approach, since they consider Conservative voters to be primarily interested in inflation, Labour voters to be interested in real disposable income, floating voters to be interested in both, and a government to employ a weighted combination of the preferences of the above interest groups. Obviously, the particular weighting chosen by a government depends both on its ideology and on its desire to maximise votes and may vary over time.[4] Van Winden (1983) suggests the use of the method of revealed preferences to unscramble the weighting scheme chosen in practice.

Unfortunately, the conventional theories discussed in Sections 7.3–7.8 ignore the insights of the Marxist view and the interest function approach. They typically still treat the electorate as a group with homogeneous preferences and thereby ignore issues of conflict and representation by the government. Further empirical work (cf. Chapter 6) and theory based on the importance of different interest groups is badly needed in political economics.

A related criticism of political economics (as for example surveyed in Frey, 1978a, b) is that the relationship between the different components of the public sector received inadequate attention. It seems proper to separate the public sector into the part which does depend on re-election for survival and the other part which does *not* depend on the electorate for its survival. The first part consists of the government (prime minister and other ministers) formed by the incumbent political party and perhaps some 'political' civil service appointments. The second part includes most of the civil servants and perhaps the monetary authorities. For convenience we will denote these two parts of the public sector by the government and state bureaucracy, respectively.[5] Although the literature surveyed in this chapter proposed various theories regarding the behaviour of the government and although the public choice literature (e.g. Niskanen, 1971; Mueller, 1979) has analysed certain aspects of the state bureaucracy, the conflicting interests between these components of the public sector have so far been ignored in the literature.

Previous studies of the *optimal* political business cycle (see Sections 7.3–7.5) focus on the political trade-off between inflation and unemployment. The approach adopted is somewhat simplistic, since the effects of real disposable income, taxation or state spending on electoral popularity are ignored and the policy instrumentation required to attain the vote-maximising strategy is not provided. This literature may therefore benefit from casting it within a complete macroeconomic framework. The emphasis on targets rather than instruments implies that empirical testing of this type of hypothesis is difficult, since these studies do not distinguish between revealing the preferences of a government and establishing a link between political popularity and economic policy (see Section 7.9). The satisficing approaches to political economics (see Section 7.7) focus on the instruments of economic policy and therefore are easier to test empirically. However the satisficing approaches are somewhat *ad hoc*, since the various reaction functions are specified independently of each other. This implies that the conflict between the state bureaucracy and government receives no attention and that the structure of economic policy does not anticipate *how* a popularity crisis is caused. Typically, public spending is raised when there is a popularity deficit, although this is hardly likely to be the correct action when the lack of popularity is caused by a balance of payments crisis or rampant inflation rather than high levels of unemployment. This argument suggests that existing approaches to political economics might benefit from first analysing the theoretical implications of the adopted political–economic system of reaction functions within a complete macroeconomic model (see Chapters 8 and 9 and van der Ploeg, 1982d), and second, using the information thus obtained in empirical work.

7.11 Conclusions

This chapter has argued for abandoning the view, prevalent in the literature on the normative theory of economic policy, of a government promoting social welfare in a benevolent manner. Instead we wish for a positive theory of government behaviour, where the government is treated as a political animal with its own preferences determined by ideology and the desire to be re-elected. We argued that a useful insight obtained from the Marxian view of the political process (Section 7.2) is the necessity of separating the electorate and the rest of the economy into conflicting interest groups and of allowing for the fact that a particular government promotes the various interests according to its own preferences. In addition the role of the state bureaucracy, the complementary part of the public sector, requires more attention. Existing operational theories of the political business cycle (Sections 7.3–7.8) badly need to be extended to allow for conflicting interest in the economy (cf. Chapter 6). Also the existing theories need to be formulated within a full-scale macroeconomic model, so that implications for key outcomes (balance of payments, disposable income, inflation, unemployment, etc.) of the political–economic strategies can be traced.

This job is performed in Chapters 8 and 9, which are more technical and may be omitted at first reading. However the macroeconomist may find these chapters useful reading, since Chapter 8 presents a complete macroeconomic model for a small open economy with exogenous government policy and Chapter 9 provides a variety of approaches to choosing the macroeconomic model with a state bureaucracy and political–economic strategies. In particular, Chapters 8 and 9 discuss the implications of political extensions for policy effectiveness and for stability of a macroeconomic model.

The final chapter of the book draws upon the theoretical ideas presented in Chapters 7, 8 and 9 to discuss the empirical aspects of political–economic policy formulation in the UK.

8

Macroeconomic analysis of a small open economy

8.1 Introduction

The concern of this book is the political implications of economic management. In articulating these implications we have made repeated references to a variety of economic variables – unemployment, inflation, income growth, balance of payments – that may be of concern to the electorate. However, in doing so, our views on the workings of the economy have remained muted. The nature of our views would determine the relationships between the different economic variables (or at least the degree of indeterminacy would be made explicit) and this in turn would shed light on the potential effectiveness of government policy and the constraints under which such policy would have to operate.

This silence on the nature of the economy (that formed the backdrop to our discussions) was largely deliberate. Our concern so far has been with the effect of economic outcomes on electoral popularity; thus, for example, we inquired about the consequences that a government's achievements with respect to unemployment, inflation, growth etc., had on its standing with voters. Since concern was primarily with outcomes, the question of what economic policies led to these outcomes did not arise. In addition, two further important questions about government behaviour remained unanswered. The time has come both to ask and to provide an answer to these two questions.

The first question is whether a government could have performed better with respect to economic and electoral outcomes by pursuing alternative policies. The next chapter is devoted to answering this question. The second question is whether the government actually attempts to manipulate the economy so as to enhance its popularity at election periods. The answer to this question is the subject of Chapter 10. It is obvious, however, that the answers to both these questions depend upon a knowledge of the channels through which economic policies influence and determine economic outcomes. The purpose of this chapter is to provide a framework for analysing the economy without political feedbacks. The strategy for doing so is to attempt to build a step-by-step picture of the economy.

The next section looks at the domestic product market. This is the home market in which goods (food, clothes, cars etc.) are traded and is in contrast to money markets where financial instruments (bonds, equities etc.) are traded. In the tradition of macroeconomic theory, we identify and analyse the different sorts of demand (from consumers, business, government and foreign buyers) for domestic products. This investigation is important because the levels of domestic output and employment depend crucially on the level of demand for domestic products.

Section 8.3 investigates behaviour in the domestic money market. Again the emphasis is on demand but this time it is the demand for money that people wish to hold both to finance current transactions (the transaction motive) and to take advantage of market movements (the speculative motive). It turns out that there is an intimate connection between the product and money markets. Income levels – determined initially through the demand for domestic products – determine the volume of transactions that a given stock of money is required to finance and this in turn determines the rate of interest. This rate, in turn, feeds back into the product market by influencing the levels of demand. An integrated analysis of the product and money markets (known as the IS–LM model) is provided in Section 8.4 and, in the context of this integrated model, Section 8.5 examines the effects of altering tax rates and/or levels of government spending.

The complications that arise when trade with other countries is considered are considered in Section 8.6, first in terms of the current account and then in terms of the capital account. Transactions in goods and services for current consumption purposes are recorded in the current account and transactions in goods and services for investment purposes are recorded in the capital account. An important conclusion that emerges from the analysis of this section is that the consequences of government policy become more unpredictable. This theme is pursued in Section 8.7 where the implications of the manner in which government debt is financed – whether through printing more money or through selling more bonds – are examined.

The important question of price and wage formation is considered in Section 8.8. The first part of this section examines the determinants – excess demand, domestic wages, foreign prices – of domestic prices. The next part of the section analyses the process of wage formation through the mechanism of the 'price-augmented Phillips curve'. This curve implies that the rate of wage inflation depends (inversely) upon the prevailing level of unemployment and (positively) upon the expected rate of price inflation. This relationship, simple though it is, has powerful consequences for the effectiveness of government policy. It turns out that this effectiveness depends crucially upon whether workers demand or do not demand complete compensation for expected price increases. It should be pointed out that the 'Phillips curve' view is not the only hypothesis to be put forward to explain the process of wage formation. Other explanations such as the 'real wage resistance' hypothesis (whereby workers try to attain a target growth rate in real wages) also exist (see Tarling and Wilkinson, 1977). We have emphasized the 'Phillips curve' hypothesis because it is the most common view and the one around which major macroeconomic controversies rage. In addition it seems particularly relevant to the experience of the last few years in most Western economies. The different aspects of the economy are put together as a complete picture in Section 8.9.

8.2 The domestic product market

Demand for domestic products comes from a variety of sources – from domestic households and businesses, from government and from foreign buyers – and in equation (8.2.1) below the total demand for domestic products, Z, is broken down into component parts:

$$Z = C^d + I^d + G^d + X = H^d + G^d + X \tag{8.2.1}$$

where C^d, I^d, G^d and X denote the total demands for domestic products by households, firms, government and foreign buyers. It should be emphasized that these are real demands, that is they relate to the quantities of goods produced and not to their money values.

The total real demand by households, C, is the sum of their demands for domestic and foreign products and this is expressed by

$$C = C^d + C^m\sigma \tag{8.2.2}$$

where C^m is the demand for foreign products by households. The argument is that domestic and foreign products, although they may satisfy the same need, are essentially different products and they are reduced to a comparable basis by means of the 'terms of trade', σ. This expresses the value of imports in terms of home-produced goods and is defined as

$$\sigma = (P^f E)/P^d \tag{8.2.3}$$

where P^f and P^d are the prices respectively of foreign and domestic products and E is the exchange rate expressed as the price of foreign currency in terms of domestic currency.

In a similar fashion, total real investment, I, and total government expenditure, G, are defined as

$$I = I^d + I^m\sigma \tag{8.2.4}$$

and

$$G = G^d + G^m\sigma \tag{8.2.5}$$

In this chapter we shall be articulating an essentially Keynesian view of the economy, one of the fundamental assumptions of which is that domestic producers are always able and willing to supply the total quantities demanded of their products. In other words, total domestic output, Q, equals total demand, Z:

$$Q = Z \tag{8.2.6}$$

The implication of this view is that both the goods and labour markets are characterised by an excess of supply over demand, so that both labour and productive capacity are available to satisfy any increases in demand. Excess supply need not necessarily characterise the goods and labour markets. Thus for example, there might be an excess supply of labour, leading to unemployment, but, through a lack of productive capacity, an excess of demand over supply in the goods market. These alternative characterisations of the state of demand and supply in the various markets are discussed in Malinvaud (1980) but do not feature in this chapter.

Turning now to total imports, M, this is the total of goods supplied by foreign producers for the domestic market and is defined as

$$M = C^m + I^m + G^m \tag{8.2.7}$$

The total supply of goods to the domestic market is then defined as the sum of imports and domestic output.

To breathe life into this framework it is necessary to ground the components of final demand in the behaviour of the different economic agents. We begin with the demand by households for goods and services which are primarily for consumption purposes.

The consumption of domestic and imported products is assumed to depend upon real disposable income, Y. In addition consumers have the opportunity to substitute between domestic and imported goods and the extent to which they would do so is assumed to depend upon σ, the terms of trade. Thus[1]

$$C^d = c_0^d + c_1^d Y + c_2^d \sigma \tag{8.2.8}$$

and

$$C^m = c_0^m + c_1^m Y - c_2^m \sigma \tag{8.2.9}$$

Hence an increase in disposable income raises consumption and a change in foreign prices relative to domestic prices causes a substitution away from the dearer products towards the cheaper products. The positive constants reflect the fact that the average propensities to consume out of income (C^d/Y) and (C^m/Y) exceed the marginal propensities (c_1^d and c_1^m). This is consistent with Keynes' own views (cf. Keynes, 1936, Book III). More complex versions of the consumption function – the relationship relating aggregate real consumers' expenditure to disposable income and other variables – are based on the permanent income hypothesis (Friedman, 1957), the relative income hypothesis (Duesenberry, 1948) and the life cycle hypothesis (Ando and Modigliani, 1963). However, since the analytical properties of our model would remain essentially unchanged under these alternative formulations, we do not consider them in this exposition.

The demand for investment goods is assumed to depend upon the level of output, Q, and upon the rate of interest, r. As before the terms of trade effect is introduced, through the variable σ, to capture the substitution between foreign and home-produced investment goods. Thus

$$I^d = i_0^d + i_1^d Q - i_2^d r + i_3^d \sigma \tag{8.2.10}$$

and

$$I^m = i_0^m + i_1^m Q - i_2^m r - i_3^m \sigma \tag{8.2.11}$$

Increases in domestic output, to meet increases in demand, call for increased capacity and hence raise demand for investment goods. On the other hand increases in the rate of interest reduce the demand for investment goods. This last effect can be explained as follows: an increase in the capital stock through investment entails an increased flow of output. The investment project will be undertaken only if the present value of this output flow, discounted at the rate of interest r, exceeds the cost of the investment, since otherwise the firm could earn greater returns by lending, at the market rate of interest, the funds it had ear-marked for investment. Since a rise in the rate of interest reduces present values, the number of profitable investment projects falls.

Exports are assumed to depend upon the level of world trade and upon relative prices captured by the terms-of-trade effect σ. However, for our purposes, the effects of world trade are subsumed into the constant term and we simply write

$$X = x_0 + x_1 \sigma \tag{8.2.12}$$

Real disposable income is defined as

$$Y = (1 - \tau) Q \tag{8.2.13}$$

where τ denotes the rate of direct taxation and Q denotes real income (equals output). Equation (8.2.13) implicitly assumes that there is no progressive taxation and that all dividends and capital gains are saved (rather than consumed).

Upon substitution of equations (8.2.1), (8.2.8) and (8.2.10)–(8.2.13) into equation (8.2.6), one obtains the following expression for real output

$$Q = \mu_1 \{A_d + G^d - i_2^d r + (c_2^d + i_3^d + x_1)\sigma\} \tag{8.2.14}$$

where $A_d = (c_0^d + i_0^d + x_0)$ denotes total autonomous demand for home products and μ_1 denotes the *multiplier for the goods market* (cf. Kahn, 1931)

$$\mu_1 = (1 - c_1^d(1-\tau) - i_1^d)^{-1} \tag{8.2.15}$$

Keynes (1936) assumed that the marginal propensity to consume was less than unity in order to have a positive multiplier. In (8.2.15) we assume $c_1^d(1-\tau) + i_1^d < 1$, which implies that $\mu_1 > 0$. An increase in autonomous or public demand raises output by more than the initial stimulus, since $\mu_1 > 1$. Also, a cut in the rate of interest, an improvement in the terms of trade (a rise in σ) or a cut in the rate of taxation raises output.

8.3 The domestic money market

The previous section determined real output in terms of the rate of interest, amongst other variables. This section seeks to explain the determination of the rate of interest. Real cash balances are the nominal balances of money divided by the price level and they thus express the purchasing power of the nominal balances. The demand for real cash balances, say L, is defined as

$$L = l_0 + l_1 Q - l_2 r \tag{8.3.1}$$

Keynes (1936, Chapter 15) argued that money was held partly for financing transactions and partly for speculative purposes, so that L would depend positively on Q and negatively on r. Thus, remembering that money is a non-interest bearing asset, when the interest rate went up agents substituted bonds for money and hence held less money. More recent approaches are based on a portfolio framework (e.g. Tobin, 1968). In this framework a total of real wealth is allocated amongst a variety of financial assets, one of which is money. Thus, unlike in the above treatment, the demand for money is not considered separate from the demand for other assets. However, such a treatment, while complicating our analysis, would not alter the main results.

Equilibrium of the money market requires that the supply of money, say M_s, equals the nominal demand for money, so that

$$M_s = PL \tag{8.3.2}$$

where P is the price level. Combining (8.3.1) and (8.3.2) yields the following relationship for the rate of interest

$$r = \frac{l_0 - (M_s/P) + l_1 Q}{l_2} \tag{8.3.3}$$

Fig. 8.1 *The IS–LM$_s$ diagram*

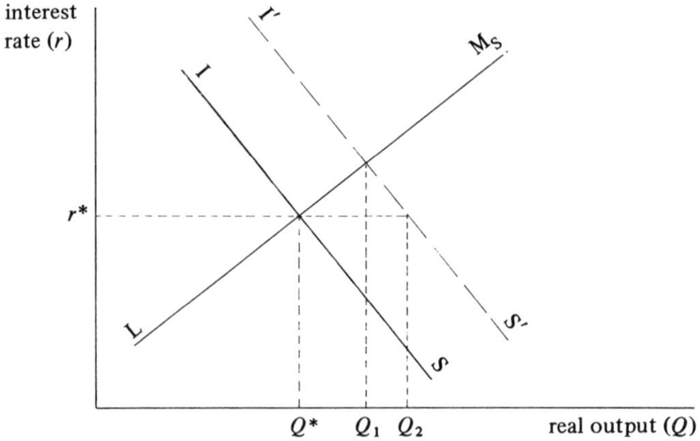

8.4 The integrated product–money market model

Equations (8.2.14) and (8.3.2) are commonly referred to as the IS-curve and LM$_s$-curve, respectively. The IS-curve shows those combinations of output and the interest rate for which the product market is in equilibrium. The IS-curve is downward sloping, since an increase in the rate of interest retards investment and therefore output. The whole IS-curve shifts upwards when autonomous or public demand is increased, taxes are cut, or the terms of trade improve. The LM$_s$-curve shows the combinations of output and the interest rate for which the money market is in equilibrium. The LM$_s$-curve is upward sloping, since an increase in output increases the transactions demand for money, leaves less funds available for speculation and therefore forces up the interest rate. Alternatively, the financing of the extra public spending by issuing new bonds would also raise the interest rate. The whole LM$_s$-curve shifts upwards when the real supply of money is increased. The above observations are summarised in the famous IS–LM$_s$ diagram (see Fig. 8.1) suggested by Hicks (1937). The intersection of the IS-curve and the LM$_s$-curve, say (r^*, Q^*), determines simultaneous equilibrium of the money and goods markets. A rise in demand, due for example to a rise in A_d, G^d or σ, or a cut in τ, shifts the IS-curve outwards to the I$'$S$'$-curve and raises output from Q^* to the new equilibrium Q_1, but not by as much as in the case of an exogenous interest rate (the case of a horizontal LM$_s$-curve). The difference between Q_1 and Q_2 is called 'the crowding out' of private investment (c.f. Blinder and Solow, 1973), because the initial boost to output raises the transactions demand for money, leaves less money available for speculative purposes and therefore pushes up the rate of interest and retards investment. Thus the relative effectiveness of fiscal and monetary policies depends on the relative steepness of the LM$_s$-curve: a near-zero interest rate elasticity of the demand for money (steep LM$_s$-curve) gives rise to no scope for fiscal management and an infinite interest rate elasticity (flat LM$_s$-curve) corresponding to the Keynesian liquidity trap leaves no scope for monetary policies.

8.5 Multipliers for fiscal policy

Upon substitution of the LM$_s$-curve (8.3.2) into the IS-curve (8.2.14) one obtains an algebraic solution for equilibrium output

$$Q = Q^* = \mu_2\{A + G^d + (i_2^d/l_2)(M_s/P) + (c_2^d + i_3^d + x_1)\sigma\} \quad (8.5.1)$$

where $A = A_d - (i_2^d l_0/l_2)$ and μ_2 denotes the IS–LM$_s$ multiplier

$$\mu_2 = (1 - c_1^d(1-\tau) - i_1^d + i_2^d l_1/l_2)^{-1} > 0 \quad (8.5.2)$$

A similar expression may be obtained for the equilibrium interest rate. The IS–LM$_s$ multiplier is less than the goods market multiplier ($\mu_2 < \mu_1$) due to the off-setting effects of crowding out of private investment (measured by the term $i_2^d l_1/l_2$). Equation (8.5.1) also shows that the multiplier for (M_s/P) is given by $(\mu_2 i_2^d/l_2) > 0$, so that an increase in the real supply of money boosts output. It also shows that the aggregate demand curve is downward sloping, since the price level (P) affects output (Q) negatively, and that an improvement in competitiveness increases output for export purposes.

An implicit assumption underlying the IS–LM$_s$ multiplier (8.5.2) is that an increase in public spending is financed by issuing bonds. An alternative is to consider the implications of a public spending stimulus for real output when it is financed by raising taxes. More precisely, to consider the effects of demanding the increase in public spending be matched by an equal increase in taxes

$$dG^d = dT \quad (8.5.3)$$

in order to keep the fiscal deficit incrementally balanced. It can be shown that under (8.5.3)

$$\frac{\partial Q}{\partial G^d} = \frac{\partial Q}{\partial T} = \mu_3 = \left[\frac{1 - c_1^d}{1 - c_1^d - i_1^d + i_2^d l_1/l_2}\right] < \mu_2 \quad (8.5.4)$$

holds. The multiplier μ_3 is called the *balanced budget multiplier* and is smaller in magnitude than μ_2, since the expansionary effect due to higher public spending is dampened by the contractionary effect due to higher taxes. Observe that in the simple case of exogenous investment ($i_1^d = i_2^d = 0$) the balanced budget multiplier is unity (e.g. Haavelmo, 1945).

8.6 The balance of payments

8.6.1 The Marshall–Lerner conditions for the balance of trade

The balance of trade which is the difference between the money value of exports and imports, say B_T, is defined as

$$B_T = P^d X - (P^f E)M \quad (8.6.1)$$

Upon substitution of equations (8.2.3), (8.2.7) and (8.2.9)–(8.2.12) into (8.6.1), one obtains the following reduced-form result for the balance of trade

$$\frac{\partial B_T}{\partial \sigma} = P^d\{x_1 - M + \sigma(c_2^m + i_3^m)\} \quad (8.6.2)$$

when Q, r, G^m and P^d are considered fixed. This result reduces to

$$\frac{\partial B_T}{\partial \sigma} = MP^d\{\eta_x + \eta_m - 1\}, \quad \eta_x = \frac{x_1\sigma}{X}, \quad \eta_m = \frac{\sigma(c_2^m + i_3^m)}{M} \quad (8.6.3)$$

near the point where the balance of trade is in equilibrium ($X = \sigma M$). In other words an increase in the relative price σ (due to a depreciation of the currency or a rise in foreign prices) improves the balance of trade if and only if the sum of the price elasticity of exports, η_x, and the price elasticity of demand for imports, η_m, exceeds unity (e.g. Kindleberger, 1963), because then the combined effects of the increase in exports and the reduction in imports of consumption goods outweighs the effect of more expensive imports. Obviously the 'elasticity' approach suffers from the drawback that the feedback from the goods and money markets upon Q and r is not considered, but this was the approach adopted in much of the early international economic literature.

8.6.2 The capital account

The balance of payments, say B, consists of the current account and the capital account and is defined as

$$B = B_c + B_k \tag{8.6.4}$$

where B_c denotes the net inflow of foreign reserves arising from current transactions and B_k denotes the net inflow of capital. Strictly speaking B_c includes B_T plus the net receipt of current income earned from the use of capital equipment abroad (including interest receipts from foreign bonds), but for simplicity this latter item is left exogenous and subsumed in the constant x_0. Therefore $B_c = B_T$ in (8.6.4). The net inflow of foreign reserves resulting from foreigners' investments in the domestic economy is supposed to be stimulated when the domestic interest rate exceeds the (expected) foreign interest rate, r_f, in domestic currency, that is

$$B_k = [k_0 + k_1(r - r^f)]P, \quad r^f = r_f + \mathrm{E}(\dot{E}/E), \tag{8.6.5}$$

where P is an appropriate domestic price level (see Subsection 8.8.1), holds (cf. Takayama 1969). One interpretation of (8.6.5) says that when the interest rate differential rises, foreigners are more likely to invest in the domestic economy and the inflow of foreign exchange increases.

One interesting assumption is *perfect capital mobility*, that is that foreign and domestic bonds are perfect substitutes. In our model it corresponds to $k_1 \to \infty$ and implies a zero interest rate differential ($r = r^f$). Obviously, under perfect capital mobility crowding out (see Section 8.4) cannot occur as the domestic interest rate is pegged to the foreign rate.

More realistic approaches model the capital account of the balance of payments within a proper portfolio framework (e.g. Turnovsky, 1977, Chapters 11 and 12), but our simple assumption (8.6.5) is quite adequate in the short run.

8.6.3 Accumulation of foreign reserves

Upon substitution of equations (8.2.3), (8.2.7), (8.2.9)–(8.2.12), (8.3.2), (8.5.1), (8.6.1) and (8.6.5) into equation (8.6.4), one obtains a complicated reduced-form expression for the balance of payments of the form

$$B = PB^*(G^d, G^m, \tau, M_s/P, \sigma, r^f) \tag{8.6.6}$$

An increase in government imports worsens the current account, whereas an increase in foreign interest rates worsens the capital account of the balance of payments $((\partial B^*/\partial G_m) < 0, (\partial B^*/\partial r^f) < 0)$. An increase in the real supply of money to the domestic market forces down domestic interest rates, which stimulates the import of investment goods, encourages the outflow of capital abroad and therefore diminishes the level of foreign reserves $((\partial B^*/\partial(M_s/P) < 0)$. Unfortunately, it is not possible to determine unambiguously the direction of the effects of G^d, τ or σ on B. For example, an increase in public spending at home or a cut in taxes on the one hand boosts output, income and imports of consumption and investment goods but on the other hand forces up the interest rate, depresses imports of investment goods and attracts the inflow of foreign funds. The output channels worsen whereas the interest rate channels improve the balance of payments position. We shall assume, given historical experience, that the output effects dominate so that a fiscal stimulus reduces the level of foreign reserves $((\partial B^*/\partial G^d) < 0, (\partial B^*/\partial \tau) > 0)$. An improvement in competitiveness has the usual Marshall–Lerner implications (see Subsection 8.6.1), but in addition the induced increase in the domestic interest rate reduces imports of capital goods, attracts foreign capital and therefore improves the balance of payments, whereas the increase in output increases imports and diminishes foreign reserves. Hence, given the assumption that the output effect dominates, the modified Marshall–Lerner conditions are less likely to hold. We shall nevertheless assume that the immediate implication of a devaluation or an increase in foreign prices is an improvement in the balance of payments position $((\partial B^*/\partial \sigma) > 0)$. Since $G^m = m_g G$, equation (8.6.6) becomes

$$B = PB^*(\overset{-}{G}{}^d, \overset{+}{\tau}, \overset{-}{M_s/P}, \overset{+}{\sigma}, \overset{-}{r^f}) \tag{8.6.6$'$}$$

where a + or − indicates the (assumed) sign of the relevant partial derivative. Domestic public spending is now even more likely to worsen the balance of payments due to the associated government imports.

There are two polar cases to the balance of payments. The first is called the *fixed exchange rate case* and simply calculates B conditional on a given σ. The second is called the *flexible exchange rate case*, which ensures an equilibrium balance of payments by varying the exchange rate and follows from solving for E such that $B = 0$. This latter case implies there is no feedback from the balance of payments to the supply of money. We will concentrate mainly on the first case.

The balance of payments is important since it determines the accumulation of the level of foreign reserves, say M_s^f, that is

$$\dot{M}_s^f = B \tag{8.6.7}$$

The level of foreign reserves forms a component of the supply of money, that is

$$M_s = M_s^d + M_s^f \tag{8.6.8}$$

where M_s^d denotes the domestic component of the nominal money stock. The next section addresses itself to the determination of the nominal stock of domestic money held by domestic residents.

8.7 The government budget constraint and monetary policy

The fiscal deficit, say D_F, plus interest payments on the public debt equals the budget deficit, say D_B, and this must be financed by the government either printing money or issuing bonds, that is

$$\dot{M}_s^d + \dot{A}^d = D_B = D_F + rA^d \tag{8.7.1}$$

where the fiscal deficit equals the excess of public spending over tax revenues

$$D_F = P^d G^d + P^f E G^m - P^d \tau Q \tag{8.7.2}$$

and A^d denotes the outstanding stock of bond debt of the domestic government. Equation (8.7.1) is called the *government budget constraint* and shows that of the five policy variables, that is M^d, A^d, G^d, G^m and τ, only four can be set independently and the fifth follows from the government budget constraint. Here we will assume G^d, G^m and τ are exogenous, until the political extensions discussed in Chapter 9 are introduced, M_s^d follows a policy rule of the form

$$\dot{M}_s^d = -sB \quad 0 \leqq s \leqq 1 \tag{8.7.3}$$

and A^d follows from equation (8.7.1). The policy rule (8.7.2) ensures that the domestic supply of money is reduced, by selling bonds on the open market to domestic agents, whenever there is a balance of payments surplus. The extent to which this is done depends on the magnitude of the parameter s. When $s = 1$ any balance of payments surplus is completely offset by a reduction in the domestic supply of money, so that the total supply of money remains constant. In this case one speaks of *complete sterilisation* of changes in foreign reserves. The above becomes clearer by noting that equations (8.6.6′), (8.6.7), (8.6.8) and (8.7.3) may be reduced to give an equation determining the change in the supply of money to the domestic market

$$\dot{M}_s = (1-s)PB^*(G^d, \tau, M_s/P, \sigma) \tag{8.7.4}$$

so that the case of complete sterilisation ($s = 1$) corresponds to a fixed supply of money to the domestic market ($\dot{M}_s = 0$).

8.8 Price and wage formation

8.8.1 Formation of domestic prices and the 'cost-of-living' index

The rate of inflation of goods produced at home, say $p^d = \dot{P}^d/P^d$, is assumed to follow the relationship

$$p^d = a_0 + a_1(Q - \bar{Q}) + a_2 w + a_3(p^f + e) \tag{8.8.1}$$

where $\bar{Q}$ denotes capacity output, $w = \dot{W}/W$ denotes the rate of wage inflation, $p^f = \dot{P}^f/P^f$ denotes the rate of inflation of goods produced by foreigners, and $e = \dot{E}/E$. Hence domestic inflation depends on excess demand for domestic goods, changes in the costs of labour inputs and on the competitive position of home producers vis à vis foreign producers. More realistic models of inflation would also assign a role to productivity in price formation, but productivity is exogenous in our model and such effects need therefore not be discussed.

Households and other agents in the domestic economy face a mixture of home-produced and foreign-produced goods, which has a price, say P, associated with it. This price P is called the 'cost-of-living' index. When the domestic agents have a (Cobb–Douglas) utility function, with domestic goods and imports as arguments, this index takes the form

$$P = P^{d\delta}(P^f E)^{1-\delta}, \quad 0 \leqq \delta \leqq 1 \tag{8.8.2}$$

(see Samuelson and Swamy, 1974). An alternative expression may be obtained by taking logarithms of equation (8.8.2) and differentiating with respect to time, that is

$$p = \delta p^d + (1-\delta)(p^f + e) \tag{8.8.3}$$

where $p = \dot{P}/P$. Similarly, the rate of change in the terms of trade is determined by

$$\frac{\dot{\sigma}}{\sigma} = p^f + e - p^d \tag{8.8.4}$$

8.8.2 *Price-expectations augmented Phillips curve*

The rate of money wage inflation, w, is determined by the price-expectations augmented Phillips curve (see Trevithick and Mulvey, 1975, for a good survey)

$$w = b_0 - b_1 U + b_2 \pi, \quad 0 \leqq b_2 \leqq 1 \tag{8.8.5}$$

where U denotes the unemployment rate and π denotes the expected rate of price inflation. Hence excess supply of labour, proxied by U, and low expected increases in the cost of living tend to reduce the rate of wage inflation. The curve is typically drawn nonlinearly (see Fig. 8.2) to capture the 'downward stickiness of wages', that is labour fiercely resists cuts in expected real wages in depressions but accepts very high wages in boom periods. Some authors (e.g. Friedman, 1968) argue that $b_2 = 1$ and interpret (8.8.5) as a Walrasian adjustment process for the expected real wages. This has important implications for the long-run trade-off between inflation and unemployment. To illustrate this point let the expected inflation rate equal the actual inflation rate in the long run and the rate of growth in labour productivity equal b_3, then in the long run the rate of growth in the share of wages in value added must be zero. In other words, the relationship

$$w - p - b_3 = \frac{\mathrm{d}}{\mathrm{d}t}(WE/PQ)/(WE/PQ) = b_0 - b_1 U + (b_2 - 1)p - b_3 = 0 \tag{8.8.6}$$

where E denotes the number of workers employed in the economy, must hold. Solving for p from (8.8.6) yields the long-run Phillips curve

$$p = \left(\frac{b_0 - b_1 U - b_3}{1 - b_2}\right), \quad w = p + b_3 \tag{8.8.7}$$

Friedman's (1968) point is that when there is no money illusion ($b_2 = 1$) there is only one unemployment rate that yields a feasible outcome, so that in the long run there is no trade-off between inflation and unemployment and the unemployment rate is fixed at the natural rate

$$U_n = \left(\frac{b_0 - b_3}{b_1}\right) \tag{8.8.8}$$

determined by frictions on the labour market. Other authors argue that it is possible for the government to buy some extra jobs by allowing the inflation rate to rise a little and justify this by a belief in a certain degree of money illusion

Fig. 8.2 *The price-expectations augmented Phillips curve*

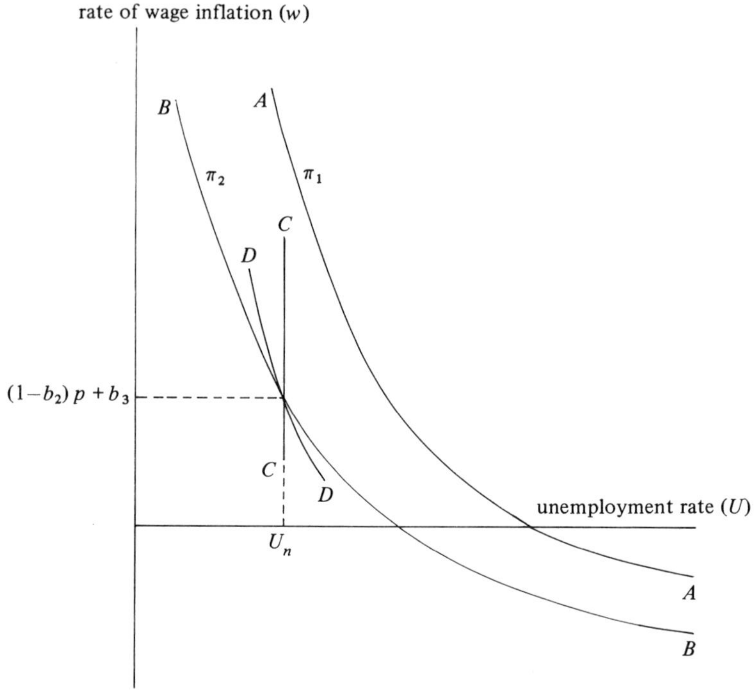

($b_2 < 1$). These different viewpoints are further illustrated in Fig. 8.2. Curves *AA* and *BB* show two short-run Phillips curves corresponding to two values for the expected rate of inflation, say π_1 and π_2. When in the long run expectations are fulfilled, say $\pi_2 = p$, the natural rate of unemployment, U_n, ensures that the rate of wage inflation equals the sum of growth in labour productivity and unanticipated increases in the costs of living ($(1-b_2)p$). The vertical curve *CC* shows Friedman's version of the long-run Phillips curve, whereas the curve *DD* shows a more Keynesian version of the long-run Phillips curve with a long-run trade-off between inflation and unemployment.

The expected rate of inflation, π, follows the adaptive expectations mechanism, that is

$$\dot{\pi} = \frac{1}{\tau_e}(p-\pi) \tag{8.8.9}$$

where τ_e is the average lag in forming expectations. Sometimes we will refer to the rational expectations hypothesis, which is defined as perfect foresight ($\pi = p$) in a deterministic world and corresponds to the case of immediate adaptation to changes in the inflation rate ($\tau_e = 0$). Equation (8.8.9) satisfies weak and strong axioms of forecasting (Turnovsky, 1974).

8.8.3 Okun's law

The final variable to be explained in this chapter is the unemployment rate, *U*. Consider the production function

$$Q = F(K, E) \tag{8.8.10}$$

where K denotes the employed capital stock and E denotes employed labour. In the short run the capital stock is assumed to be fixed, so that (8.8.10) may be linearised as follows

$$Q = q_0 + q_1 E \tag{8.8.10$'$}$$

The unemployment rate is then determined by Okun's law

$$U = L - E = u_0 - u_1 Q \tag{8.8.11}$$

where L is the exogenous supply of labour,

$$u_0 = L + q_0/q_1 \quad \text{and} \quad u_1 = 1/q_1.$$

8.8.4 The reduced-form price–wage sector

Upon substitution of equations (8.8.1), (8.8.5) and (8.8.11) into equations (8.8.4) and (8.8.3), one obtains the differential equation determining the development of the terms of trade over time

$$\frac{\dot{\sigma}}{\sigma} = \alpha_0 - \alpha_1 Q - \alpha_2 \pi + \alpha_3 (p^f + e) \tag{8.8.12}$$

where $\alpha_0 = a_0 - a_1 \bar{Q} + a_2(b_0 - b_1 u_0)$, $\alpha_1 = a_1 + a_2 b_1 u_1$, $\alpha_2 = a_2 b_2$ and $\alpha_3 = 1 - a_3$, and the equation determining the rate of inflation of the 'cost-of-living' index

$$p = \beta_0 + \beta_1 Q + \beta_2 \pi + \beta_3 (p^f + e) \tag{8.8.13}$$

where $\beta_i = \delta \alpha_i$, $i = 0, 1, 2$ and $\beta_3 = 1 - \delta \alpha_3$. Hence, increases in output or the expected rate of inflation raise the rate of domestic inflation and worsen the terms of trade. An increase in the rate of world inflation increases domestic inflation, *via* the increased costs of imports, but nevertheless improves competitiveness. A maintained devaluation implies a once and for all increase in the level of domestic prices and the terms of trade.

8.9 The complete model

The reduced-form model of the small economy discussed in this chapter may now be summarized by the three differential equations governing the evolution of the real supply of money to the domestic market, that is

$$\dot{L} = (1 - s)B^* - p^* L \tag{8.9.1}$$

the terms of trade, that is

$$\dot{\sigma} = \{\alpha_0 - \alpha_1 Q^* - \alpha_2 \pi + \alpha_3 (p^f + e)\}\sigma \tag{8.9.2}$$

and the expected rate of price inflation, that is

$$\dot{\pi} = \frac{1}{\tau_e}(p^* - \pi) \tag{8.9.3}$$

respectively, and the static equations determining output, that is equation (8.5.1) or

$$Q = Q^*(\overset{+}{L}, \overset{+}{\sigma}; \overset{+}{G^d}, \overset{-}{\tau}) \tag{8.9.4}$$

the 'real' balance of payments, that is equation (8.8.6′) or

$$B/P = B^*(\overset{-}{L}, \overset{+}{\sigma}; \overset{-}{G}^d, \overset{+}{\tau}, \overset{-}{r}^f) \tag{8.9.5}$$

and the rate of price inflation, that is equation (8.8.13) or

$$p = p^*(\overset{+}{L}, \overset{+}{\sigma}, \overset{+}{\pi}; \overset{+}{G}^d, \overset{-}{\tau}, \overset{+}{p}^f + e) \tag{8.9.6}$$

respectively, where a + or − indicates the sign of the corresponding partial derivative. The above reduction used equations (8.5.1), (8.5.2), (8.7.4), (8.8.9), (8.8.12) and (8.8.13) and gives a reduced-form model for the endogenous variables L, σ and π (and Q, B and p) in terms of the policy variables G^d, τ, e and s and the uncontrollable exogenous variables p^f, r^f and the parameters (representing uncontrollable exogenous forces such as the volume of world trade).

8.9.1 Case: perfect capital mobility

As remarked in Subsection 8.6.2 perfect capital mobility arises when agents are indifferent between domestic and foreign bonds with the same return. This may not be a bad approximation for a modern Western economy such as the United Kingdom, since the financial network provided by the City of London provides a system of nearly perfect capital markets. This assumption implies that the domestic interest rates are pegged to the foreign interest rates and that there is no scope for an independent monetary policy. More precisely, the multiplier relationships (8.5.1) and (8.5.2) (or (8.9.4)) are replaced by (8.2.14) with $r = r^f$ and (8.2.15) (or $\partial Q^*/\partial L = 0$), so that effectively there is no crowding out and there is more scope for demand management. In addition the real supply of money does not influence, under perfect capital mobility, the 'real' balance of payments or the rate of price inflation ($(\partial B^*/\partial L) = (\partial p^*/\partial L) = 0$), so that equation (8.9.1) governing the evolution of the real supply of money becomes redundant.

8.9.2 Case: purchasing power parity

There have been cases in history when a government implements a simple policy rule for the rate of change in the exchange rate in order to maintain purchasing power parity.[2] In other words the exchange rate is adjusted so as to maintain a constant ratio of the foreign price level to the domestic price level, which may be formalised by the rule

$$e = p - p^f = p^d - p^f \tag{8.9.7}$$

Hence, foreign goods are made more expensive by depreciating the exchange rate whenever the domestic inflation rate exceeds foreign interest rates. The upshot of this policy rule is that the terms of trade (σ) remain constant and, from the point of view of our model, equation (8.9.2) becomes redundant.

8.9.3 Case: perfect anticipation of changes in the inflation rate

The final case we shall consider is rational expectations of the inflation rate. This is achieved when trade unions immediately adapt their expectations of the inflation rate to the true rate ($\pi = p^*$). Under this assumption equation (8.9.3) becomes redundant and equation (8.8.13) (or (8.9.6)) is replaced by

$$p = \{\beta_0 + \beta_1 Q^* + \beta_2(p^f + e)\}/(1 - \beta_2) \tag{8.9.6′}$$

The implication of perfect anticipation of the inflation rate is that the effects of changes in output or competitiveness on the rate of inflation are higher than before, since these effects work themselves out immediately.

8.10 Conclusions

This chapter has proposed a simple macroeconomic model for explaining employment, disposable income, inflation and the balance of payments. This is an essential exercise, since, as the first part of this book demonstrated, a government's popularity depends partly on the outcomes of these economic variables. The remainder of the book is concerned with adding political factors to the economic analysis in order to explain the behaviour of the public sector. To the political economist this seems a natural undertaking, because the conventional type of macroeconomic model (as discussed in this chapter) lacks a satisfactory explanation of government policy. This is curious given the enormous efforts devoted to providing satisfactory explanations of consumption or investment behaviour and the fact that the government takes up as much as fifty per cent of the gross domestic product in certain Western economies. The next two chapters attempt to correct this imbalance by providing various explanations of government behaviour.

9

Political aspects of macroeconomic analysis

9.1 Introduction

The orthodox theory of economic policy views the government as a benevolent dictator who implements policy in an attempt to promote social welfare. It is concerned with how a government *ought* to behave, so it has a *normative* character. The orthodox theory ignores the fact that a government has objectives of its own manifested in its ideology and its attempts to secure survival (re-election), which may well differ from the social welfare objective. *Positive* theories of how a government *actually* behaves are needed and provided by political economics (e.g. Kalecki, 1943; Nordhaus, 1975; Lindbeck, 1976; Frey, 1978b). The modification of macroeconomic theory (see Chapter 8) to allow for positive theories of government behaviour is the subject of this chapter.

Existing theories of political economics suffer from at least six defects (see Chapter 7). Firstly, most studies relate popularity to economic performance in an *ad hoc* manner and therefore lack a satisfactory theory of voting behaviour. Secondly, the nation is seen as one group with homogeneous preferences and different interest groups are not discussed (cf. Chapter 6). Thirdly, the public sector is usually not separated into the component which does *not* depend on the electorate for survival, e.g. the state bureaucracy and monetary authorities, and the part which does depend on re-election for its survival, the government. In practice there will be conflict between these components of the public sector, which so far has been ignored. Fourthly, previous studies of the optimal political business cycle (e.g. Sections 7.3, 7.4 and 7.5) focus on the political trade-off between inflation and unemployment and ignore the effects of disposable income, level of taxation and balance of payments on electoral popularity (see Chapters 4 and 5). Furthermore, these studies do not discuss the policy instrumentation necessary to attain the optimal political cycle. Fifthly, previous studies of political–economic reaction functions for state spending and taxes (see Section 7.7) specified these *independently* of each other and without reference to a complete macroeconomic model (such as Chapter 8 discusses). This means that the conflict between the state and government receives no attention and that the signs on the coefficients of the reaction functions cannot be properly assigned. Finally, previous analysis of the stability of political–economic systems (e.g. Fassbender, 1981) have failed to take account of the discontinuous nature of reaction functions based on satisficing theory.

This chapter attempts to remedy the above deficiencies by extending the macroeconomic model of Chapter 8 with a full political–economic structure. Section 9.2

considers the behaviour of the state bureaucracy and means by which the government can control the expansion of state spending. The introduction of this constraint on the state into the analysis of Chapter 8 sets the scene for reconciling the conflicting interests of various pressure groups in society (i.e. active private sector agents, public sector workers, unemployed, rentiers and bureaucrats). Section 9.3 shows how the ratio of the fiscal deficit to national income may be chosen to obtain a Pareto-optimal outcome for the various interest groups. The theory of qualitative political choice developed in Chapter 3 and the empirical insights obtained in Chapters 4 and 5 are used in Section 9.4 to show how a government might manipulate the tax rate over the course of the election period in order to maximise votes at the forthcoming election *and* secure a satisfactory balance of payments position. Extensions to strategic voting and maximisation of the uninterrupted length in office are also provided. The interactions between ideological and re-election objectives are discussed in Section 9.5. An interdependent system of political–economic reaction functions based on satisficing theory, used in conjunction with the model of Chapter 8, is formulated in Section 9.6, which also discusses the comparative statics of the system and the principle of effective political–economic assignment. The implications of the rational expectations hypothesis for the political business cycle are discussed in Section 9.7.

9.2 Behaviour of the state bureaucracy

9.2.1 Strict control of the state

In Section 7.10 of Chapter 7 we argued that the previous literature ignored the conflict between the government and bureaucracy components of the public sector. The government may have certain ideas about the planned level of expenditures to be undertaken by the state bureaucracy, but it is not clear at all that the civil servants will be prepared to cut down state projects when told to do so by the government. The reasons underlying this type of behaviour of civil servants may be found in the literature on the managerial theory of the firm (e.g. Koutsoyannis, 1979). Civil servants simply run the state and are not interested in cutting their own size, since they relate their own prestige to the number of employed civil servants and the number of (prestigious) state projects implemented. This hypothesis of a budget-maximising bureaucracy may also be found in the public choice literature (e.g. Niskanen, 1971; Mueller, 1979), although this literature typically relates to individual departments rather than to the state bureaucracy as a whole.[1]

Given the desire always to expand, the government gains control over the state bureaucracy by setting guide lines for total planned public expenditures, say G^p. This may be formalised by the following constraint on the state bureaucracy

$$G \leqq G^p \tag{9.2.1}$$

When the *planned* fiscal deficit (see equation 8.7.2)) is not allowed to exceed a certain fraction, say ξ, of the national income, that is

$$D_F^p = P^d(G^p - \tau Q) \leqq \xi P^d Q \tag{9.2.2}$$

one speaks of *strict control of the state bureaucracy.* Combining equations (9.2.1) and (9.2.2) yields the reduced-form constraint on the state bureaucracy

$$G - \tau Q \leqq \xi Q \tag{9.2.3}$$

The hypothesis of budget-maximising bureaucrats would ensure that the above constraint on the state holds with equality, although in practice there may be some over-shooting due to unanticipated events persuading the government to allow a bigger state expansion.

The magnitude of the parameter ξ indicates the degree to which the government is prepared to finance a large state. A constraint of the form (9.2.3) has been important for some time in the British political debate. For example, the Conservative administration under Mrs Thatcher had a range of 1.5–4.5 per cent in mind for the value of ξ. A more Keynesian administration would probably operate with a somewhat higher value of ξ. The parameter ξ reflects therefore the ideological nature of the government, although ξ may also be affected by stabilisation considerations. For example, when there is too high inflation and large balance of payments deficits a government may decide to use a very low value of ξ (see also Subsection 3.4 of this chapter).

When proper account is taken of the constraint on the state bureaucracy, the properties of the macroeconomic model considered in Chapter 8 alter dramatically. It is now clear that *either* the level of public spending *or* the rate of taxation is a policy variable, since one of these policies follows from the behaviour of the civil servants. Here we will assume that the government sets the tax rate and this forms a constraint on the size of the state. Upon substitution of (9.2.3) into the outcome of the *purely economic* IS–LM$_s$ model (8.5.1)–(8.5.2), one obtains the *public sector* version of the IS–LM$_s$ model giving real output as

$$Q = Q^* = \mu_2^s\{A + (i_2^d/l_2)(M_s/P) + (c_2^d + i_3^d + x_1)\sigma\} \tag{9.2.4}$$

where μ_2^s denotes the public sector IS–LM$_s$ multiplier

$$\mu_2^s = \{1 - c_1^d(1-\tau) - i_1^d + i_2^d(l_1/l_2) - (\xi + \tau)/(1 + m_g)\}^{-1} > \mu_2 > 0 \tag{9.2.5}$$

The multiplier for output with respect to increases in autonomous demand or the supply of money and improvements in the terms of trade has increased since the expansion in output is reinforced by the increase in the size of the permitted state bureaucracy. Relaxation of the permitted fiscal deficit ratio, as measured by ξ, raises as expected the size of the multiplier. An increase in the marginal propensity to import by the government (m_g) causes import leakage whenever output is increased and therefore reduces the size of the multiplier. A reduction in the tax rate now reduces the size of the multiplier (assuming $(1 + m_g)^{-1} > c_1^d$) because of the associated reduction in the size of the state!

The special case of a balanced fiscal deficit ($\xi = 0$) corresponds to the balanced budget multiplier, which may alternatively be expressed in the form (8.5.4).

Alternatively, the tax rate may be set in response to the public spending outcomes which would yield the following equation for real output

$$Q = \frac{A + \{1 - c_1^d(1 + m_g)\}G^d + (i_2^d/l_2)(M_s/P) + (c_2^d + i_3^d + x_1)\sigma}{1 - c_1^d(1 + \xi) - i_1^d + i_2^d(l_1/l_2)} \tag{9.2.6}$$

The special case of a balanced fiscal deficit ($\xi = 0$) corresponds to the balanced budget multiplier case and yields equation (8.5.4). Equations (9.2.4) and (9.2.6) show that either G^d or τ may be eliminated from the model and the other may be used by the government to satisfy other objectives of economic policy.

9.2.2 Autonomous state bureaucracy

Some may find the hypothesis of strict control of the state bureaucracy unrealistic given the strong powers of persuasion and manipulation found in many civil servants. Perhaps the alternative hypothesis of an autonomous state bureaucracy is more justifiable when one adopts the view that the implementation of state projects is often pre-determined and takes some time to complete, whilst it is difficult to scrap projects once the decision to build has been made. For this alternative hypothesis the *permanent income model*, previously developed in studies of the aggregate consumption function (see Friedman, 1957), of state expenditures comes in useful (cf. Chrystal and Alt, 1979a, 1981b).

The permanent income hypothesis assumes that state spending is a certain fraction of permanent income to the public sector. Since in the long run government income must be proportional to total real income in the domestic economy, Q, the above may be formalised by

$$G = \alpha Q^p \tag{9.2.7}$$

where Q^p denotes permanent real income to the economy. Permanent income may be viewed as a weighted average of all previous incomes, that is

$$Q^p = \int_0^\infty \mathrm{T}(k) Q(t-k)\,\mathrm{d}k \tag{9.2.8}$$

where the weightings must satisfy

$$\mathrm{T}(k) \geqq 0,\ k \geqq 0 \quad \text{and} \quad \int_0^\infty \mathrm{T}(k)\,\mathrm{d}k = 1.$$

Choosing exponential weighting, say $\mathrm{T}(k) = \beta \exp(-\beta k)$, one obtains the permanent income model for state expenditures

$$\dot{G} = \beta(\alpha Q - G),\ \beta \geqq 0 \tag{9.2.9}$$

where $1/\beta$ may be interpreted as the average implementation lag of state projects.

State spending, as explained by equation (9.2.9), is no longer dependent on short-run changes in the rate of taxation or of real output, but instead depends simply on the trend value of output. Empirical evidence for such a hypothesis may be found in Chrystal and Alt (1981a, b). However no theoretical foundation is provided (see Subsection 9.3.4). Two implications of the permanent income model of the state are that a government finds it more difficult to use state spending as a political instrument, since state spending very much follows its own course (independent of taxation policy), and that the bureaucrats prevent the use of state spending as a counter-cyclical instrument. In other words under the permanent income hypothesis most of the government action must come from the revenue rather than from the expenditure side of the public sector.

9.2.3 *Gradual control of the state*

An intermediate position between the strict control of the state and the autonomous state hypotheses may be obtained by allowing taxes to have not an immediate but a long-run impact on the size of the state bureaucracy. This may be modelled by the *gradual control of the state* hypothesis

$$\dot{G} = \beta\{(\xi + \tau)Q - G\} \tag{9.2.10}$$

where the long-run share of government in the national income equals the sum of the tax rate and the permitted fiscal deficit ratio.

In the remainder of this chapter we shall make use of each of the three hypotheses regarding state behaviour. We shall *either* investigate how the strict control hypothesis may be used to provide a theoretical foundation for the autonomous hypothesis *or* employ the gradual control hypothesis. The first approach is used in Sections 9.3, 9.4 and 9.5 and the second approach is used in Section 9.6.

9.3 Reconciliation of competing interests in the economy

9.3.1 *The interest function approach*

The interest function approach says that the government represents the interests of various pressure groups in society and formulates economic policy accordingly (cf. Section 7.10 of Chapter 7). Any classification of interest groups is bound to be arbitrary, but we believe it important at least to distinguish between (i) active private sector agents, (ii) unemployed private sector agents, (iii) rentiers (e.g. financial institutions and persons receiving an income fixed in money terms), (iv) civil servants and (v) bureaucrats. Groups (ii) and (iii) combined constitute the inactive private sector agents. Van Winden (1983) aggregates our groups (iv) and (v), which when combined constitute the state. In the terminology of van Winden, each social group's interests may be represented by an elementary interest function showing the group's utility. We shall assume that the elementary interest function for the active private sector agents (workers and capitalists) depends on their real disposable income, say $U_p(Y_p)$, for the unemployed inversely on the unemployment rate, $U_u(-U)$, and for the rentiers inversely on the rate of inflation, $U_r(-p)$.[2] Strictly speaking, it is perhaps better to represent the economic interests of the rentiers by the sum of dividend payments and capital gains,

$$\{rA^d - p(A^d + M_s)\}$$

where the second term reflects the erosion of private sector wealth due to inflation. Since our analysis in this section is concerned with the short run, A^d and M_s may be regarded as fixed and, since we assume (for simplicity) perfect capital mobility (see Subsection 8.9.1), r is determined by foreign interest rates, we may proxy the loss in disposable income of rentiers by the rate of inflation. The civil servants are workers employed by the state and their interests are represented by their real disposable income, say $U_c(Y_s)$. The top civil servants are the bureaucrats, who are primarily interested in the size of the public sector, say $U_b(G)$. This illustrates the idea that bureaucrats are keen to expand the size of their own offices in terms of employees and expenditures for prestige motives. The chosen structure of the elementary interest functions is to a certain extent arbitrary, although we feel the above fits in best with the macroeconomic model of Chapter 8.[3] One could, if one wanted, extend the elementary interest functions suggested above for groups (i), (ii), (iii) and (iv) by including the quantity of goods provided by the (welfare) state to the representative member of each interest group. The emphasis on using total disposable income as the main interest of each group implies that equal weights are attached to the numerical strength of the interest group and the real disposable income of the representative members. In other words we assume perfect substitution between jobs and after-tax income to the representative agent.

The above elementary interest functions are taken into consideration when the government decides on its economic policy. We shall assume that the government represents the interests of the groups in society by maximising the collective interest function, say

$$J = \rho_1 U_p(Y_p) + \rho_2 U_u(-U) + \rho_3 U_r(-p) + \rho_4 U_c(Y_s) + \rho_5 U_b(G) \tag{9.3.1}$$

where the weights ρ_i satisfy ($\rho_i \geqq 0$, $\Sigma_{i=1}^{5} \rho_i = 1$) and denote the weights the government attaches to each interest group, subject to the constraint on the state bureaucracy, say (9.2.3) (assuming strict control), and the constraints on economic behaviour (Chapter 8). The weights ρ_i will also be referred to as the power parameters and depend to a certain extent on the number of non-apathetic agents in group i. A Conservative administration might have rather high values for ρ_1 and ρ_3 whereas a Labour government might have higher values for ρ_2, ρ_4 and ρ_5, so that Conservatives endeavour to cut inflation and boost the private sector in order to serve their clients (rentiers and private sector) whereas Labour aim to cut unemployment and boost the state sector. This procedure essentially produces a compromise between the conflicting interests of the different groups with the particular outcome depending on the relative importance the government attaches to each group. It can be shown that the above ensures a Pareto-optimal outcome, so that the government's role may be seen as the reconciliation of conflicting interests and the creation of a co-operative bargain.[4]

Some might argue that the collective interest function (9.3.1) should be replaced by a vote function. This does not seem satisfactory, since some interest groups may be in a better position than others to have their wishes implemented by the government. However, when (and only when) the government faces severe re-election problems the weights ρ_i may be determined by attempts to gain votes (cf. Section 9.4).

9.3.2 Disposable income of private and state sector workers

Before we can move on to explain the optimal allocation strategy for the government, we need to explain disposable income for the private and the state sector (Y_p and Y_s). Let the proportion of total public expenditure that is the public sector wage bill,[5] say W_s, be b_3, so that

$$W_s = b_3 G, \quad 0 < b_3 < 1 \tag{9.3.2}$$

Hence the real disposable income of the civil servant group equals

$$Y_s = (1 - \tau)W_s = (1 - \tau)b_3 G \tag{9.3.3}$$

and of the active private sector equals

$$Y_p = Y - Y_s = (1-\tau)(Q - b_3 G) \tag{9.3.4}$$

For later reference, it is useful to explain the effects of changes in the tax rate or the permitted budget deficit ratio on disposable income. We will use the public sector IS–LM$_s$ model (9.2.4)–(9.2.5) and the constraints on the state (9.2.3). For the disposable income of the civil servants one finds the following multipliers under strict control of the state bureaucracy (see Subsection 9.2.1)

$$\frac{\partial Y_s}{\partial \tau} = b_3 \mu_2^s Q\{(1+m_g)^{-1}(\xi+\tau)^2 - c_1^d(1-\tau)^2 + (1-i_1^d)[(1-\tau)-(\xi+\tau)]\} \tag{9.3.5}$$

and

$$\frac{\partial Y_s}{\partial \xi} = b_3(1-\tau)Q\{1+(\xi+\tau)\mu_2^s(1+m_g)^{-1}\} > 0 \tag{9.3.6}$$

Hence an increase in the permitted fiscal deficit ratio allows a bigger state sector, more employment of civil servants and therefore a rise in the state sector's disposable income. Tax cuts boost the disposable income of the *representative* civil servant, but at the same time imply a smaller state sector, fewer civil servants and perhaps a reduction in the total disposable income of the civil servants. This, *inter alia*, shows that our analysis might gain from considering these two factors separately in the elementary interest function of civil servants. For most plausible parameter values the employment-generating effects dominate and we therefore assume $(\partial Y_s/\partial \tau) > 0$.[6]

The effects on total disposable income for the whole economy are

$$\frac{\partial Y}{\partial \tau} = \mu_2^s Q\{(1+m_g)^{-1}(1+\xi) + i_1^d - 1\} \tag{9.3.7}$$

and

$$\frac{\partial Y}{\partial \xi} = \mu_2^s Q(1+m_g)^{-1}(1-\tau) > 0 \tag{9.3.8}$$

As before relaxation of the fiscal deficit increases overall disposable income. In the extreme case of the Balanced Budget Theorem ($m_g = \xi = i_1^d = 0$), raising the tax rate boosts the economy sufficiently to offset *exactly* the increase in taxes paid by the representative agent in the economy. A fiscal deficit or an accelerator effect in the investment function implies that a cut in the tax rate reduces overall disposable income, although government imports and crowding out might counteract this effect.

Finally, consider the effects on private sector disposable income. A tax cut is seen to cause an increase in disposable income for the private sector at the expense of the public sector (and to leave total disposable income virtually unaffected). A suitable approximation may therefore be

$$\frac{\partial Y_p}{\partial \tau} \doteqdot -\left(\frac{\partial Y_s}{\partial \tau}\right) \tag{9.3.9}$$

An increase in the permitted fiscal deficit ratio cuts both ways for Y_p, since on the one hand it boosts the economy and on the other hand it increases the share of the state bureaucracy at the expense of the private sector.

9.3.3 *Political–economic allocation using the collective interest function*

We may now use the results obtained for disposable income in conjunction with Okun's law (8.8.11) and the price equation (8.8.13) to obtain the reduced-form collective interest function. Since we are interested in the day-to-day running of the economy, we make the short-run assumption of fixed expectations ($\tau_e = \infty$) and given degree of competitiveness (P^f and E fixed) in addition to the assumption of perfect capital mobility. This leads to the reduced-form collective interest function

$$J(\tau) \tag{9.3.10}$$

where the effectiveness of the tax rate in promoting collective interest is measured by

$$J' = \{\rho_4 U_c' - \rho_1 U_p'\}\left(\frac{\partial Y_s}{\partial \tau}\right) + \{\rho_2 U_u' u_1 - \rho_3 U_r' \beta_1 + \rho_5(\xi + \tau) U_b'\}\left(\frac{\partial Q}{\partial \tau}\right) \tag{9.3.11}$$

when we assume $(\partial Y_p/\partial \tau)$, $(\partial Y_s/\partial \tau)$ and $(\partial Q/\partial \tau)$ follow from equations (9.3.9), (9.3.5) and (9.2.4).

Increasing the rate of taxation (τ) or raising the permitted budget deficit ratio (ξ) boosts output *via* an expansion of the state but induces inflationary pressures, so that these may be viewed as policies for promoting the interests of the unemployed and bureaucrats at the expense of the interests of rentiers. An increase in taxes also raises the disposable income of public sector workers (civil servants) as a whole, although the average after-tax income of a representative member of this group is reduced, at the expense of private sector workers (see Subsection 9.3.3). An increase in the permitted fiscal deficit ratio is like 'manna from heaven' to both the public sector workers and the bureaucrats, since it leads to higher national output, a bigger share of the state in national income and therefore increases both the number of public sector jobs and the number of prestige state projects implemented, whereas the active private sector agents have mixed feelings about such a strategy. From the above it is clear that *as regards the policies for taxation and the fiscal deficit*, the interests of rentiers and private sector workers are aligned with each other but in conflict with the interests of civil servants, bureaucrats and the unemployed.

Before formulating its collective strategy, the government balances the interests of the various groups carefully. To the outside observer the actual outcome of government policy may appear a-political, but within the government many struggles may have occurred in preparing the final strategy. In our model it corresponds to finding the tax rate that balances the conflicting interests, i.e. τ such that $J' = 0$. The government may also choose the deficit ratio, ξ, to satisfy interests, but we will assume that this policy variable is determined by ideological motives, sound monetary management and/or stabilisation tactics (e.g. to secure a balance of payments equilibrium).

Consider a hypothetical administration which is *only* interested in promoting the interests of rentiers and diminishing the powers of bureaucrats (high ρ_3, low ρ_5 and $\rho_1 = \rho_2 = \rho_4 = 0$). In this case the government chooses the tax rate so that the

Fig. 9.1 *Optimal allocation between conflicting interest groups*

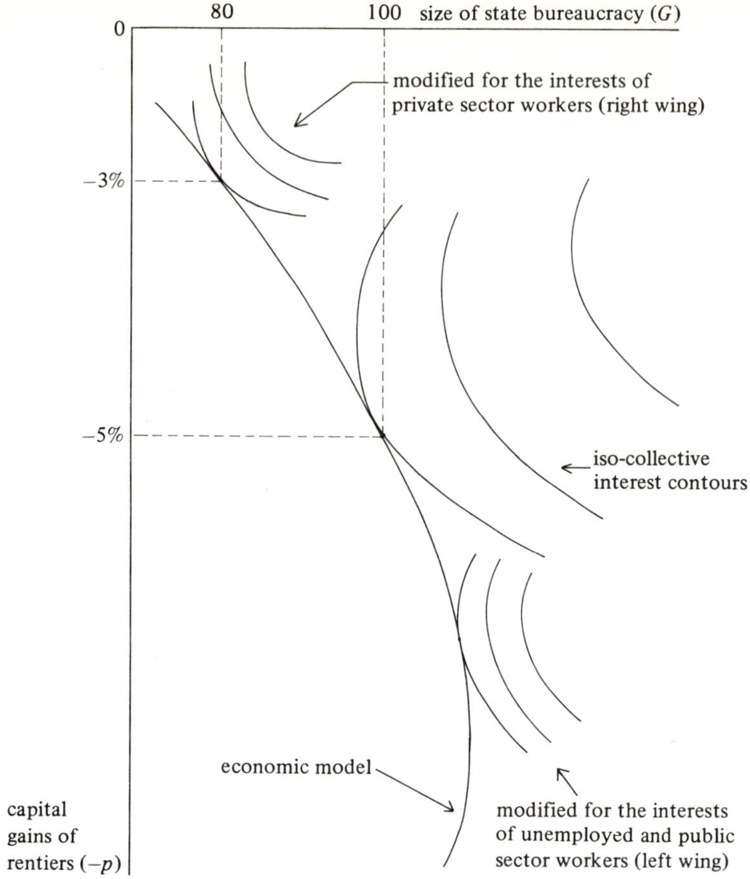

marginal rate of collective substitution between capital gains (proxied by *minus* the inflation rate, $-p$) and the size of the state bureaucracy, $(\rho_5 U'_b)/(\rho_3 U'_r)$, equals the rate of economic substitution, $\beta_1/(\xi + \tau)$. In diagrammatic terms the government chooses the allocation where the iso-collective interest contours are tangential to the economic model (yielding say, $G = 100$ and $p = 5$ per cent in Fig. 9.1). When this government also decides to pay some attention to the interests of the private sector workers or to become more right-wing by reducing the power of bureaucrats relative to rentiers even further, this effectively corresponds to employing a lower marginal rate of substitution and the iso-collective interest contours therefore become flatter. The revised optimal allocation is obtained by a cut in taxation and yields lower inflation and a reduced state sector ($Y_p = 80$ and $p =$ 3 per cent in Fig. 9.1), so that the re-allocation of resources to the private sector workers and rentiers occurs at the expense of the bureaucrats. A more left-wing administration may be much more concerned about the interests of the unemployed and public sector workers than the government just considered. This would tend to make the iso-collective interest contours steeper yielding higher public spending and more inflation (see Fig. 9.1). The result is achieved by rises in taxation to finance the expansion of the state and the resulting boom in employment, so that a left-wing government ends up promoting the interests of the unemployed and public sector workers at the expense of rentiers and private sector workers.

The political trade-offs portrayed in Fig. 9.1 were obtained for taxation policy, but could just as well have been obtained by taking the tax rate as fixed and using the permitted fiscal deficit ratio as the reconciliatory measure.[7] Such an approach is perhaps more realistic, since it is much more reasonable to assume that the fiscal deficit is the outcome of the day-to-day struggle between the various interest groups as the tax rate is rather sticky. The analysis would then require a minor modification to allow for the interests involved in running an economy properly, which is perhaps best achieved by introducing the 'economy' as a sixth interest group with an elementary interest function depending on the balance of payments (say $U_e(B^*)$). A higher permitted fiscal deficit expands the economy, sucks in more imports and damages the balance of payments position (see equation (8.6.6′)), so that the purely economic interests are in harmony with the interests of rentiers (and perhaps private sector workers) but in conflict with the interests of bureaucrats, civil servants and unemployed. The next section considers an example of manipulating the fiscal deficit ratio rather than the tax rate.

9.3.4 Reconciliation of competing interests under the zero-multiplier hypothesis

So far we have assumed that the government anticipates the employment-generating effects of government expenditures. The zero-multiplier hypothesis relaxes this by assuming instead that the government takes output as given. This may occur because *either* the government is 'naïve' *or* the private sector is smart and markets clear immediately. The latter case is particularly relevant when the policy neutrality proposition of the New Classical School holds (see Section 9.7). The zero-multiplier hypothesis may also be relevant in terms of the first factor, since here we are primarily concerned with the day-to-day running of the public sector. We shall assume that the conflict between the various groups is directed at the budget rather than the tax rate. It then follows that with logarithmic elementary interest functions, the optimal permitted fiscal deficit implies the following pattern of government expenditures[8]

$$G = \alpha Q, \ \alpha = \xi + \tau = \left[\frac{\rho_4 + \rho_5}{b_3(\rho_1 + \rho_4 + \rho_5)}\right] \tag{9.3.12}$$

Hence when state sector interests in the form of public sector jobs or average disposable income and prestige state projects are more heavily weighted compared with the interests of active private sector agents, the permitted fiscal deficit and the share of government in the national income rises. A lower tax rate means that less finance is available, so that the permitted fiscal deficit ratio must rise by an equal amount.

It is clear that *ex post* the share of the public sector is determined by the relative power structure, that is by the weights ρ_1, ρ_4 and ρ_5 and by no other economic outcomes. This is very interesting, since it implies we have found a *theoretical* underpinning for the permanent income hypothesis underlying the autonomous state bureaucracy (see Subsection 9.2.2). Equation (9.3.12) would then give the ratio of G to Q^P, i.e. α, and the speed of implementing state expenditures, β, in equation (9.2.9) would be very fast. In other words after the conflicting interests regarding the fiscal deficit have been resolved, i.e. *ex post*, tax cuts boost output and the public sector multipliers for output with respect to autonomous demand, say $\mu_2^{ss} = \{\mu_2^s | \xi + \tau = \alpha\}$, and competitiveness are larger than the a-political multipliers derived in Section 8.5 of Chapter 8. The *reconciliated public sector* multipliers of output and disposable income with respect to the tax rate are

$$\frac{\partial Q}{\partial \tau} = -c_1^d \mu_2^{ss} Q < 0 \tag{9.3.13}$$

and

$$\frac{\partial Y}{\partial \tau} = -\{1 - i_1^d + i_2^d (l_1/l_2) - \alpha(1 + m_g)^{-1}\} \mu_2^{ss} Q < 0 \tag{9.3.14}$$

so that *ex post* a tax cut boosts both output and real disposable income.

We shall assume from now on that state expenditures and the fiscal deficit are set in the manner just discussed and we shall concentrate on how the other policy variables may be determined.

9.4 Re-election efforts and the optimal political business cycle

9.4.1 The vote function and the balance of payments position reconsidered

After having considered the day-to-day running of an economy with different interest groups, it is appropriate to consider medium-term economic policy. Given that the fiscal deficit was determined by reconciling the interests of active private sector agents and the public sector, it seems reasonable to manipulate demand by satisfying the interests of unemployed and rentiers and other objectives of economic policy. In line with the ideas of Subsection 9.2.2, we shall assume that the government manipulates the tax rate to control output (Q) and that therefore public spending follows from the interest function model (9.3.12).

Since the government (in the form of the incumbent political party) depends on being re-elected for its political survival, re-election must be an important objective of economic policy. We shall assume, for the purpose of this section, that the government is wholeheartedly devoted to securing a maximum number of votes at the forthcoming election (perhaps modified by actions to look after the interests of the 'economy') and manipulates the tax rate accordingly. One might argue that the maximisation of votes cast in favour of the government is unrealistic, since any lead over the opposition would be sufficient to secure re-election. Such a viewpoint might lead to theories of economic policy based on ideology (see Sections 9.5 and 9.6). Here, maximisation of votes is nevertheless considered, because the ruling party may attempt to flatter itself by being as popular or having as many seats in Parliament as possible or alternatively may attempt to safeguard itself against any unexpected vote-losing events. This puts this section in the tradition of the literature discussed in Section 7.3 of Chapter 7, although we modify the tradition by allowing the government also to regulate demand to obtain a satisfactory level of foreign reserves.

Before we can discuss what policy such a government would adopt, we must recall what determines voting patterns. From Part I of this book we know that the main factors are economic performance and social class. We shall assume (for simplicity) that the actual outcome of votes is mainly determined by economic outcomes (cf. Chapters 3, 4 and 5). Rewriting the theoretical vote function (3.4.5) (or (4.3.3)) in continuous time, we obtain

$$l^{\mathrm{R,O}}(T) = \int_0^T \left[\exp(\rho t) \sum_i \gamma_i x_i(t)\right] \mathrm{d}t \qquad (9.4.1)$$

for the lead of the ruling over the main opposition party. The parameter ρ is the rate of decay of voters' memories and T denotes the length of the election period. Any events prior to the current election period are ignored and, perhaps more important, rational anticipation of future events by voters is ruled out (see however Section 9.7). This assumption of myopic voting, established *inter alia* in the empirical literature (see Part I), is crucial to the analysis of this section. The parameter ρ is like a backward (rather than a forward) discount rate and in this sense resembles Pigou's 'defective telescopic faculty'.

To make the vote function operational, we need to explain the economic variables that enter (9.4.1). For this it is perhaps simplest to refer to Table 5.2 in Chapter 5, where we found that the inflation rate, the unemployment rate, real disposable income, the balance of payments and the level of taxation were all important in judging the government's economic performance. Upon substitution of these variables into (9.4.1), one finally obtains the predicted majority over the main opposition party

$$l^{\mathrm{R,O}}(T) = \int_0^T \exp(\rho t) \left[\gamma_0 - \gamma_1 p - \gamma_2 U + \gamma_3 Y - \frac{\gamma_4}{2} B^{*2} - \gamma_5 \tau Q\right] \mathrm{d}t \qquad (9.4.2)$$

In the *optimal* political business cycle discussed in this section, the government would maximise $l^{\mathrm{R,O}}(T)$ as given by equation (9.4.2). Observe that the special case $\gamma_3 = \gamma_4 = \gamma_5$ corresponds to Nordhaus (1975) who focussed only on the political trade-off between inflation and unemployment without reference to a complete macroeconomic model (see Section 7.3 of Chapter 7).

The fact that Nordhaus incorporates the unemployment rates squared seems rather *ad hoc.* If any nonlinearity should be introduced, an inverse nonlinearity (e.g. U^{-2}) seems more appropriate (cf. Pissarides, 1980). Instead a distinction between 'symmetric' and 'a-symmetric' economic variables may be worthwhile. For example, lower levels of unemployment, inflation and taxation are desirable however low the outcome whereas higher levels are undesirable. The reverse argument holds for disposable income. However, *both* large balance of payments surpluses *and* deficits are undesirable to those running the economy. For a perpetual deficit diminishes the level of foreign reserves in an intolerable manner whereas a perpetual surplus feeds into the supply of money and eventually violates monetary targets. An equilibrium balance of payments seems to be an objective of government policy, even if this is *not* reflected in the preferences of the electorate.

The above argument provides the rationale for including the balance of payments, which is the only symmetric variable, in a squared form. We feel this is a *crucial* modification to Nordhaus (1975), since one of the reasons for the lack of empirical evidence found for the Nordhaus-type cycle, at least for the United Kingdom (see Section 7.9 of Chapter 7), might have been the dominating concern wth the balance of payments position. In other words 'the stimulus of the balance of payments was so urgent that the balance of payments cycle may have swamped the political cycle' (see Nordhaus, 1975, p. 187).

In maximising (9.4.3) the government faces the model constraining economic behaviour. The model may be summarised by the dynamic equations (8.9.1)–(8.9.3) governing the evolution of the real supply of money, degree of competitiveness and expectations, the reconciliated public sector IS–LM_s model (9.2.4)–(9.2.5) and (9.3.12) describing real output, equations (8.2.13), (8.8.11) and (8.8.13) giving disposable income, unemployment and inflation and the following equation for the balance of payments position

$$B^* = B^{**}(\overset{-}{L}, \overset{+}{\sigma}; \overset{+}{\tau}, \overset{-}{r}^f) \tag{9.4.3}$$

where ** denotes that B^* is revised to take account of the results in Subsections 9.2.1 and 9.3.4.[9] The vote-maximising tax strategy is difficult to analyse unless we make specific assumptions regarding the dynamic structure of the economy. We make the reasonable assumption of perfect capital mobility (see Subsection 8.9.1), which ensures that the real supply of money does not affect outcomes due to pegged interest rates and renders equation (8.9.1) redundant. Subsections 9.4.2 and 9.4.3 then consider the special cases of purchasing power parity (see Subsection 8.9.2) and perfect foresight (see Subsection 8.9.3), respectively.

9.4.2 Political exploitation of adaptive expectations

Consider a government maximising votes at the forthcoming election by manipulating the tax rate in the world characterised by perfect capital mobility and purchasing power parity. The problem is defined as

$$\text{Max} \int_0^T \exp(\rho t) V(\pi;\ \tau,\ r^f) \tag{9.4.4}$$

subject to the constraint

$$\dot{\pi} = \frac{1}{\tau_e}[p^{**}(\pi;\ \tau,\ r^f) - \pi] \tag{9.4.5}$$

where the partial derivatives are given by

$$\frac{\partial V}{\partial \pi} = -\gamma_1 \frac{\partial p^{**}}{\partial \pi} < 0$$

$$\frac{\partial p^{**}}{\partial \pi} = \beta_2/(1-\beta_3) > 0$$

$$\frac{\partial V}{\partial \tau} = \left\{\left[\gamma_1 \frac{\beta_1}{1-\beta_3} - \gamma_2 u_1\right] c_1^d - (\gamma_3+\gamma_5)[1 - i_1^d - \alpha(1+m_g)^{-1}] - \gamma_4 b_4 B^* + \gamma_5 c_1^d\right\} \mu_1^{ss} Q$$

and

$$\frac{\partial p^{**}}{\partial \tau} = -\beta_1 c_1^d \mu_1^{ss} Q < 0$$

where b_4 is positive and increases with the marginal propensities to import and μ_1^{ss} equals μ_2^{ss} without the crowding out term (cf. (8.2.15)). Tax cuts have an undetermined effect on popularity, since the boost in popularity due to better unemployment figures, higher disposable income and the lower tax level of taxation may be swamped by higher inflation and a draining of foreign reserves. However low expectations of inflation unambiguously improve political popularity. Since expectations are sluggish, the government strategy will be to dampen expectations over the course of the election cycle. This idea becomes clear upon solving the above problem formally by means of Pontryagin's Maximum Principle (see Bryson and Ho, 1969, for a good exposition of optimal control techniques).

Consider the Hamiltonian functional

$$H = \exp(\rho t) V(\pi;\ \tau,\ r^f) + \chi \frac{1}{\tau_e} [p^{**}(\pi;\ \tau,\ r^f) - \pi] \tag{9.4.6}$$

where χ is the adjoint variable corresponding to equation (9.4.5). The stationarity condition $(\partial H/\partial \tau) = 0$ may be solved for χ to give

$$\chi = -\tau_e \exp(\rho t)(\partial V/\partial \tau)/(\partial p^{**}/\partial \tau) \tag{9.4.7}$$

and the solution must also satisfy the adjoint equation

$$\dot{\chi} = -\left(\frac{\partial H}{\partial \pi}\right) = -\exp(\rho t)\left(\frac{\partial V}{\partial \pi}\right) + \frac{\chi}{\tau_e}\left(\frac{1-\beta_2-\beta_3}{1-\beta_3}\right) \tag{9.4.8}$$

Upon differentiating (9.4.7) with respect to time and substituting χ and $\dot{\chi}$ into (9.4.8), one obtains the differential equation

$$\dot{X}_1 = \left[\frac{1}{\tau_e}\left(\frac{1-\beta_2-\beta_3}{1-\beta_3}\right) - \rho\right] X_1 + \frac{1}{\tau_e}\left(\frac{\partial V}{\partial \pi}\right) \tag{9.4.9}$$

in terms of the variable $X_1 = (\partial V/\partial \tau)/(\partial p^{**}/\partial \tau)$. Upon substituting the partial derivatives of (9.4.4)–(9.4.5) into (9.4.9), one obtains the differential equation

$$\dot{B}^* = \left[\frac{1}{\tau_e}\left(\frac{1-\beta_2-\beta_3}{1-\beta_3}\right) - \rho\right][B^* - X_2] - X_3 \tag{9.4.10}$$

where

$$X_2 = \left\{\left[\gamma_1\left(\frac{\beta_1}{1-\beta_3}\right) - \gamma_2 u_1\right] c_1^d - (\gamma_3 + \gamma_5)[1 - i_1^d - \alpha(1+m_g)^{-1}] + \gamma_5 c_1^d\right\} \Big/ (\gamma_4 \beta_4)$$

and

$$X_3 = \left(\frac{\gamma_1 \beta_2 \beta_1 c_1^d}{\gamma_4 b_4 (1-\beta_3)}\right)$$

Solving (9.4.10) gives the optimal balance of payments trajectory

$$B^*(t) = B^*(0) - [B^*(0) - B_T^*] \exp\left\{\left[\frac{1}{\tau_e}\left(\frac{1-\beta_2-\beta_3}{1-\beta_3}\right) - \rho\right](t - T)\right\} \tag{9.4.11}$$

Fig. 9.2 *Concern with vote-maximisation and the balance of payments position*

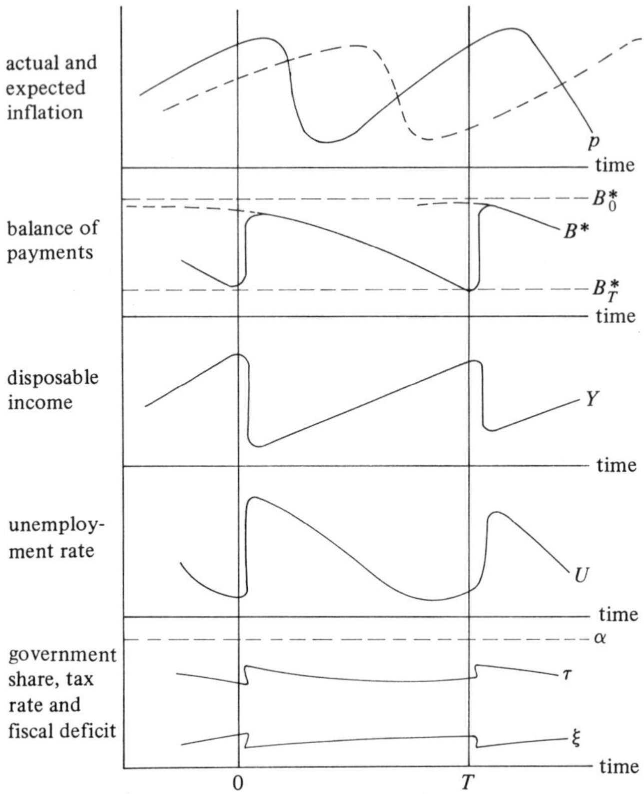

where the balance of payments attained on election eve follows from $\lim_{t\uparrow T} \chi(t) = 0$ or $X_1 = 0$, and is given by

$$B_T^* = \lim_{t \uparrow T} B^*(t) = X_2 \tag{9.4.12}$$

and the balance of payments attained immediately after the election (ending the previous period) is approximately given by

$$B^*(0) \cong B_0^* = \frac{+\gamma_1\beta_2\beta_1 c_1^d}{\gamma_4 b_4\left[\frac{1}{\tau_e}(1-\beta_2-\beta_3)-\rho(1-\beta_3)\right]} + X_2 > B_T^* \tag{9.4.13}$$

Hence, from (9.4.13) and (9.4.10) the balance of payments deteriorates over the election period owing to the buying of votes by means of gradual cuts in the tax rate. The remaining economic outcomes follow from the implied trajectory for the tax rate and are drawn in Fig. 9.2.

Immediately after an election the new government raises the tax rate to a high level, which implies an instantaneous loss in popularity due to higher unemployment and cuts in disposable income (though these are partially offset by an improved balance of payments position). However the main objective of this strategy is to obtain a reduction in the rate of inflation, which cannot be achieved instantaneously because of the gradual nature of adaptation to changes in the costs of living, and subsequently to lower expectations also. The timing of the strategy over the election period is crucial as can be seen from the top panel of Fig. 9.2. The optimal strategy is to choose the tax rate so that the expected rate of inflation is lowest *on* election eve. This tactic depresses wage settlements and actual inflation just before an election, which gives scope for popular reflationary measures towards election eve. In this sense the government invests in low levels of expectation. The vote-maximising strategy relies on 'cheating' the electorate by lumbering it (and the next administration) with the inflationary consequences of a myopic policy (see Section 9.7). This type of recurring political decision-making has been called the optimal political business cycle. Observe that the share of government spending is unaffected by the vote-maximising tactics in our model, since the loss in finance due to cuts in taxes manifests itself in higher fiscal deficits.

The extent to which a government is prepared to force down the level of foreign reserves (the tax rate and unemployment rate) increases as the importance of unemployment, the level of taxation and disposable income to the electorate increases and the importance of inflation diminishes. An increase in the importance of the balance of payments objective reduces the magnitude of the surplus or deficit on election eve, so that in the case of surplus demand is stimulated by cutting the tax rate and in the case of a deficit, demand is dampened.

The magnitude of the cycle is measured by $(B_0^* - B_T^*)$. An overwhelming concern with the balance of payments (high γ_4) very much swamps the optimal political business cycle. We also note that with an electorate which does *not* care about inflation at all there is no reason to have a vote-maximising cycle, since expectations are irrelevant then. This is a particularly serious critique, because the rentier fraction of the electorate is likely to be small in size and therefore popularity may not be very strongly affected by inflation (see Chapters 4 and 5). A low value of $[(1/\tau_e)(1 - \beta_2 - \beta_3) - \rho(1 - \beta_3)]$ implies that (i) the magnitude of the cycle increases and (ii) the government implements most of the popular policies near election eve, because an electorate with a high rate of memory loss does not remember much of the earlier policies anyway and an economy with little compensation for increases in the cost of living and slow formation of expectations does not care too much about post-election inflationary consequences. The extreme case of perfect foresight ($\tau_e = 0$) completely destroys the cycle.

9.4.3 Manipulation of competitiveness

The results of the previous section relied essentially on the adaptive expectations mechanism. Let us abandon this assumption and have perfect foresight ($\tau_e = 0$) instead (cf. Section 9.7). The political cycle as discussed in the previous section then disappears, but other cycles may be possible. Here we give an example based on manipulating competitiveness. We assume instead of purchasing power parity a regime of fixed exchange rates (see Subsection 8.6.3) and maintain the vote-maximising hypothesis. Because we do not wish to obtain a political cycle which depends crucially on the electorate being concerned with inflation (as in Subsection 9.4.2), we assume $\gamma_1 = 0$. The problem is to choose the tax rate to maximise the political criterion (9.4.2) subject to equation (8.9.2) describing the developing of the terms of trade.

Observe that as before a cut in the tax rate improves unemployment, disposable income and the level of taxation at the same time as lowering the balance of payments. An improvement in competitiveness unambiguously improves political popularity. The rate of change in the terms of trade depends inversely upon the inflation rate, which in turn increases with stimulatory tax cuts and improvements in competitiveness, so that the terms of trade adjust upwards when competitiveness is bad or the tax rate is high. Since the structure is similar to the problem of Subsection 9.4.2, an analogous story can be told.

On the morning after an election the victor cuts inflation by using a high rate of taxation to dampen the economy, which should be interpreted as an 'investment' in improving competitiveness. Towards the end of the election period the unpopular policy is gradually replaced to obtain better unemployment and disposable income figures. On election eve the level of competitiveness is best even though the rate of domestic inflation may be high. The worsening of competitiveness is thereby postponed until after election eve. Over the election period taxes and unemployment fall whereas disposable income, inflation and the fiscal deficit rise. Uncompetitiveness ($1/\sigma$) follows a path which has the same shape as the π-path in the top panel of Fig. 9.2 and is smoother than the other paths.

The above type of political manipulation of competitiveness is not always worthwhile. For example, when the electorate does care about inflation an improvement in competitiveness does not necessarily boost popularity, owing to the induced inflationary pressures. This is made particularly clear when one considers the implications of the J-curve for the balance of payments. The J-curve arises when competitiveness affects exports more realistically after a time lag. The short-run effect of an improvement in the level of competitiveness is then a worsening of the balance of payments because of the induced inflation at home, while the full beneficial impacts on the balance of payments do not occur until exports adjust. In such a situation a myopic vote-maximising government may be inclined to dampen the economy and/or appreciate the currency in order to gain votes on a ticket of reduced inflation.

9.4.4 Strategic voting and far-sighted governments

The discussion in Sections 4 and 5 of Chapter 7 on strategic voting and on the government maximising the expected uninterrupted length in office can be suitably modified to fit the model discussed in this chapter.

An electorate can penalise a government for deliberately causing economic cycles for political reasons by strategically changing its voting pattern *on* election day (cf. MacRae, 1977). The preferences of the electorate may remain the same at all points of time before the election, but on election day the voters must increase the importance of inflation to persuade the government to abandon the reflation of demand in order to have the same outcome on election day as just after the election. Such a strategy would eventually eliminate the optimal political business cycle, since it might take several election periods for the government to realise that it cannot get away with manipulating votes. For example, in the case of

Subsection 9.4.2 the electorate simply raises the relative weight of inflation on election eve in the criterion function (9.4.2) from γ_1 to

$$\left[1+\frac{\beta_2}{\left[\frac{1}{\tau_e}\left(\frac{1-\beta_2-\beta_3}{1-\beta_3}\right)-\rho\right]}\right]\gamma_1>\gamma_1 \qquad (9.4.14)$$

and thereby changes the boundary condition to ensure $B_T^* = B_0^*$.

When a government maximises the uninterrupted length in office and the electorate does not have any memory ($\rho = \infty$), the government maximises

$$\sum_{k=1}^{\infty} Z_k, \quad Z_1 = p(T), \quad Z_k = p(kT)Z_{k-1} \qquad (9.4.15)$$

where $p(T)$ denote the expected number of votes attained during the election at time T and Z_k denotes the probability of being k uninterrupted terms in office. Frey and Ramser (1976) assume that *elections are held continuously* and therefore approximate (9.4.15) by

$$\int_0^{\infty} Z(k)\,\mathrm{d}k, \quad Z_0 = p(0), \quad \dot{Z} = \{p(kT)-1\}Z \qquad (9.4.16)$$

It is now a straightforward exercise to show that the optimal strategy for a government corresponds to the steady state optimum obtained by maximising

$$\int_0^{\infty} \exp(-\hat{\rho}t)\left[\gamma_0-\gamma_1 p-\gamma_2 U+\gamma_3 Y-\frac{\gamma_4}{2}B^{*2}-\gamma_5\tau Q\right]\mathrm{d}t \qquad (9.4.17)$$

where $\hat{\rho}$ now denotes a *forward* discount rate equal to the probability of not being re-elected (i.e. $\hat{\rho} = 1-\rho$). This shows that objectives slightly different from vote-maximisation (e.g. maximising the uninterrupted length in office) may yield non-myopic socially-optimal strategies and no political business cycles.

9.5 Maximising ideology subject to a re-election constraint

The optimal political business cycles derived in the previous section assumed that a government maximised the expected number of votes at the forthcoming election. This is not necessarily realistic, since a simple majority would be sufficient to secure re-election and a government may wish to promote its own ideological objectives rather than the preferences of the electorate (see Section 7.6 of Chapter 7). Instead a government might maximise its own ideology subject to a number of constraints to ensure re-election, control of the state bureaucracy and feasibility of key economic target variables.

The government's problem may be formalised by choosing the tax rate to maximise discounted ideology

$$i = \int_0^{\infty} \exp(-\hat{\rho}t)I(p, U, Y, B^*, \tau Q)\,\mathrm{d}t \qquad (9.5.1)$$

subject to the constraints describing economic behaviour and the re-election constraints

Fig. 9.3 *Social (ideological) and political weighting schemes*

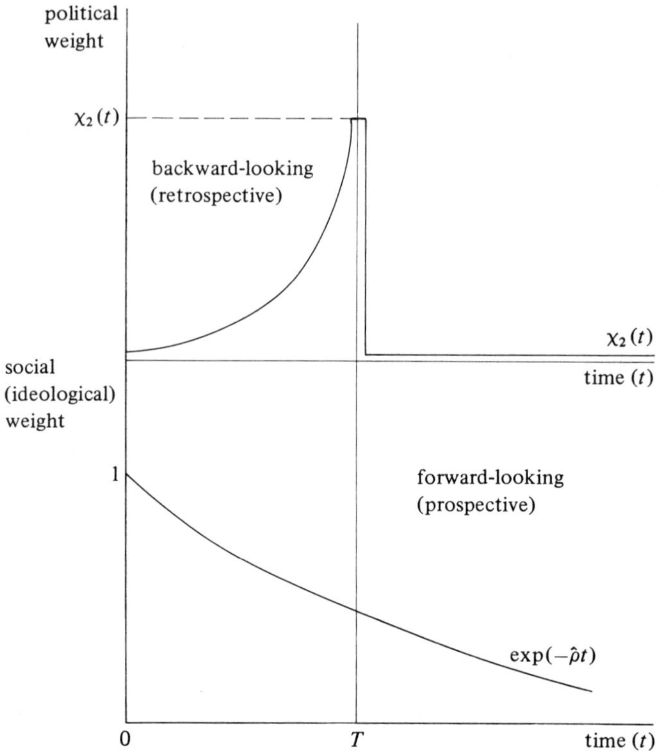

$$l^{\mathrm{R,O}}(kT) \geqslant 0.5 + \epsilon, \quad k = 1, 2, 3, \ldots \tag{9.5.2}$$

where $l^{\mathrm{R,O}}$ is given by

$$\dot{z} = [\gamma_0^{\mathrm{R}} - \gamma_1^{\mathrm{R}} p - \gamma_2^{\mathrm{R}} U + \gamma_3^{\mathrm{R}} Y - \gamma_4^{\mathrm{R}} B^{*2} - \gamma_5^{\mathrm{R}}(\tau Q)] - \rho z,$$

$$l^{\mathrm{R,O}}(t) = z(t) \exp(\rho t) \tag{9.5.3}$$

(cf. (9.4.2)) and ϵ denotes the popularity margin. The parameter $\hat{\rho}$ denotes the forward-looking discount rate employed by the government in discounting its own ideology and ρ is a backward-looking discount rate used by the electorate (see Fig. 9.3).

Assume the conditions of Subsection 9.4.2 and that the government is only interested in securing the first election ($k = 1$). The solution then follows, using Pontryagin's Maximum Principle (see Bryson and Ho, 1969), from the differential equation (cf. (9.4.9))

$$\dot{X}_1^I + \hat{\chi}_2 \dot{X}_1^R = \frac{1}{\tau_e}\left(\frac{1 - \beta_2 - \beta_3}{1 - \beta_3}\right)(X_1^I + \hat{\chi}_2 X_1^R)$$

$$+ \hat{\rho} X_1^I - \rho X_1^R - \frac{1}{\tau_e}\left(\frac{\beta_2}{1 - \beta_3}\right)(\gamma_1^I + \hat{\chi}_2 \gamma_{-1}^R) \tag{9.5.4}$$

where $X^I = (\partial I/\partial \tau)/(\partial p^{**}/\partial \tau)$, $X^R = (\partial V/\partial \tau)/(\partial p^{**}/\partial \tau)$, $\hat{\chi}_2 = \exp(\hat{\rho}t)\chi_2$ and

$$\chi_2(t) = \chi_2(T)\mathrm{H}(t-T)\exp\{\rho(t-T)\}$$

Here χ_2 denotes the adjoint variable corresponding to state equation (9.5.3) for government popularity and H(k) denotes the Heaviside function ($\mathrm{H}(k) = 0, k \leqq 0$, $\mathrm{H}(k) = 1, k > 0$). The problem may be decomposed by first finding the post-election and then the pre-election strategy. After the election ($t > T$) the political weight, χ_2, is zero and the optimal strategy is simply the ideological welfare optimum (cf. Phelps, 1967). The derivation of the post-election strategy may be determined independently of the pre-election objectives, which is a simple consequence of Bellman's principle of dynamic programming. For the pre-election strategy we have three possibilities. The first case is a non-binding election constraint (9.5.2), so that the shadow price on the popularity margin, $\chi_2(t)$, is zero for all t. The government then simply chooses economic policy to maximise its own welfare (9.5.1) and the ideological welfare optimum pertains all the time. The second possibility is a bottle-neck election, so that the shadow price, $\chi_2(T)$, is strictly positive and the long-term ideology is frustrated by short-term election problems. The magnitude of $\chi_2(T)$ gives the increase in ideological welfare which the government obtains from a relaxation of the required political lead at the forthcoming election, i.e. $\chi_2(T) = (\partial i/\partial \epsilon)$, and which is therefore called a shadow price. This information is useful when there is a wind-fall gain in popularity, for example as a result of winning the World Cup, since it shows by how much the government can implement its own ideology without losing the election. The third possibility is that there exists no $\chi_2(T)$ which ensures a feasible outcome *and* $l^{\mathrm{R,O}}(T) \geqq 0.5 + \epsilon$, so that the government cannot manipulate votes sufficiently to secure a re-election.

The second possibility is the most interesting one and will be further analysed for the case of indifference between the welfare of different generations, that is the 'golden rule' case ($\hat{\rho} = 0$) and no loss of memory ($\rho = 0$). Choosing the same functional form for the current measures of ideology and popularity as in Sub-section 9.4.1, one obtains the optimal balance of payments trajectory (9.4.10)–(9.4.13) with $\rho = 0$ and $\{\gamma_i = \gamma_i^I + \hat{\chi}_2\gamma_i^R, i = 1, 2, \ldots 5\}$. The tax rate therefore gradually reduces towards election eve, on election eve a myopic optimum of a weighted combination of ideological and political welfare is attained, and immediately afterwards the tax rate is increased to the purely ideological welfare optimum. A left-wing government is probably more interested in unemployment and rather less in inflation (high γ_2, low γ_1), whereas a right-wing government is typically more interested in inflation and less in unemployment (high γ_1, low γ_2). Taking account of these differences in ideology and assuming that the preferences of the electorate are somewhere in the middle, it follows that a left-wing government forces down unemployment more during the first election period, although not as low as it would like to, owing to frustration of ideology by re-election efforts, than a right-wing government and allows higher inflation rates. Similarly, the ideological objectives relating to disposable income and public spending will be modified when the oncoming election is a bottle-neck.

The general case with some memory loss or some ideological discounting of future generations gives valuable insights into the dynamic trade-offs between ideology and re-election objectives. Although it is tedious, owing to the presence of time-varying parameters, to obtain an analytical expression for the optimal trajectories, it can be proved that the shadow price on popularity χ_2, increases with time (cf. Fig. 9.3) and therefore the weights γ_i will become increasingly dominated by the γ_i^R as the election approaches. The result is that the government implements a fairly ideological strategy in the early periods of its term in office and as the election approaches the government adjusts its ideological actions in order to secure re-election.

9.6 Satisficing popularity, ideology and economic policy

9.6.1 Political–economic reaction functions

In Subsection 7.7.1 of Chapter 7 it was argued that a government might not always implement *optimal* political–economic strategies of the type discussed in Sections 9.2, 9.3, 9.4 and 9.5. Instead of *ex ante* optimisation an *ex post* behavioural or satisficing approach was judged to be more realistic in practice. Such an approach is implicit in the methodology of the Zürich School (see Subsection 7.7.2). The object of this section is to formalise a system of political–economic reaction functions based on a modified version of the Zürich School, introduce the system into the purely economic model of Chapter 8 and analyse the static and dynamic interactions between the political formulation of policy and economic behaviour.

The main factors we wish to incorporate in an analysis of economic policy are (i) re-election efforts (cf. Section 9.4), (ii) conflict with the state bureaucracy and ideology, and (iii) concern with the smooth functioning of the economy. Criteria (i) and (iii) are captured by the political lead of the government over the opposition modified for the balance of payments objective (9.4.2). An illustrative three-tier system of political–economic reaction functions is defined by a rule for the tax rate

$$\dot{\tau} = \{\Lambda_1 \mathrm{H}(-l^{\mathrm{R,O}}) + \Lambda_2 \mathrm{H}(l^{\mathrm{R,O}})\} l^{\mathrm{R,O}}, \ \Lambda_1 \geqq 0 \tag{9.6.1}$$

and a rule for the level of public spending

$$\dot{G} = \beta\{-\Lambda_3 \mathrm{H}(-l^{\mathrm{R,O}}) + (\xi + \tau)Q - G\}, \quad \Lambda_3 \geqq 0, \quad \beta \geqq 0 \tag{9.6.2}$$

where $\mathrm{H}(l^{\mathrm{R,O}})$ denotes the Heaviside dummy which is zero unless $l^{\mathrm{R,O}} > 0$ (cf. Subsection 7.7.2) and $l^{\mathrm{R,O}}$ should be interpreted as the difference between the actual political lead and the desired lead (say 8 per cent). Equations (9.6.1) and (9.6.2) may be interpreted as continuous-time versions of the type of empirical political–economic reaction functions investigated by Wright (1974), Frey (1978a, b) or Frey and Schneider (1978a, b). They are meant to replace the optimal tax rate portrayed in Fig. 9.2 and the gradual control of the state hypothesis (9.2.10) and serve merely as an illustration of the behavioural approach.

The reaction function for the tax rate shows that when there is a popularity deficit, the government, whatever its ideology, reduces the tax rate at the speed Λ_1 in order to reduce unemployment and the level of taxation, raise disposable income and thereby increase the chances of re-election. Of course such a strategy assumes that the lack in popularity is not caused by too high inflation or, possibly, that the electorate is not very concerned with inflation. Alternatively, the proportion of rentier voters should be small. When the government enjoys a popularity surplus, it also enjoys some political slack which may be used for ideological purposes. A left-wing government may be inclined to raise taxes, which is a relatively unpopular policy necessary to finance more (ideological) state projects. The ideology of a right-wing government might force it to reduce taxes in an attempt to minimise state intervention and provide incentives. Thus a left-wing and a right-wing administration use $\Lambda_2 > 0$ and $\Lambda_2 < 0$, respectively. In this sense (9.6.1) is an extension of the analytical reaction function employed in Fassbender (1981), where a government uses an excess popularity to increase taxes regardless of its ideology. Another major extension is the government's concern over the level of foreign reserves. Where there are large deficits (surpluses), the government may reduce (increase) imports by dampening (reflating) the economy. This is achieved by increasing (reducing) the tax rate.

It is a difficult and long process to persuade the state bureaucracy to undertake and implement new state projects (see Section 9.2). We therefore adopt the view that the adjustment of state spending to the desired level is sluggish and takes on average $1/\beta$ periods to complete. The desired level of state spending is determined by re-election, ideology and balance of payments considerations. When the balance of payments is in equilibrium and popularity is satisfactory, the political–economic reaction function reduces to a rule for controlling the state bureaucracy (see equation (9.2.10)). This rule shows how the ideology of a government manifests itself in the attitude to the bureaucracy. The long-run limit on the ratio of state spending to output equals the sum of the long-run desired fiscal deficit ratio, ξ, and the tax rate, τ. A left-wing government tends to increase the relative size of the state, since it typically allows a greater deficit (high ξ) and in periods of excess popularity it finances more state spending by raising the tax rate. A right-wing government acts in an opposite manner, hence it tends to reduce state intervention. Observe that the reaction functions for the tax rate and state spending are specified, in contrast to previous approaches, as an *interdependent* system of policy formulation as the tax rate acts in the long run as a control on the size of the state bureaucracy. When the level of foreign reserves diminishes too rapidly, the government holds back government spending in an attempt to reduce both private and public sector imports. The intensity of this stabilisation component of the rule is measured by γ_4.

The elements of the reaction function for state spending discussed so far capture the attempts to maintain the feasibility of key target variables and the promotion of ideology. These policy components carry on regardless of the popularity of the government, but when re-election chances are low the government undertakes additional state projects to improve popularity.

To close the model we need to link the system of reaction functions to an economic model. This will be the model described in Chapter 8 with the assumptions of perfect foresight, perfect capital mobility and purchasing power parity (see Section 8.9). The advantage of these assumptions is that we can concentrate on the dynamics of the political–economic reaction functions only[10] and, in particular, analyse the *discontinuous* nature of political–economic reaction functions based on satisficing theory. This second aspect has been ignored in the previous literature (e.g. Fassbender, 1981). We also borrow the implicit assumption of the

Zürich School that the electorate has no memory and judges the government simply by its current performance ($\rho = \infty$).

9.6.2 *Comparative statics*

The equilibrium of the system, say (τ^*, G^*), satisfies

$$\{\tau, G | l^{\mathrm{R,O}} = 0, \ (\xi + \tau)Q = G\} \tag{9.6.3}$$

so that at the equilibrium popularity has reached its desired level and strict control on the budget of the state bureaucracy is achieved. Observe that in the long run the balance of payments may not be in equilibrium, but it may be that the permitted fiscal deficit ratio is chosen to ensure a stationary level of foreign reserves in the long run. It is interesting to examine the comparative statics of the equilibrium strategies with respect to the permitted public sector fiscal deficit ratio, ξ, and with respect to the desired lead over the opposition.

This may be done with the aid of Fig. 9.4. The RR-curve shows the combinations of G and τ for which a satisfactory vote outcome is attained ($l^{\mathrm{R,O}} = 0$). This curve is almost always upward-sloping, since a higher level of state spending requires a higher tax rate to offset the increase in popularity. The RR-curve shifts upwards when the government desires a greater lead over the opposition, since with unchanged state spending tax cuts are required to obtain the increase in popularity. The II-curve shows the combinations of G and τ for which the ideology objective is attained, that is for which the desired control of the state is achieved ($(\xi + \tau)Q = G$). It is also upward-sloping, since a higher tax rate permits the finance of more state spending, and shifts upwards when the permitted fiscal deficit ratio, ξ, is increased.

The equilibrium strategies, (τ^*, G^*), are given by the intersection of the RR-curve and the II-curve. The comparative statics properties of the equilibrium depend critically on the relative steepness of these two curves. When the RR-curve is steeper than the II-curve, an increase in the desired political lead (or a decrease in the permitted fiscal deficit ratio) reduces the equilibrium levels of state spending and the tax rate, because the cut in the tax rate causes an increase in popularity (or a reduction in the size of the state) and the lower level of state spending offsets the resulting tighter control on the bureaucracy (or increase in popularity). When the II-curve is steeper than the RR-curve an increase in the popularity margin or a decrease in the permitted fiscal deficit ratio increases the equilibrium levels of the tax rate and state spending, because now state spending is used to increase popularity and the tax rate is used as an instrument of finance. When a tax cut improves popularity under *the strict control of the state hypothesis* (see Subsection 9.2.1), the RR-curve is steeper and tax cuts are used to improve popularity rather than to control the size of the state. The above holds when the inequality

$$\left[-\gamma_1\left(\frac{\beta_1}{1-\beta_2-\beta_3}\right)+\gamma_2 u_1-\gamma_5\right]\ [(1+m_g)^{-1}-c_1^d] - (\gamma_3+\gamma_5)\left[1-i_1^d-\frac{1+\xi}{1+m_g}\right]+\gamma_4 b_4 B^* < 0 \tag{9.6.4}$$

Fig. 9.4 *Phase diagrams for the political–economic system of reaction functions*

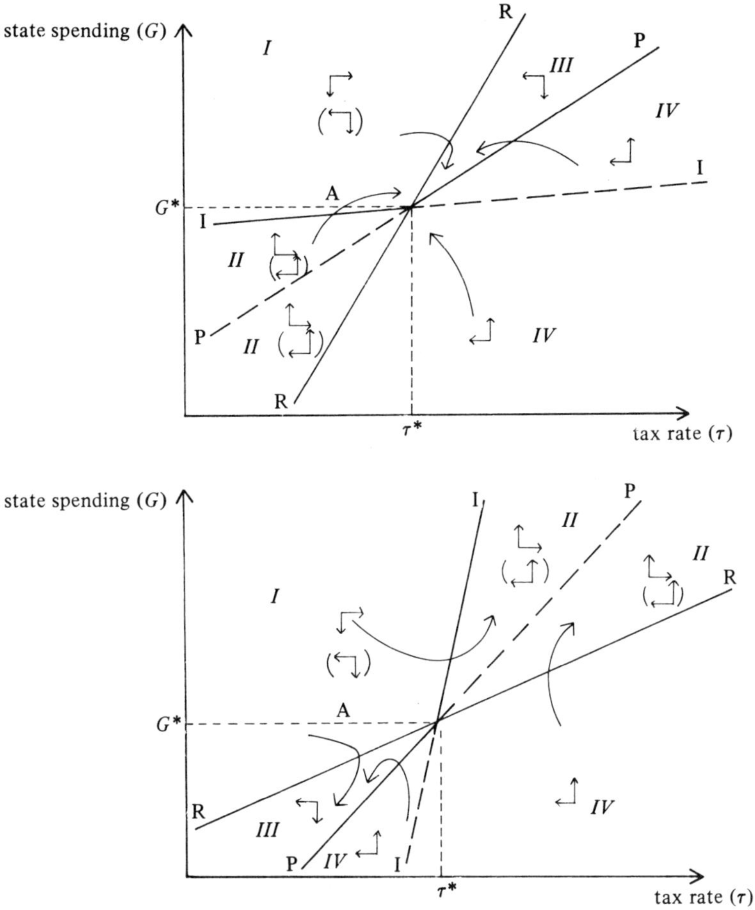

Key: Region I – popularity surplus and too large state ($\dot{G} < 0$, $\dot{\tau} > 0$ ($\dot{\tau} < 0$))
II – popularity surplus and too small state ($\dot{G} > 0$, $\dot{\tau} > 0$ ($\dot{\tau} < 0$))
III – popularity crisis and too large state ($\dot{G} < 0$, $\dot{\tau} > 0$)
IV – popularity crisis and too small state ($\dot{G} > 0$, $\dot{\tau} < 0$)

Note: The diagrams have been drawn for the left-wing political–economic system and, if different, the outcome for the right-wing system is denoted in brackets. For simplicity, the curves in the diagrams have been drawn linearly.

is satisfied. The RR-curve is therefore steeper than the II-curve when the electorate attaches relatively more value to improving the balance of payments (when in deficit) and lowering the inflation rate and the level of taxation than to decreasing the outcome of the unemployment rate. When the electorate values disposable income very much and the government operates with a high permitted fiscal deficit ratio, (9.6.4) is likely to be violated and there are strong incentives to use the tax rate as an instrument of finance in the equilibrium.

9.6.3 The principle of effective political–economic assignment

Fig. 9.4 also shows the PP-curve, that is the combinations of G and τ for which $\dot{G} = 0$ holds with a popularity deficit. It can be shown that the slope of the PP-curve is somewhere between the slopes of the RR-curve and the II-curve. The II-curve shows the G and τ for which there is a popularity surplus and $\dot{G} = 0$ holds, whereas the RR-curve shows the G and τ for which $\dot{\tau} = 0$ holds. These three curves combined allow an examination of the stability of the system of reaction functions.

Fig. 9.4 shows how the (τ, G)-space may be divided into four regions each with a different phase direction, which allows Fig. 9.4 to be interpreted as a version of Poincaré's phase diagram. For example, Region *III* is one of popularity crisis and a too-large size of the state sector. This calls for a cut in the tax rate and lower levels of state spending. To illustrate the adjustment process, it is probably best to distinguish the two cases above first for a left-wing and then for a right-wing administration. When (9.6.4) holds for a left-wing system ($\Lambda_2 > 0$), any displacement from the equilibrium, say to point A in Region *I*, causes a popularity surplus and a too large state. This prompts the government to cut state spending and raise the tax rate, so that the system eventually moves into Region *II* (or *III*) with a popularity surplus (crisis) and a too small (big) state and therefore state spending and the tax rate are raised (reduced). This adjustment process moves the system away from the equilibrium. A right-wing system ($\Lambda_2 < 0$) moves away from the equilibrium irrespective of the relative steepness of the RR-curve and the II-curve. Typically, a right-wing administration tends to reduce the tax rate (and state spending) *ad infinitum* until removed from office.

Thus a left-wing system is stable when the electorate attaches rather more importance to the removal of balance of payments deficits, low inflation rates and low levels of taxation than to high disposable income (if $\xi > m_g - i_1^d$) and low unemployment figures whereas a right-wing system is always unstable.[11] It is important to notice that these results are independent of the speeds of adjustment used in the reaction functions (Λ_i, β) and depend only on the preferences of the electorate and the structural parameters describing the economy (see (9.6.4)). More specifically, the stability of the left-wing system relies on the tax rate being more effective in influencing popularity than state spending is

$$\frac{(\partial l^{\mathrm{R,O}}/\partial \tau)}{(\partial X/\partial \tau)} > \frac{(\partial l^{\mathrm{R,O}}/\partial G)}{(\partial X/\partial G)} \tag{9.6.5}$$

where $X = (\xi + \tau)Q - G$. When state spending has a comparative advantage over the tax rate in influencing popularity and by implication a comparative disadvantage in influencing the fiscal deficit (i.e. (9.6.5) does not hold), the left-wing system is unstable.[12] However, this does not mean that a left-wing system of reaction functions with a different assignment structure is also unstable.

This section so far has only accounted for political dynamics and ignored the intrinsic dynamics of the economy (equations (8.9.1), (8.9.2) and (8.9.3)). Analysis of political–economic systems which allows for both political and economic dynamics should prove a useful direction for future research.

9.7 Implications of rational expectations for the political business cycle

9.7.1 Assumptions of the New Classical School of macroeconomics

In Section 8 of Chapter 7 we noted the contradiction between the neutrality position of the New Classical School of macroeconomics and the political business cycle. The objection to the economic manipulation of votes may be summarised as follows (cf. McCallum, 1978). When there are rational expectations, the systematic exploitation of dynamic trade-offs would be 'seen through' and this would render the manipulation of votes impossible. We have already seen in Section 7.4 of Chapter 7 and in Subsection 9.4.4 of the present chapter that the voters by changing their preference on election eve can punish a government for causing political–economic instability, but here we focus on rational expectations of government policy and *unchanged* preferences of the electorate (as represented by the popularity function (9.4.2) of Subsection 9.4.1). Before we can commence a serious analysis of the critique of the New Classical School, we need to expose its twin assumptions of self-regulating markets and rational expectations.

Consider therefore a discrete-time version of the reduced-form price equation (8.8.13)

$$\hat{P}_t - \hat{P}_{t-1} = \beta_0 + \beta_1 Q_t + \beta_2(\hat{P}^e_{t/t-1} - \hat{P}_{t-1}) + \beta_3(p_f + e)_t + \epsilon^m_t \qquad (9.7.1)$$

where $\hat{P}_t$ denotes the logarithm of the price level at time t, $\hat{P}^e_{t/t-1}$ denotes the expected value of $\hat{P}_t$ formed at time $t-1$ and ϵ^m_t is an independently distributed error term in the model. The error term ϵ^m_t captures shocks in the labour and goods markets and is induced to capture the stochastic implications of the rational expectations hypothesis. For simplicity we adopt the view that exchange rates are formed according to the purchasing power parity hypothesis (8.9.7), so that $p^d = p = p^f + e$ holds. When used in conjunction with an innocent assumption of homogeneity in equation (8.8.1), that is $a_3 = 1 - a_2$, it follows that equation (9.7.1) may be rewritten as

$$\hat{P}_t - \hat{P}_{t-1} = \hat{\beta}_0 + \hat{\beta}_1 Q_t + b_2(\hat{P}^e_{t/t-1} - P_{t-1}) + \hat{\epsilon}^m_t \qquad (9.7.2)$$

where $\hat{\beta}_i = \beta_i/(\delta a_2)$ and $\hat{\epsilon}_t = \epsilon^m_t/(\delta a_2)$. An essential feature of the New Classical School is rapid market clearing, which in terms of our equation (9.7.2) implies that there is no money illusion ($b_2 = 1$) in the wage equation (8.8.5). This feature can be made more transparent by inverting the 'Phillips curve' (9.7.2) for the case $b_2 = 1$, that is

$$Q_t = Q^n + (\hat{P}_t - \hat{P}^e_{t/t-1})/\hat{\beta}_1 - \hat{\epsilon}^m_t/\hat{\beta}_1 \qquad (9.7.3)$$

where $Q^n_t = -\hat{\beta}_0/\hat{\beta}_1$ denotes the natural level of output. The interpretation of the aggregate supply equation (9.7.3) is that when prices are higher than expected firms supply more output, which corresponds to stochastic market clearing. When Okun's law (8.8.11) is used to interpret equation (9.7.3) in terms of unemployment, that is

$$U_t = U^n - u_1(\hat{P}_t - \hat{P}^e_{t/t-1})/\hat{\beta}_1 + u_1 \hat{\epsilon}^m_t/\hat{\beta}_1 \qquad (9.7.4)$$

where U^n denotes the natural rate of unemployment, the interpretation is as follows. When prices are higher than expected, real wages are lower than expected, the supply of labour diminishes, the unanticipated cheapness of labour induces additional demand for workers and consequently the level of unemployment diminishes. The above argument clearly shows the implicit assumption of self-regulating markets when there is no money illusion in wage formation or when workers are unable to transmit increases in the expected cost of living into increases in wages (cf. Friedman, 1968).

Let us now consider the second main hypothesis of the New Classical School, that is the rational expectations hypothesis (REH), since without a theory of unanticipated and anticipated components of price inflation the aggregate supply equation is incomplete. The REH is meant to replace the adaptive expectations hypothesis (AEH), which in discrete time may be written as (cf. equation (8.8.9))

$$\Delta(\hat{P}^e_{t/t-1} - \hat{P}_{t-1}) = \frac{1}{\tau_e}[\hat{P}_{t-1} - \hat{P}^e_{t-1/t-2}] \qquad (9.7.5)$$

where Δ is the difference operator. Under adaptive expectations agents revise their expectations in the light of *past* errors of expectations and in this sense agents simply extrapolate past behaviour. The New Classical School has raised two related objections to the AEH. The first is that under the AEH it is possible for agents to make *systematic* mistakes. For example, when the rate of price inflation is accelerating expectations systematically underestimate the actual rate of price inflation. Another example is the Nordhaus (1975) model of the political business cycle, where election period after election period private sector agents make the same mistake of under-estimating the actual inflation rate towards the end of the election period and are therefore systematically fooled by the government's vote-maximising strategy. The second objection to the AEH is that private sector agents only consider the past trajectory of the relevant variable and ignore information other than past rates of inflation. For example, private sector agents might know the true structure of the economy, the game played by the government and all variables that enter the economic model. Furthermore, they might use this information to form their expectations. In response to these objections the New Classical School adopted the REH originally formulated by Muth (1961), which in terms of our model may be summarised by the mathematical expectation

$$\hat{P}^e_{t/t-1} = \mathrm{E}(\hat{P}_t/\Omega_{t-1}) \qquad (9.7.6)$$

where Ω_t denotes the information set available to agents at time t. The REH has two properties, which are relevant for the policy neutrality results of the New Classical School. Firstly, the forecasting errors of rational expectations conditional on the available information set, say ϵ_t^F, have zero mean, that is

$$\mathrm{E}(\epsilon_t^F) = \mathrm{E}(\hat{P}_t - \hat{P}^e_{t/t-1}) = 0 \qquad (9.7.7)$$

and secondly they will be uncorrelated with their own past (e.g. Begg, 1982).

9.7.2 Ineffectiveness of political–economic policy rules

Let us assume that the government can manipulate unemployment directly *via* the public sector IS–LM$_s$ model (9.2.4)–(9.2.5), the behaviour of the fiscal deficit (9.3.12) and Okun's law by simply changing the tax rate. Then a discrete-time version of the type of vote-maximising strategy discussed by Nordhaus (1975) (see Section 7.3 of Chapter 7) or in Section 9.4 of the current chapter may be represented by the political–economic policy rule (cf. MacRae, 1977)

$$U_t = v_{1t}(\hat{P}_{t-1} - \hat{P}_{t-2}) + v_{2t} + \epsilon_t^p \qquad (9.7.8)$$

where ϵ_t^p denotes the independently-distributed error term with zero mean in controlling the economy. Equation (9.7.8) represents in a sense the aggregate demand schedule caused by the vote-maximising strategy. Upon taking expectations of both sides of equation (9.7.4), one finds that the anticipated unemployment rate equals the natural rate

$$U_{t/t-1}^e = U^n \qquad (9.7.9)$$

Equating the right-hand sides of equations (9.7.4) and (9.7.8), taking expectations with respect to Ω_{t-1} and subtracting yields the following expression for the forecasting error

$$\epsilon_t^F = \hat{P}_t - \hat{P}_{t/t-1}^e = \hat{\epsilon}_t^m - \frac{\hat{\beta}_1}{u_1}\epsilon_t^p \qquad (9.7.10)$$

which clearly shows that forecasting errors under the REH are independently distributed with zero mean. Upon substitution of the result (9.7.10) into equation (9.7.4), one obtains

$$U_t = U_{t/t-1}^e + \epsilon_t^p = U^n + \epsilon_t^p \qquad (9.7.11)$$

Hence the unemployment rate cannot deviate systematically from the expected/natural rate of unemployment under the influence of a conventional demand management package, since agents anticipate the policy rule (9.7.8) correctly, modify their wage bargains accordingly, therefore avoid making mistakes and render any political–economic strategy ineffective. Under the REH the Phillips curve is vertical *even* in the short run which is what is meant by the policy neutrality proposition of the New Classical School. It can be shown to hold for a very wide class of linear structures of effective demand and policy rules (e.g. Pesaran, 1983).

However the above conclusion does not necessarily deny the existence of any political–economic strategy, since the policy neutrality proposition breaks down under reasonable extensions of the above model. These issues are further explored in the remainder of this section.

9.7.3 Breakdown of the policy neutrality proposition

There are at least five reasons for economic policy to become ineffective; these are outlined below.

Firstly, the assumption of self-equilibrating markets may be unrealistic. The most obvious example of this is the existence of money illusion, which may alternatively be interpreted as the inability of workers to compensate themselves for anticipated increases in the cost of living (i.e. $b_2 < 1$ in equation (8.8.5)). This is a common feature of imperfectly competitive labour markets with conflict between trade unions and firms (see van der Ploeg, 1982e). More precisely, the stochastic market-clearing assumption (9.7.4) is replaced by

$$Q_t = Q^n + (\hat{P}_t^* - \hat{P}_{t/t-1}^e)/\hat{\beta}_1 - \hat{\epsilon}_t^m/\hat{\beta}_1 \qquad (9.7.4')$$

where $\hat{P}_t^*$ denotes the steady-state market clearing value of $\hat{P}_t$, and extended with the partial adjustment mechanism

$$\hat{P}_t - \hat{P}_{t-1} = \beta_4(\hat{P}_t^* - \hat{P}_{t-1}), \quad 0 < \beta_4 \leqq 1 \qquad (9.7.12)$$

where β_4 is the adjustment coefficient (cf. Buiter, 1980). Solving (9.7.12) for $\hat{P}_t^*$ and substituting the result into (9.7.4') gives

$$Q_t = Q^n + \hat{\beta}_1^{-1} [(\hat{P}_t - \hat{P}_{t/t-1}^e) + (\beta_4^{-1} - 1)(\hat{P}_t - \hat{P}_{t-1}) - \hat{\epsilon}_t^m] \qquad (9.7.13)$$

which is in a similar form to the Phillips curve with money illusion. Non-instantaneous market clearing therefore gives scope for discretionary policy (see also Begg, 1982, for a more Keynesian approach relying on sticky nominal wages to markets in disequilibrium under the REH). A less obvious example of self-equilibrating markets relates to the market for foreign exchange. For example, when the purchasing power parity hypothesis is replaced by a fixed exchange rate régime one would use equation (9.7.1) instead of (9.7.2) with a coefficient on the expected inflation term equal to $\beta_2 = \delta a_2 b_2$. Even when $b_2 = 1$ the expected inflation rate is not completely compensated as some of the goods sold on the home market are imported ($\beta_2 < 1$). The result of this is that the government does have leverage on domestic output under the REH and political–economic strategies become feasible.

Secondly, the assumption of complete information underlying the REH may be unrealistic. For example, assume that private sector agents believe erroneously that the government adopts the neutral strategy

$$U_t = v_3 + \epsilon_t^p \qquad (9.7.8')$$

whereas the government actually adopts the political–economic policy rule (9.7.8). In this case the relationship for the forecasting error (9.7.10) is no longer valid, since $U_{t/t-1}^e$ is erroneously given by v_3. Instead the forecast error satisfies

$$\epsilon_t^F = \hat{\epsilon}_t^m - \frac{\hat{\beta}_1}{u_1} [\epsilon_t^p + v_{1t}(\hat{P}_{t-1} - \hat{P}_{t-2}) + v_{2t} - v_3] \qquad (9.7.14)$$

Since the forecasting errors no longer have zero mean, systematic mistakes are possible and the government may find it possible to engage in a vote-maximising strategy. This example raises the question of how agents acquire the information on the government's political–economic strategy. Although there are (Bayesian) schemes for learning the information required for the REH (see, e.g., Cyert and De Groot, 1974), these schemes merely present a scheme for learning the parameters in the policy rule (v_{1t} and v_{2t}) but do not give clear guidance on the *structure* of the economy and the policy rule.

Thirdly, the government may possess an informational advantage over the private sector. For example, the existence of overlapping nominal wage contracts gives the government an informational advantage over the private sector as wages are fixed for, say, two periods (see, e.g., Fischer, 1977). Hence the private sector is stuck to a contract for two periods, which gives the government scope for manipulation of demand even though the policy may be fully anticipated.

Fourthly, the neutrality proposition of the New Classical School relies on certainty equivalence. In other words the structure of the economy and the policy rule must be linear and the parameters must be known exactly. Nonlinear models and stochastic parameters are typical in applied econometrics and often give scope for demand management.

Fifthly, even when the government is unable to secure systematic deviations from the natural levels of output and unemployment the government may be able to affect the natural levels themselves by supply-side policies. When the government is not able to do this one speaks of *super-neutrality*, but most members of the New Classical School would admit this to be unrealistic. For example, a government may by reducing taxes increase incentives or by increasing housing subsidies increase labour mobility and therefore raise the natural level of real output. Another example relies on the real balance effect in the consumption equation (Patinkin, 1956). Since monetary policy can increase inflation directly, it erodes real wealth, depresses consumption and therefore depresses the natural levels of output by crowding out private sector investment.

9.8 Conclusions

The purely macroeconomic model of Chapter 8 was closed by incorporating either optimising or satisficing behaviour. By optimising in the short run the government functions as an agent implementing a Pareto-optimal outcome for conflicting interest groups. The government does this by maximising the collective interest function, a weighted average of the elementary interest functions, subject to the constraints implied by (the economy and) the strict control of the state hypothesis. The weights in the collective interest function reflect the power structure in the economy and depend on the ideology of the incumbent political party. The outcome for the fiscal deficit (or tax) ratio therefore depends on struggles between the various interest groups (active private sector agents, rentiers, public sector workers, unemployed and bureaucrats) and the success of each of these groups in having their own interests promoted by the government. In the *day-to-day* running of the public sector the government faces a fixed tax rate and probably ignores the employment-generating effects of state spending. The resulting maximum of the collective interest function yields an autonomous state bureaucracy, so that the share of the state spending in total spending is a constant depending on the ideology and relative power structure of the interest groups. In the medium term, say over the course of an election period, the government can manipulate the tax rate. It was assumed the government does this to win votes and/or steer the economy towards a satisfactory balance of payments position. As long as there are lags in economic behaviour there is no strategic voting, and the government maximises votes at the forthcoming election (rather than the uninterrupted length in office), a political business cycle will result. The examples of political manipulation of adaptive expectations and changes in international competitiveness were discussed, but tax indexation can also be exploited politically (van der Ploeg, 1982d). The extensions to maximisation of party ideology subject to re-election constraints apply a prospective discount scheme for evaluating ideology and a retrospective discount scheme for evaluating the government's performance to show that as a bottle-neck election approaches the promotion of ideology is gradually replaced by re-election efforts.

The satisficing approach rejects the *ex ante* optimising approach in favour of an *ex post* reaction to a political or economic crisis. It leads to an *interdependent* system of the political–economic reaction functions for state spending and the tax rate, which ensures corrective actions when there is a balance of payments crisis or when popularity is insufficient and promotes the ideological targets (based on gradual control of the state) all the time. Using a theorem for the stability of 'patched-up' systems, the stability of a left-wing system was established. This stability result relies on the tax rate having a comparative advantage (disadvantage) over state spending in influencing popularity (the fiscal deficit).

Where there is perfect foresight or more generally rational expectations the introduction of a political cycle will be unsuccessful, but this neutrality result only holds in the unrealistic presence of rapid market clearing, linear structures, certainty equivalence, complete information and rapid learning.

The theoretical analysis of this chapter suggests various political–economic links, but in practice there may be many others. Many other lags in economic behaviour, for example in investment, could be exploited. Other political motives, such as public revenue motives for having high inflation (see Burton *et al.*, 1981), may arise in practice. The electorate or the number of interest groups could be further disaggregated to include the social classes of Chapter 6, local authorities, trade unions, central bank behaviour, etc. For example, Frey and Schneider (1981) have commenced a study of the conflict between the bank and government and Gärtner (1981) investigated political reasons for the leaders of a centralised trade union to recommend wage rises. These studies are only a first step. Further analysis inevitably leads to a game-theoretic approach (cf. van der Ploeg, 1982c) and to the problem of dynamic inconsistencies. The relationship with the rational expectations approach requires further attention. Finally, empirical tests must be performed within the context of a full-scale political–economic model, owing to the dependence of policy on the structure of the economy and politics. The hypothesis of the benevolent dictator, assumed in studies of revealed preferences (e.g. Friedlaender, 1973), versus the political–economic view of the government should be tested. These empirical matters are the subject of the next chapter.

Appendix: Stability of economic systems 'patched-up' by political manipulation

This appendix investigates the stability properties of the system of reaction functions (9.6.1)–(9.6.2). Unfortunately, conventional stability criteria (e.g. Routh-Hurwicz criterion, Lyapunov method) cannot be applied owing to the discontinuous nature of the Jacobian of the system (9.6.1)–(9.6.2). Instead the classical (or Carathéodory) approach to the analysis of discontinuous differential equations will be used. This approach has previously been applied to the analysis of disequilibrium growth models (Ito, 1980) and to the derivation of feedback control strategies with switching régimes.

The space $\mathbf{R}^2$ may be divided into two régimes, an ideological régime, say $\mathbf{R}_I = \{(\tau, G)/l^{\mathrm{R,O}}(\tau, G) \geqq 0\}$, and a régime 'patched-up' by re-election strategies, say $\mathbf{R}_P = \{(\tau, G)/l^{\mathrm{R,O}}(\tau, G) \leqq 0\}$, such that $\mathbf{R}_I \cup \mathbf{R}_P = \mathbf{R}^2$ and $\mathbf{R}_I \cap \mathbf{R}_P = \{(\tau, G)/\eta(\tau, G) = l^{\mathrm{R,O}}(\tau, G) = 0$ where $\eta(\tau^*, G^*) = 0\} = S$ is a connected line. For each of these régimes the system (9.6.1)–(9.6.2) satisfies the Lipschutz condition and has a Jacobian, say $\mathbf{J}_I(\tau, G)$ for $(\tau, G) \in \mathbf{R}_I$ and $\mathbf{J}_P(\tau, G)$ for $(\tau, G) \in \mathbf{R}_P$, which is continuous. The two régimes are smoothly connected, that is $\mathbf{J}_I(\tau, G) = \mathbf{J}_P(\tau, G)$, for all $(\tau, G) \in S$, and have a unique common equilibrium, (τ^*, G^*). Using the above facts, the following theorem (adapted from Ito, 1980) may be proved:

The system (9.6.1)–(9.6.2) is locally asymptotically stable if

(1) the two solutions on the boundary point towards the same régime (in order to connect a solution coming in with the one coming out), that is the inequality

$$\left\{\begin{pmatrix}\eta_1\\ \eta_2\end{pmatrix}' \mathbf{J}_I \begin{pmatrix}\eta_2\\ -\eta_1\end{pmatrix}\right\} \left\{\begin{pmatrix}\eta_1\\ \eta_2\end{pmatrix}' \mathbf{J}_P \begin{pmatrix}\eta_2\\ -\eta_1\end{pmatrix}\right\} > 0$$

must be satisfied at the equilibrium, and

(2) the system is locally asymptotically stable around the equilibrium for each of the two régimes, that is trace $(\mathbf{J}_i^*) < 0$, det $(\mathbf{J}_i^*) > 0$, for $i = I$ and $i = P$ must be satisfied.

The first condition is satisfied, since it is easily checked that the scalars in curly brackets are equal and therefore their product is positive. The second condition is first examined for a left-wing government ($\Lambda_2 > 0$) and then for a right-wing government ($\Lambda_2 < 0$). When $\Lambda_2 > 0$, trace $\mathbf{J}_I < 0$, trace $\mathbf{J}_P < 0$ are satisfied always and det $\mathbf{J}_I > 0$, det $\mathbf{J}_P > 0$ are satisfied only if the inequality (9.6.4) holds. When $\Lambda_2 < 0$, trace $\mathbf{J}_I < 0$ if β is sufficiently large, trace $\mathbf{J}_P < 0$, det $\mathbf{J}_I > 0$ if (9.6.4) is *not* satisfied and det $\mathbf{J}_P > 0$ if (9.6.4) is satisfied.

Thus when $\Lambda_2 > 0$ the system is locally asymptotically stable only if (9.6.4) holds and when $\Lambda_2 < 0$ the system is always unstable. The above holds only when there is a balance of payments surplus.

10

Political aspects of British economic policy

10.1 Introduction

In this chapter we use the ideas developed in Chapters 7, 8 and 9 to examine the political aspects of economic policy making in Britain over the past twenty years. The next section begins with a consideration of two views on the nature of political influences on policy formulation. Both perspectives, in our opinion, suffer from grave deficiencies, and an attempt to analyse British economic policy taking into account the critical points raised in this section is contained in the remainder of the chapter.

Our general plea is for an approach which looks more closely at the nature of the institutional framework within which policy is made and which also examines, in greater detail than hitherto, the nature of the policy options available. Section 10.3 is concerned with the organisation of economic policy in Britain and points out some of the contradictions that may exist between the different branches of government. Section 10.4 reviews the economic performance in the context of which policy has been made. A detailed look at movements in government expenditure under different administrations is the concern of Section 10.5 and Section 10.6 similarly examines government revenues. Incomes policies and the possibility of conflicts between the interests of government and the interests of private sector agents are the concern of Section 10.7, and Section 10.8 concludes the chapter.

10.2 Empirical studies of endogenous government behaviour in Britain

In this section we consider critically some of the empirical work which, in the British context, attempts to explain movements in certain economic variables that can be regarded as the instruments of government policy. Some of the explanations that are advanced for such movements accord well with the discussions in Chapters 7 and 9 of this book. The intertemporal variation in the instruments of policy may be explained in terms of a government's desire to implement its ideology as well as to seek re-election, both these desires being constrained by the need to adopt policies to stabilise the economy (see, for example, Frey and Schneider, 1978b and 1982). Other authors, however, (Chrystal and Alt, 1979a, b; 1981a, b) deny the existence of any political influences, either ideological or contained in the desire for re-election, on the major instruments of policy. There would thus appear to be a divergence of opinion on whether or not economic policy-making in Britain is politically influenced. (It should be emphasised that political influences are defined – as they have been throughout this book – in the widest possible sense to include both ideological influences and the influence of the ballot box.)

It is the contention of this section that this difference in opinion on empirical matters arises mainly because these are highly aggregative studies which make little attempt to explore the institutional framework within which policy is made and implemented. As will be argued below, the range of policy options considered by these studies is very narrow, instruments are ascribed to government which are not really within its control, no account is taken of conflicts within government or of conflicts between government and private sector agents and, finally, the ideological position of the various parties is not properly articulated. The succeeding sections of this chapter attempt to take some of these factors into account. We begin in this section, however, with a brief review.

Frey and Schneider (1978b and 1982) formulate a model in which a government distinguishes between two states of the world, one in which it has a popularity deficit (that is its standing in the polls is less than what it, at that moment, regards as desirable) and the other in which it has a popularity surplus. In periods of popularity deficit, the government would alter its policy instruments so as to increase its popularity. In periods of popularity surplus the government would alter its policy instruments so as to implement its ideology. In making policy changes, whether to increase popularity or to implement its ideology, the government would be constrained by balance of payments considerations and by the fact that public sector costs rise faster than the general level of costs (see Section 10.5 for a discussion of this relative price effect).

The policy instruments considered were government expenditures (disaggregated into current expenditures on goods and services, investment expenditures, transfer payments through grants and transfer payments through subsidies) and government revenues (defined as the total of government receipts from direct and indirect taxation and other income). The ideological differences between the different parties were captured by the differing proportions of each of these instruments in gross domestic product (cf. Subsection 9.2.1 of the previous chapter), with the expectation that these would be lower for a Conservative government than for a Labour government. The desired lead was hypothesised to vary inversely with the distance in time away from a general election and in the study it was set to vary from − 8 per cent (just after an election to) + 8 per cent (just before an election). The equations were estimated on quarterly data and a sample regression from Frey and Schneider (1982), for the total of real, current and capital expenditures, is reproduced below.

$$
\begin{aligned}
\text{EXPENDITURES}(t) = {} & \left.\begin{array}{l} 0.16 \\ + 0.02^{*} \text{ Lead-deficit } (t-1) \\ \quad (2.70) \\ + 0.83^{*} \text{ adjustment to value desired} \\ (28.07) \text{ for re-election } (t-1) \end{array}\right\} \begin{array}{l}\text{in case of}\\ \text{re-election}\\ \text{effort}\end{array} \\
& \left.\begin{array}{l} + 0.01^{*} \text{ Conservative ideology } (t-1) \\ \quad (2.11) \\ + 0.03^{*} \text{ Labour ideology } (t-1) \\ \quad (3.66) \\ + 0.53^{*} \text{ adjustment to value desired} \\ (25.60) \text{ for ideological reasons } (t-1) \end{array}\right\} \begin{array}{l}\text{in case of}\\ \text{ideologically}\\ \text{orientated}\\ \text{policy}\end{array}
\end{aligned}
$$

$$
\left.\begin{array}{l} + \underset{(3.6)}{0.02^*} \text{ balance of current account} \\ + \underset{(5.90)}{0.02^*} \text{ real wage rate } (t-1) \end{array}\right\} \begin{array}{l}\text{economic}\\ \text{and}\\ \text{financial}\\ \text{constraints}\end{array}
$$

figures in parentheses are t-values $\bar{R}^2 = 0.99$
1958:1 to 1976:3

In a situation of popularity deficit a government increases its expenditures to improve its re-election chances; on the other hand with a popularity surplus a Conservative government aims for a lower share of public expenditure in gross domestic product than does a Labour government.

Contrasting with this view of economic policy making is that of Chrystal and Alt (1979a, b; 1981a, b) whereby political influences are unimportant and government expenditures may be explained by a permanent income hypothesis. A sample regression is reproduced below

$$
\begin{aligned}
\text{EXPENDITURES}(t) = & -2.623 \\
& + \underset{(3.06)}{0.0806^*} \text{ real GNP}(t) \\
& + \underset{(14.01)}{0.759^*} \text{ Expenditures } (t-1)
\end{aligned}
$$

figures in parentheses are t-values $\bar{R}^2 = 0.99$
1958:1 to 1976:3

Frey and Schneider (1982) compare the forecasting performances of the two models for the period 1976:4 to 1979:3 and conclude that their model yields superior forecasts compared to the 'permanent income' explanation of public expenditures.

However, there are several deficiencies inherent in this approach to explaining variations in economic policy. First, the expectation is that a government will always increase expenditure to meet a crisis, regardless of the origins of the crisis. This is at variance with the behaviour of British governments over the past two decades, which have for example imposed incomes policies when they regarded inflation as the source of crisis and reflated when they regarded unemployment as being too high. This defect follows quite naturally from the limited range of policy options considered. The second defect is that by considering broad aggregates the approach misses some of the subtle differences in ideology between the Conservatives and Labour. Thus in the past both Conservative and Labour governments have cut public expenditure, but they have emphasised different items (see Section 10.5). The third defect is that instruments are ascribed to government which are not really within its control. Thus, for example, a government can vary its tax rates or the rates that it pays on benefits but it cannot control the amount of its tax revenues or the amount that it pays on, say, unemployment benefits (see Sections 10.5 and 10.6). The first approach, that of investigating the political aspects of tax rates, has been adopted in the theoretical framework of Chapter 9, whereas the empirical studies of Frey and Schneider and Chrystal and Alt (cf. Section 10.2) focus mistakenly on total tax revenues. Finally, Chapters 7 and 9 demonstrate that government policy is not the output of a homogeneous entity and instead relies upon the reconciliation of a number of interests within government (see Section 10.3) and between government and other agents (see Section 10.7). The remainder of this chapter attempts to examine British economic policy taking these points into account.

10.3 The organisation of British economic policy

The making of economic policy in Britain is not the prerogative of any single department, and several ministries have economic functions and contribute to the formulation and implementation of policy in their areas of responsibility. Thus, to name but a few, there are the Departments of Energy, Trade, Industry, Employment, each dealing with a specific area of economic life. However, standing above this welter of economic ministries, through its overall responsibility for government expenditures and the allocation of funds between departments, is the Treasury.

On the political side, the Treasury is headed by the Chancellor and he is assisted in his tasks by two, sometimes three ministers, one of whom, the Chief Secretary to the Treasury, usually has Cabinet rank. On the civil service side, the head of the Treasury is the Permanent Secretary and he is assisted by a range of second secretaries, below whom are deputy secretaries and under secretaries. The division of the Treasury, as indeed of every ministry, into the political and the non-political wing raises the possibility of conflicts between politicians and civil servants over the making of policy (cf. Chapter 9).

At the risk of caricature, we may describe this potential conflict as stemming from two sources. First, ministers and bureaucrats may believe in the same economic paradigm but may differ as to the degree to which a particular policy, on the need for which they are both agreed, should be followed. An example of this would be the Butskellite consensus of the 1950s and 1960s, according to which demand management, through the regulation of public expenditures and taxes, was the instrument of policy and the maintenance of full employment, constrained by balance of payment considerations, its objective. The second possibility is that ministers may come to power with a view of the economy which is at variance with the established civil service view. This situation could give rise to disagreements about the appropriate instruments of economic policy and perhaps even about its objective. An example of this sort of conflict would be the 'monetarist experiment' of the present Conservative government. Mrs Thatcher's government of 1979 was the first post-war British government which was not committed to full employment policies. Indeed, by downgrading high employment and upgrading control of inflation as objectives of policy, Mrs Thatcher reversed the postwar consensus on the economic role of government. Concomitant with this reversal of objectives was also the spurning of traditional demand management policies in favour of an almost exclusive reliance on policies designed to control the money supply. Attempts to reduce the money supply would of course have fiscal implications, since the government's borrowing requirements would have to be reduced and this in turn would require cuts in public expenditure and perhaps therefore a smaller public sector.

The manner in which such conflicts might be resolved would of course depend on their origins. When disputes arose in the context of an agreed view of the economy it is possible that the civil servants in the Treasury would have the dominant say. This is because the Treasury deals with both more technical and more abstract issues than those dealt with by other departments. This would place the conventional type of politician at a disadvantage *vis-à-vis* Treasury officials. According to the doctrines that prevailed in the Treasury in the late 1960s (described in Brittan 1969), a rate of unemployment of 2 per cent was regarded as satisfactory. If the balance of payments position was reasonable, politicians would be allowed the political kudos of an unemployment rate lower than 2 per cent. If, on the other hand, the balance of payments was not satisfactory, the Treasury was prepared to countenance rates of unemployment in excess of 2 per cent, with the proviso that devaluation would be recommended if unemployment rose considerably.

When the conflict is more fundamental, the government could try to alter the power structure within the civil service, either by injecting new talent from outside or by upgrading civil servants more in harmony with the government's view. The appointment of outside advisers to economic ministries on a large scale was a feature of the Labour government of 1964 and was prompted by the fear that the civil service, after more than a decade of uninterrupted Conservative rule, would thwart a 'radical' government. The utility of such outside appointments is however diminished by the fact that, though such appointments might contribute to the making of policy, the execution of policy would depend upon the co-operation of other departments and this they would not know how to obtain. The present Conservative government has adopted the alternative strategy of restructuring the Treasury more to its liking. This has been effected in a variety of ways – through the appointment of a sympathetic Chief Economic Adviser, through the appointment to key positions of Treasury officials who are sympathetic to the government's economic thinking, and finally through a reallocation of influence between Treasury departments so that more traditional groups (like the forecasting group) are downgraded in terms of importance with a corresponding rise in the importance of officials dealing with monetary policy.

Turning one's attention outwards there is also the complexity of the Treasury's relationship with the other economic ministries, and here too there is scope for conflict. The involvement of both the Treasury and the Department of Employment in the formulation and implementation of incomes policies illustrates the scope for this conflict. The Department of Employment has, as its natural constituency, the labour force and, in deciding on the appropriate wage settlements, would be more inclined to countenance exceptions to the incomes policies' norm. The Treasury, on the other hand, without any such interests, would be less inclined to make exceptions.

Conflicts may also arise in the Treasury's relationship with the Bank of England. These conflicts are partly institutional. The Bank enjoys an independent income from the interest on securities held by its Banking Department and is therefore more generously staffed than the Treasury. Moreover, the Governor of the Bank of England, unlike the Permanent Secretary to the Treasury, has the right to express publicly his views on economic affairs. However, conflicts may also arise through differences in objectives between the Treasury and the Bank. Just as the Treasury is primarily interested in the government's expenditures and revenues, the Bank wishes to ensure the smooth functioning of the foreign exchange market and the market for government securities. Consequently the Bank, in the days of pegged exchange rates, would be anti-devaluation and, with floating exchange rates, would be more anxious to smoothe out fluctuations in the foreign exchange market. On the domestic front, the Bank would pay close attention to the government's borrowing requirement and this might bring it into conflict with the Treasury's demand management policies (see Brittan, 1969, pp. 48–49).

Thus a government's economic policy is not the output of a homogeneous entity but evolves through the resolution of conflict both within a central policy-making department like the Treasury and also between the central department and other departments. The next section examines how this has affected Britain's economic performance.

10.4 Economic performance in Britain, 1964–1981

In the previous section we discussed the manner in which economic policy making was organised in Britain. We now turn to a discussion of the objectives of policy and examine whether, in the British context, policy has been systematically directed towards particular areas.

In terms of economic performance, Figs 10.1, 10.2, 10.3, and 10.4 summarise Britain's performance with respect to growth, unemployment, inflation and the balance of payments for the period 1964–1981. The picture that emerges is a dismal one, with low and sluggish rates of growth (averaging 2.0 per cent over the period) and rising rates of inflation and unemployment, averaging 10.0 per cent and 3.8 per cent respectively. Over the same period, Britain's economic performance was far worse than that of most other OECD countries (see Caves and Krause, 1980). Thus, over the period 1967–1978, gross domestic product in Britain grew at an annual average rate of 2.3 per cent, while the corresponding average for all OECD countries was 3.8 per cent. Interestingly enough, this performance deteriorated over the latter part of this period. Although all the OECD countries suffered from the oil crisis and its aftermath, Britain's performance worsened in that its annual growth was only 1.1 per cent over the period 1973–1978, less than half of the annual average of 2.5 per cent for all OECD countries.

The sluggishness of Britain's economy is confirmed by the behaviour of growth in employment, productivity and manufacturing production (see Table 10.1). Unemployment rates grew from about 1.4 per cent in 1964–1965 to about 2.5 per cent in 1973–1974 and then to about 5.5 per cent in 1978–1979, reaching 11 per cent by 1981. Over the period 1964–1981 the working population grew by 3 per cent while the employed labour force declined by just over 6 per cent. Underlying the falling levels of employment there was a decline in employment in manufacturing of 28 per cent over the period. This was accompanied by an increase in productivity over the whole economy of 37 per cent and in manufacturing by 48 per cent. Manufacturing output peaked in 1973, fell for two successive years and by 1979 was still 4 per cent below its peak value. By 1981 manufacturing output was barely above the 1967 level. The decline in manufacturing employment, however, far outstripped the decline in output (17.5 per cent over 1973–1981), so that productivity rose quite sharply.

Performance regarding the control of inflation has also been disappointing. In

Fig. 10.1 *Rate of growth in GDP over corresponding quarter in previous year, 1964–1981*

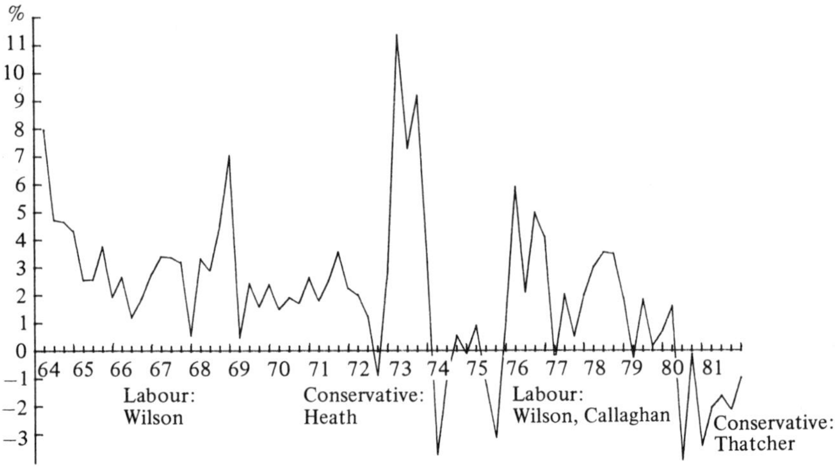

Source: Economic Trends Annual Supplement, 1983.

Fig. 10.2 *Percentage rate of unemployment, 1964–1981*

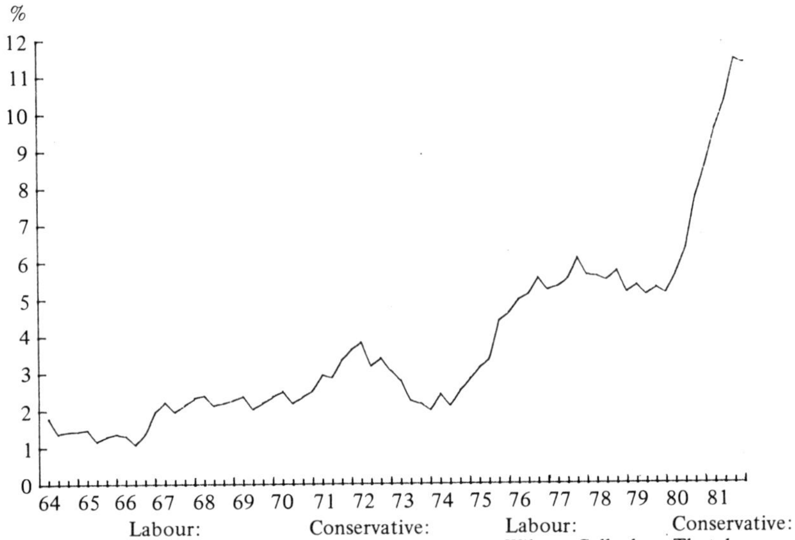

Source: Economic Trends Annual Supplement, 1983.

1967 Britain had a lower rate of inflation than all the OECD countries (except West Germany) and the British rate of 2.5 per cent was comfortably below the OECD average of 3.1 per cent. After 1967 all countries experienced more inflation, but the acceleration was much faster in Britain, so that the OECD average rate of inflation was consistently lower than the British rate for the next 12 years. This difference was most pronounced in 1975, when Britain achieved an inflation

Fig. 10.3 *Percentage rate of change in the retail price index over corresponding quarter in previous year, 1964–1981*

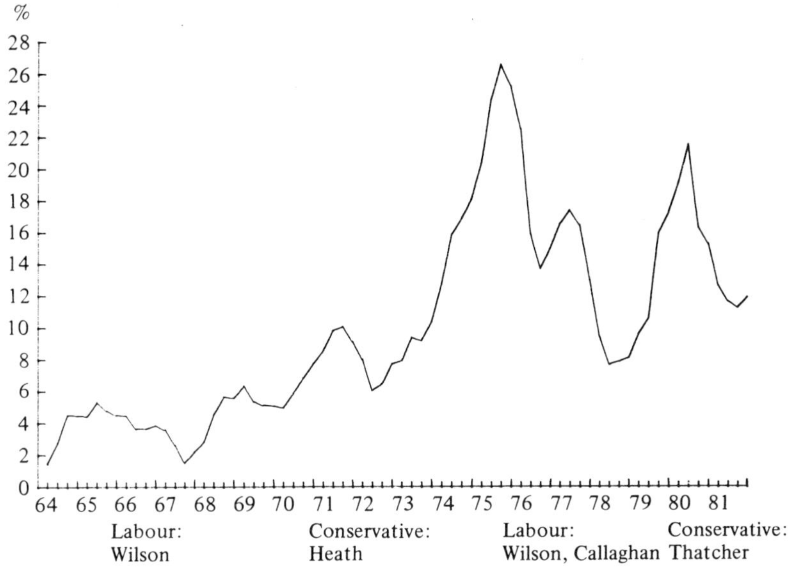

Source: Economic Trends Annual Supplement, 1983.

Fig. 10.4 *The balance of payments, 1964–1981*

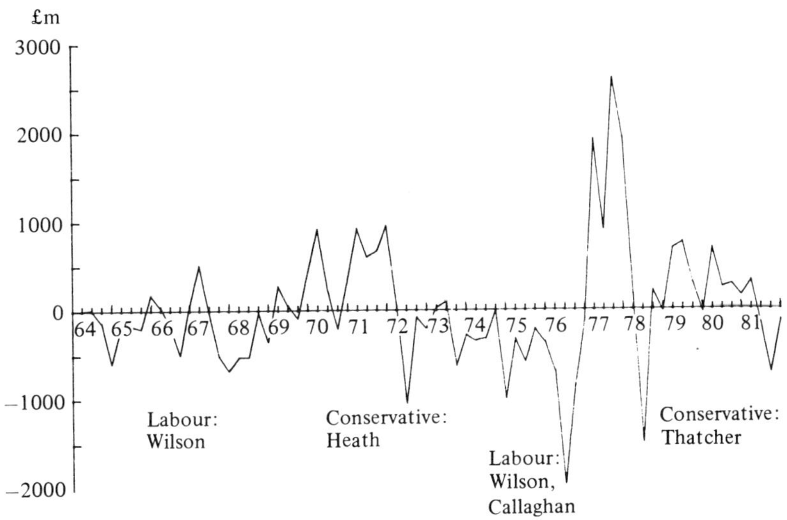

Source: Economic Trends Annual Supplement, 1983.

rate of 24.2 per cent, more than twice the average OECD rate. Over the entire period only Italy's performance was as bad as Britain's.

Britain's performance on the external front was more satisfactory. The period 1964–1967 was characterised by stop–go policies to regulate demand, leading to

Table 10.1 *Indexes of employment, productivity and manufacturing production in the United Kingdom, 1964–1981 (1975 = 100)*

Year	Total employed labour force	Employment in manufacturing	Output per employee (whole economy)	Output per employee (manufacturing)	Manufacturing production
1964	100.2	112.5	81.3	74.5	83.4
1965	101.1	113.9	82.8	75.6	85.8
1966	101.5	113.9	83.9	77.0	87.3
1967	100.2	110.7	86.6	79.7	87.9
1968	99.7	109.9	90.7	86.0	94.1
1969	99.7	111.3	92.5	88.0	97.6
1970	99.3	111.1	94.5	88.6	98.0
1971	97.7	107.5	97.4	90.6	97.5
1972	98.1	104.0	100.1	95.8	100.0
1973	100.2	104.5	103.6	104.1	108.4
1974	100.6	104.7	101.5	102.6	106.6
1975	100.0	100.0	100.0	100.0	100.0
1976	99.4	96.9	103.0	105.4	101.4
1977	99.6	97.1	105.0	107.1	103.0
1978	99.9	96.4	108.6	108.3	103.8
1979	100.2	95.1	110.0	109.8	104.1
1980	98.3	89.8	109.0	105.9	95.4
1981	93.6	80.8	111.7	110.3	89.4

Source: Economic Trends Annual Supplement, 1981.

balance of payments deficits whenever the economy began rapid growth. The devaluation of sterling in 1967 led, from 1969 onwards, to considerable improvements in the balance of payments and it was not till 1972 that large deficits reappeared. These deficits continued until 1976, undermining confidence in sterling, so that it declined considerably in value. Over 1977–1979, the balance of payments again started showing a surplus.

With this background we turn to a discussion of three major components of economic policy *viz.* government expenditures and revenues and policies to restrain inflation.

10.5 Economic policy in Britain: government expenditures

In the context of Britain's economic performance, detailed in the previous section, it is pertinent to enquire into the nature of economic policies pursued over this period and examine the extent to which they contributed to this performance. We begin first with a discussion of general government expenditures.[1] In doing so we shall often be concerned with movements in government expenditures relative to gross domestic product (both evaluated in current prices, the latter calculated at 'factor cost'). Two factors serve to determine this share. The first factor is the growth of government output relative to national output; if the growth of government output is greater than the growth of national output, then the share of government expenditures in GDP will rise and *vice versa*. This effect is referred to as the 'volume effect'. The other factor is concerned with prices. If the relative prices at which government expenditures are valued rise faster than the prices at which GDP as a whole is valued, then the share of government expenditures in GDP will rise and, provided this 'price effect' is strong enough, this rise may occur in spite of an opposite movement *via* the volume effect. The effect of relative prices in increasing the share of government in total expenditures is due to lower productivity growth for the public authorities relative to the rest of the economy.

A problem with discussing the role of government expenditures as an instrument of economic policy is the control over the many agencies responsible for implementing the programmes which constitute the government's expenditure policy. This problem was referred to in the previous chapter in the context of a theoretical model in which the elected and non-elected branches of government might have conflicting interests over the implementation of spending programmes. However there may even be conflict between the elected components of government. A good example of such conflict, in the British context, may be found in the conflict between the central government and local authorities. When the central government expands expenditure, it has to suffer the economic and political consequences of the adverse effects of such expenditure increases on the balance of payments and the rate of inflation. The adverse macro consequences of expenditure increases do not however rebound on local authorities. On the other hand, increases in local taxes (rates) to finance such expenditures do make local authorities unpopular with their constituents. This lays the basis for a conflict of interests, with local authorities wishing to maximise their expenditures, by maximising the amount of the rate support grant from the central government and hence minimising the level of local taxes. The central government would have, of course, precisely the opposite interests. Although the above discussion caricatures the intensity of conflicting interests between central government and local authorities, it does provide another example of the difficulty of regarding a government's expenditure policy as a homogeneous entity being implemented smoothly towards a definite end.

The Treasury in fact admits that the mechanism of rate support grants constitutes 'strong influence' rather than 'control'. In respect of capital expenditures, however, control by the central government over local authorities is more secure. This is mainly due to the inability of local authorities to raise loans without central government sanction. Broadening the discussion to the public sector, investment in nationalised industries presents special problems of control. The problem here is not so much that the system of control is inadequate or vitiated by conflicts of interests but that such investment programmes are subject to market forces and hence are unsuitable as instruments of demand management.

This general problem of controlling public expenditures is cited as a possible cause for the gradual expansion of the public sector. Thus Sandford and Dean (1970) argue that since local authorities' expenditure functions bear no relation to their revenue-raising abilities, the system facilitates over-expansion. Demographic factors are also cited as reasons for public sector growth; if for example demographic trends produce an increasing proportion of school-age children, then maintaining a given quality of service would imply an expansion of educational

Fig. 10.5 *Government expenditures as a percentage of GDP, 1964–1981*

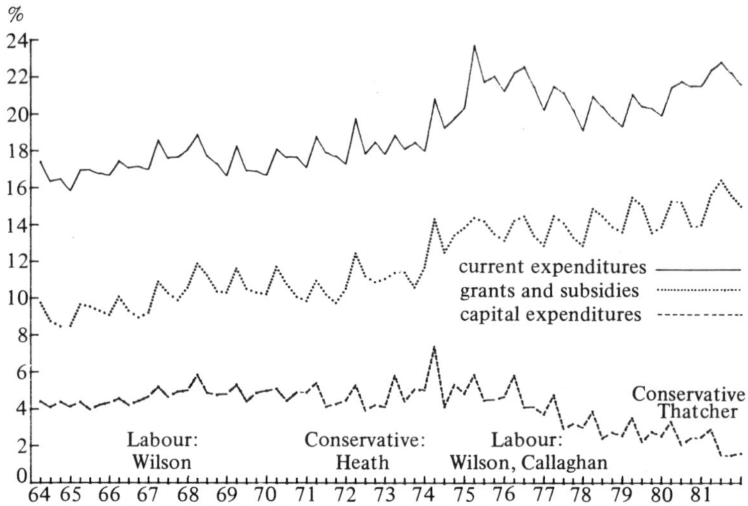

Source: Economic Trends Annual Supplement, 1983.

services. Wagner's law provides an explanation for the increasing expansion of state activities in terms of 'the pressure for social progress and the resulting changes in the relative spheres of private and public economy' (Musgrave and Peacock, 1967, p. 8); Peacock and Wiseman (1961) provided an explanation for the same phenomenon in terms of 'social disturbances' which force governments temporarily to assume greater responsibilities, but which have displacement effects leaving some of the increase as permanent.

With this background we turn to a discussion of trends in government expenditure in the United Kingdom over the period 1961–1981. These trends may be analysed with respect to the main components of expenditure, namely current expenditures on goods and services, capital expenditures and transfers. Fig. 10.5 charts the movements of general government current and capital expenditures on goods and services and on transfer payments, all as a percentage of GDP at factor cost.

The stability of the ratio of government current expenditures on goods and services to GDP is immediately striking. Between the peak years of 1975–76 and the trough years of 1964–65, there was no significant change in this respect, in the government's claim on national resources. This stability could of course be due to the offsetting movements in the volume and relative price effects and Table 10.2 examines the volume growth of government expenditures relative to real growth in GDP for the four governments (Wilson, Heath, Wilson/Callaghan, Thatcher) of the period 1964–1981.

The smallest expansion of government relative to national output occurred under Wilson and the largest (if one ignores the recent recession) under Heath. This was in spite of the Heath government's intention to reduce substantially previous plans for public spending and to permit taxation to be reduced. By the budget of 1971, however, the Chancellor, worried by rising unemployment (the number

Table 10.2 *Growth in current general government expenditures on goods and services and in GDP (all at 1975 prices). Percentage change over sub-periods*

	Wilson 1964–1970	Heath 1970–1974	Wilson–Callaghan 1974–1979	Thatcher 1979–1981
Current government expenditures	8.4	12.3	7.6	2.2
GDP	13.6	11.8	7.7	-4.3

Source: Economic Trends Annual Supplement, 1983.

unemployed rose by over 12 per cent between the first quarters of 1970 and 1971), proposed a reflationary budget, and the desire to use public spending as an instrument to control the rising levels of unemployment gained further strength as the life of the government progressed. This was of course a classic instance of a government of a particular ideological persuasion following, for economic and political reasons, policies that negated its ideology. On the other hand, the early Wilson administration pursued a policy of relative deflation, despite its ideological commitment to expansion, in order to solve the balance of payments crisis. One could interpret such actions as being motivated either by a re-election constraint or, more simply, by a balance of payments constraint (see Chapters 5 and 9). Both the early Wilson and the Heath administration therefore provide examples of frustration of ideology due to re-election constraints (Chapters 7 and 9). The Labour administration of 1974–1979 provides an instance of a government ideologically committed to high employment levels but forced to follow deflationary policies through pressures exerted on it through an outside agency – the IMF. Finally, the Thatcher government represents an administration which, for better or for worse, follows policies which are broadly consistent with its ideological position of reducing the role of the state in economic affairs. Many factors combine to explain Mrs Thatcher's persistence with ideology. Firstly, there is the personality factor – Mrs Thatcher has disowned the existing tradition of consensus politics and, to a far greater extent than her predecessors, has projected herself as a strong-willed leader pursuing a well-defined ideology. Secondly, this strategy has not been damaging to its popularity, both because the Labour party, in its present state of disarray, has not been able to exploit the unemployment issue and because Mrs Thatcher – with the assistance of a Conservative-biased popular press – has been able to alter the substance of the economic debate (cf. Chapter 5) and thereby to upgrade control of inflation and downgrade the maintenance of high employment levels as priorities of political-economic policy.

Further insight into the behaviour of the different governments is provided by examining the composition of government expenditure (see Table 10.3). Irrespective of party affiliation there has been a trend towards reducing expenditures on military defence as a proportion of total government expenditures. This trend has coincided with the decline in Britain's own position in international affairs, the granting of independence to former colonies and the gradual reduction in military commitments

Table 10.3 *The composition of current general government expenditure on goods and services at current prices as a percentage of total expenditure*

	Wilson 1964-1970	Heath 1970-1974	Wilson-Callaghan 1974-1979	Thatcher 1979-1981
Defence	30	26	23	23
Health	20	20	22	23
Education	19	20	21	20
Other	31	34	34	34
	100	100	100	100

Source: National Income and Expenditure, successive issues.

Table 10.4 *Public and private investment as a percentage of GDP*

	Year	General government investment	Public corporations investment	Private investment
Wilson	1964	4.8	4.1	11.8
	1965	4.8	4.1	11.9
	1966	5.1	4.4	11.4
	1967	5.6	4.8	11.1
	1968	5.8	4.3	11.7
	1969	5.7	3.8	12.2
Heath	1970	5.6	3.9	12.3
	1971	5.2	3.8	12.3
	1972	4.9	3.2	12.8
	1973	5.7	3.2	13.2
Wilson/Callaghan	1974	5.9	3.8	13.0
	1975	5.3	4.2	12.3
	1976	4.9	4.2	12.1
	1977	3.8	3.8	12.8
	1978	3.2	3.4	13.9
Thatcher	1979	3.1	3.4	14.0
	1980	2.8	3.5	14.0
	1981	2.2	3.3	13.2

Source: Economic Trends Annual Supplement, 1983.

abroad. However, it could be plausibly argued that expenditure on health and education is determined by social and demographic factors and that such marginal changes in these expenditure shares that have occurred between governments have been relatively free of ideological overtones.

There is much more evidence that the government has, to a certain extent, used its capital expenditures as an instrument of policy. This usage shows up first of all in variations in the level of public investment relative to GDP (Table 10.4). A casual inspection of Table 10.4 shows some counter-cyclical pattern to general government

Table 10.5 *Growth in the volume of general government investment. Percentage change over sub-periods*

	Wilson 1964–1970	Heath 1970–1974	Wilson/Callaghan 1974–1979	Thatcher 1979–1981
General government investment of which:	30.2	5.8	-35.0	-37.0
dwellings	17.0	-10.0	-4.0	-43.0
other new building	40.6	11.5	-52.2	-40.0
plant and machinery	42.0	22.2	-17.5	-4.8
vehicles	47.8	12.2	0	-13.3
Growth in GDP	13.6	11.8	7.7	-4.3

Source: National Income and Expenditure, successive issues.

investment so that it moves in a direction opposite to that of private investment. No inter-party differences in preference for public investment emerge from the figures. The halcyon days of social capital formation appeared to be the years of Wilson and Heath, and under the most recent Labour and Conservative governments public investment (as a proportion of GDP) has gone into decline. This proposition can be examined more closely by looking at the growth of public investment in volume terms, under the different governments of the period 1964–1981. Table 10.5 illustrates very dramatically the cuts in social capital formation that have occurred since 1974.

In many respects social capital is a very tempting target for governments concerned with reducing public expenditure, as the Labour government of 1974–1979 was, and the present Conservative government continues to be. In the first place there is no obvious reduction in the level of services provided to the public through cuts in capital expenditure and, in the second place, owing to the practice of contracting out work to private operators, there is a minimal loss of public sector employment. An interesting feature of the Labour administration's cuts is that investment in dwellings got off relatively lightly whereas, under the present Conservative government, investment in dwellings has come in for the heaviest punishment. It is clear that the construction of public sector dwellings is determined more by ideological forces rather than by re-election or economic considerations, since the early Wilson government expands dwellings despite a popularity and balance of payments crisis and the Heath government cuts expenditure on dwellings despite a fall in popularity due to rising unemployment. However, we have the additional reason that the greater provision of public housing to meet housing needs promotes the electoral chances of the Labour party, and the spread of owner occupation benefits the Conservative party (cf. the class-based analysis of voting in Chapter 6).

Grants and subsidies by the government however showed an increase (as a percentage of GDP) over the period 1964–1981. The reasons for this increase can be traced to social and economic policy. Social security benefits have been a method

Table 10.6 *Weekly rate of the principal national insurance benefits (1975 prices)*

	Unemployment[a] benefit	Retirement[b] pensions	Family[c] allowances	Sickness benefit	Widow's pension	
March 1964	8.31	13.76	0.99	8.31	8.31	
January 1965	9.43	15.63	0.94	9.43	9.43	
October 1967	9.65	16.11	0.86	9.65	9.65	
April 1968	9.30	15.60	1.55	9.30	9.30	Wilson
October 1968	9.15	15.30	1.83	9.15	9.15	
November 1969	9.67	16.07	1.74	9.67	9.67	
September 1971	9.98	16.49	1.49	9.98	9.98	
October 1972	10.31	17.00	1.37	10.31	10.31	Heath
October 1973	10.17	17.43	1.24	10.17	10.72	
July 1974	10.79	20.36	1.13	10.79	12.54	
April 1975	9.88	18.57	1.51	9.88	11.7	
November 1975	10.37	19.76	1.40	10.37	12.43	
November 1976	10.48	19.38	1.22	10.48	12.44	Wilson/Callaghan
November 1977	10.58	19.59	1.80	10.58	12.58	
November 1978	10.48	20.39	3.99	10.48	12.97	
November 1979	10.50	21.04	4.54	10.50	13.22	
November 1980	10.16	21.52	4.68	10.16	13.36	Thatcher
November 1981	9.89	21.04	4.62	9.89	13.02	

a Men, single women and widows.

b Married couple; deflated by pensioners index, all other items deflated by retail price index.
Source: Economic Trends Annual Supplement, 1983.

c Two children.

Source: Annual Abstract of Statistics, successive issues.

of redistributing income, while subsidies also help in combating inflation. Variations in the real value of the weekly rate of the principal national insurance benefits are shown in Table 10.6.

If any pattern can be discerned in the numbers of Table 10.6 it is that both the Labour governments that succeeded Conservative administrations began by disbursing large increases in the real value of benefits. Thereafter they allowed the real value to decline, but never for more than a year, before resuming a more modest growth. The largest step increase in the standards of living of those on social security occurred with the advent of the first Wilson government, when the real value of unemployment and sickness benefits, widows' pensions and retirement pensions rose by over 13 per cent. Subsequently, however, the real value of benefits was allowed to decline and in November 1969 unemployment benefits stood at the rates prevailing (in constant prices) two years before while the retirement pensions were actually lower than the October 1967 rate. The Heath government saw modest rises in the real value of benefits and these benefits were magnified by the incoming Labour government, which awarded real increases of 6 per cent to the unemployed and almost 17 per cent to the retired. Thereafter the pattern of the Wilson government of 1965 was repeated, with the real value of benefits being allowed to fall sharply before resuming a moderate growth. Under the Thatcher government the real value of unemployment benefits was allowed to fall for two successive years so that an unemployed man enjoyed a lower level of benefit in November 1981 than he would have over a decade earlier. This suggests that the Thatcher administration puts relatively less weight on the unemployed as an interest group (cf. Chapter 9).

10.6 Economic policy in Britain: government revenues

The development of British economic policy with respect to the government's control of its revenues can be analysed in terms of revenues from direct taxation and revenues from indirect taxation. Movements in government revenues from direct and indirect taxation as a percentage of GDP are shown in Fig. 10.6. Direct taxation can be further considered in terms of personal taxation and company taxation.

As regards personal taxation there is the possibility of genuine ideological differences between the Labour and Conservative parties. The heart of this difference would appear to lie in disagreements about the disincentive effects of higher tax rates. Thus, while on the one hand, an increase in the marginal rate of income tax may reduce incentives to work, on the other hand the consequent increase in average rates may induce people to work more in order to maintain a given post-tax income. Price (1978) notes that there was a marked difference in income tax policy in the Labour years of 1964–70 and the years before and after. In general Conservative policy was characterised by reductions in income tax rates and higher tax thresholds, while the Labour policy of a buoyant public sector required increases in the standard rate of income tax and an erosion of the real value of allowances. These details are set out in Table 10.7.

Under the Wilson (1964–70) government, the real value of tax allowances declined steadily for the first four years. Accompanying this were a rise in the basic rate of tax in the 1965 budget and two successive rises in the highest rate of tax

Fig. 10.6 *Government revenues as a percentage of GDP, 1964–1981*

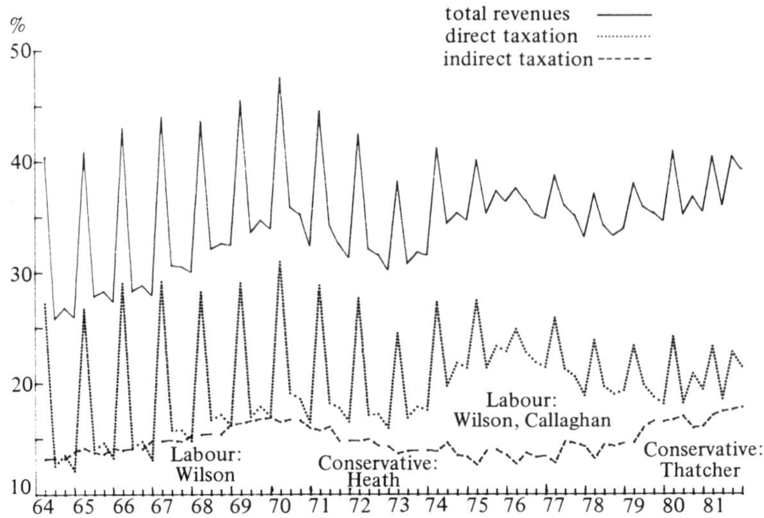

Source: Economic Trends Annual Supplement, 1983.

in the 1965 and 1966 budget. However, the pre-election budget of 1970 saw a 7 per cent rise in the real value of allowances over the 1969 budget levels. The Heath government began in the 1971 budget by increasing the real value of allowances, cutting the basic and lowest rates of income tax by 1.94 percentage points and by cutting the highest rate of income tax by almost 16 percentage points. Although the rates of income tax were left unchanged, substantial increases in the level of allowances were awarded in the reflationary budget of 1972. The Wilson–Callaghan government of 1974–1979 continued the Labour tradition of eroding the real value of allowances (between the 1974 and 1978 budgets this fell by 31 per cent) and raising tax rates, although the pre-election budget contained the substantial concession of a 25 per cent rate of tax for lower income bands. Mrs Thatcher's government lowered the basic rate, increased the rate of tax on lower incomes and substantially reduced the rates on high incomes. Since in the Conservative philosophy there is an inverse relation between tax rates and work incentives, this might mean that, in the Conservative view, the importance of work incentives was confined to people in the higher income brackets and the benefits accruing to such persons was, to an extent, paid for by imposing higher tax rates on lower incomes and by allowing the real value of allowances to decline considerably. Indeed, in the 1981/82 financial year, the real value of allowances stood at their lowest value for the period 1963–83. It could be argued that, from a political point of view, the problem is one of visibility. The hand that takes away by cutting the real value of allowances operates stealthily whereas the hand that gives by cutting rates of income tax is clearly visible to a grateful public.

The influence of political ideology is also apparent in the sphere of company taxation, though perhaps this influence is not as obvious as it is with regard to personal taxation. Up to the budget of 1958, profits retained by companies were taxed at a lower rate than profits distributed to shareholders. This discrimination

Table 10.7 *The real value of allowances and statutory rates of tax*

		Personal taxes				Company taxes		Indirect taxes
		£(1975 prices)	%	%	%	%	%	%
		threshold	lowest rate	basic rate	highest rate	on retentions	on distributions	purchase tax/VAT
	1964-65	1862	15.60	30.14	88.75	56.25		10-25
	1965-66	1836	15.60	32.08	91.25	40.00	64.75	10-25
	1966-67	1767	15.60	32.08	96.25	40.00	64.75	11-27.5
Wilson	1967-68	1725	15.60	32.08	91.25	42.50	66.22	11-27.5
	1968-69	1647	15.60	32.08	91.25	45.00	67.69	12.5-50
	1969-70	1650	23.33	32.08	91.25	42.50	66.22	13.75-55
	1970-71	1767	32.08	32.08	91.25	40.00	64.75	13.75-55
	1971-72	1789	30.14	30.14	75.44	40.00	63.25	11.25-45
Heath	1972-73	1940	30.14	30.14	75.44	40.00	63.25	11.25-75
	1973-74	1794	30.00	30.00	75.00	52.00		10
	1974-75	1758	33.00	33.00	83.00	52.00		10
	1975-76	1505	35.00	35.00	83.00	52.00		8
Wilson-Callaghan	1976-77	1506	35.00	35.00	83.00	52.00		8
	1977-78	1381	34.00	34.00	83.00	52.00		8
	1978-79	1234	25.00	33.00	83.00	52.00		8
Thatcher	1979-80	1094	25.00	30.00	60.00	52.00		15
	1980-81	1097	30.00	30.00	60.00	52.00		15
	1981-82	980	30.00	30.00	60.00	52.00		15
	1982-83	1027	30.00	30.00	60.00	52.00		15

Source: Price (1978) and *Annual Abstract of Statistics*, 1983.

in favour of retained profits was ended in the 1958 budget, when a single tax on profits was introduced. (This reform followed from the majority recommendation of the Royal Commission on Taxation of Profits and Income.)

The Wilson government of 1965 introduced changes which were ideologically consistent with the Labour government's socialist position. The old system of discriminating against distributed profits was revived, although under a different guise. There was now to be a uniform rate of corporation tax which applied to all company profits, whether distributed or not. However, dividends, having already been taxed as a part of total company profits, were to be taxed again at the standard rate of income tax, with companies responsible for deducting this at source. At the same time both long-term (on assets held for more than a year) and short-term capital gains were made subject to a capital gains tax of 30 per cent. The Labour reforms therefore hurt the rentier class (cf. Chapter 9) in two ways – through the system of double taxation of dividends and through the taxation of long-term and short-term capital gains.

The Conservative government of 1970 announced, on its return, that it would end discrimination against profit distribution, though the system for doing so was not introduced until 1973, after considerable debate and discussion. Under the new system of Advance Corporation Tax (ACT), companies make an advance payment, at the standard rate of income tax, on their distribution of dividends. This advance payment was to be essentially an income tax payment by companies on behalf of their shareholders, for the corporation tax paid in advance counted against the companies' eventual corporation tax liabilities. These reforms of 1973 achieved two objectives. Firstly, the separation of the company and the personal tax systems, initiated by the 1965 budget, was confirmed. Secondly, because companies could set the advance corporation tax against their mainstream tax liabilities, the discrimination between distributed and undistributed profits was removed.

The preceding paragraphs describe the different attitudes (and consequently the different legislation) of the Labour and Conservative governments to company taxation. Mayer (1982), in examining how the average corporate tax rates (corporation tax liabilities divided by historic cost-accounting profits) have varied for a sample of 276 firms over the period 1965–1976, finds that they fall from a peak of 40 per cent in 1965 (start of the Wilson government) to around zero per cent in 1974 (end of the Heath government). Since these changes may be due either to changes in the tax system and its associated rates and reliefs or to the performance of the companies in the sample, he decomposes the changes in the average rate into changes due to each of these factors. Mayer's conclusion is that the dramatic fall in the average corporation tax rate paid by his sample of firms can be traced to the set of reliefs and incentives introduced between 1971 and 1974 by the Heath government. The rise in investment allowances in 1971 and 1972, the introduction of stock relief and the small companies rates in 1973 and the advance corporation tax system of the same year explains the dramatic fall of 40 percentage points in the average rate of corporation tax between 1970 and 1974.

What emerges from the above discussion is therefore a clear difference in the attitude of Labour and Conservative administrations towards company taxation. Conservative policy has been to minimise the tax liabilities of companies – particularly smaller businesses – whereas Labour policy has been to ensure that companies made a positive contribution to government revenues. In terms of the theory of interest groups developed in Chapter 9, this means that the Conservatives (Labour) give rather more (less) weight to business corporations and the rentier class.

Turning to the question of indirect tax rates, prior to the introduction of Value Added Tax (VAT) in 1973 there existed a number of purchase tax rates, and Table 10.7 shows the lower and upper limits of these rates. As Price (1978) notes, though purchase tax increases were occasionally used in contractions, its absolute and relative impact on a restricted range of goods was a drawback recognised by all Chancellors; thus 'in Conservative periods this acted as an incentive to reduce and standardise rates and in Labour periods as a disincentive against increases'. The Wilson government introduced, in its 1966 budget, the selective employment tax, levied as a flat-rate surcharge on employers' national insurance contributions. This tax was to be refunded to all industries except services and construction, the logic being to transfer manpower from the service industries to manufacturing. This tax was abolished by the Conservative government (in two steps, in 1971/72 and 1973/74) as a part of a wider programme to introduce VAT. In 1973/74, VAT at a rate of 10 per cent was introduced, with a broader and more uniform tax base than the earlier purchase taxes which were more selective in their impact. The rate of VAT was reduced by the Labour government from 10 per cent to 8 per cent, thus demonstrating a Labour party preference of raising revenues from direct rather than indirect taxation. A preference in precisely the opposite direction was revealed by the Conservative government of 1979 who raised the rate of VAT from 8 per cent to 15 per cent. This may be interpreted as the Labour party representing the interests of the unemployed and lower income groups in society, since these groups typically consume a much greater proportion of their income than other groups in society.

10.7 Incomes policies in Britain

In the previous sections we considered, in the British context, the political influences that acted upon the formulation of government expenditure and revenue policies. In this section we turn to another important component of post-war British economic policy which has strong political overtones. This is the area of policies designed to restrain the level of wage and pay settlements, these policies being commonly referred to as incomes policies.

Although incomes policies made their appearance on the British economic scene with the wage-freeze of 1948–1950, it is only over the last twenty years or so that they have become a standard part of every government's economic policy package. Over the past two decades both Conservative and Labour governments, prompted either by political ideology or by economic necessity, have accepted the need for policies for pay restraint. The exception to this is Mrs Thatcher who, on ideological grounds, has eschewed such policies, in the belief that wage settlements are best left to the judgement of the market place. However, it is debatable whether Mrs Thatcher really constitutes an exception to the general run of governments who pursue policies on incomes, since the government, by virtue of being a major employer in the economy, cannot help but take a stance on public sector pay, and this indeed Mrs Thatcher's government has done.

The acceptance, by both major parties, of the need for incomes policies would appear to rest on the commonly shared belief that the private sector is capable of securing economic growth with full employment and external equilibrium only if it is able to generate sufficient profits. This in turn requires that private business be unencumbered by large wage claims which, if passed on as high prices, would only make British products uncompetitive and which, if not passed on as higher prices, would diminish profits and hence discourage investment. The rationale for incomes policies would thus be the redistribution of income away from workers to capitalists, a redistribution which, in turn, through higher levels of investment and competitiveness, would serve as an engine for growth.

This interpretation accords well with the views of Kalecki (cf. Section 7.2 of Chapter 7) who argued that governments would not maintain full employment, even if they knew how to do so, because under high levels of employment, the growing self-assurance of workers, who could not be fired from their jobs, would act to undermine the social position of the employers. Reinterpreting Kalecki, one could plausibly argue that post-war governments, under the shadow of Keynes, have been publicly committed to full employment policies. However, the measure that they have adopted, in the context of high levels of employment, to protect the position of the capitalist class, is that of restricting the growth in the standards of living of the working class. This attempt to restrict wages, and hence by implication to protect profits, may have been undertaken partly in the belief that, given the dominant role of private enterprise in the British economy (a role that no serious political party wished to change), profits were necessary for a flourishing economy. It may also have been undertaken partly through a natural affinity between the ruling party (for example the Conservatives) and the capitalist class, but whatever the reasons such policies have served to alter the distribution of income and, with it, the balance of economic power, against the interests of the working class.

It is interesting to note, and this will be discussed in detail later, that although incomes policies have often had the support of trade union officials and leaders, they have been resisted strenuously by the rank and file members. At the same time there have been periods in the recent past when governments have spurned the use of incomes policies. Both the Heath government of 1970 and the Thatcher government of 1979 came to power on the principle of non-intervention in wage negotiations. Mr Heath of course reversed his policies within two years of taking office. Mrs Thatcher has proved more obdurate and, on the Kalecki interpretation, has attempted to subdue workers through high levels of unemployment rather than to follow the 'consensus' policy of earlier governments of ensuring high employment levels and then organising redistributions in favour of profits through incomes policies.

The salient characteristics of the nature of incomes policies operating in Britain are reproduced in Table 10.8. Three features of these policies deserve comment. Firstly, there is the form of the pay restraint adopted by the particular incomes policies; then there is the question of whether or not these policies were backed by legal sanctions and finally there is the issue of the attitudes adopted by the trade unions and their members towards these policies.

The form of pay restraint adopted has usually taken the form of establishing norms for pay increases subject to certain exceptions and, more unusually, the form

Table 10.8 *Pay policies, 1948–1979*

Policy period	Party in power	Restrictions on pay	Exceptions	Method of implementation	Institutional arrangements	Role of the institution
1948–50	Labour	Zero norm	(i) To maintain established differentials (ii) Low pay (iii) Productivity[a]	Voluntary	None	None
1956–57	Conservative	None	None	Voluntary, seeking wage restraint, via price constraint	Council on Prices, Productivity and Incomes ('The 3 Wise Men')	To keep under review changes in prices, productivity and incomes, and report thereon
1961–63						
Stage 1 (1961–62)	Conservative	Zero norm	None	Voluntary, with Government pressure on public sector, Wage Councils, etc.	None	None
Stage 2 (1962–63)	Conservative	'Guiding light' of 2–2½%, raised to 3–3½%	(i) Exceptional contributions to productivity (ii) Labour mobility	Voluntary	National Incomes Commission	To consider the particular circumstances of cases referred to it by the Government, having regard for the national interest; no substantive powers were taken nor did the Government take powers to implement the findings

Table 10.8 (*cont.*)

1965-69					
Stage 1 (1965-66) Labour	3-3½%	(i)Direct contributions to productivity by employees (ii)Labour mobility (iii)Low pay (iv)Where it was in the national interest to restore differentials between groups of workers doing similar work	Voluntary, with voluntary wage vetting scheme by the TUC	National Board for Prices and Incomes	To examine particular cases in order to advise whether the behaviour of prices or of wages, salaries or other money incomes was in the national interest as defined by the Government after consultation with management and unions; the role was largely advisory
Stage 2 (1966-67) Labour	Freeze for 6 months followed by a zero norm for 6 months	None initially, but certain exceptions later restored	Compulsory		
Stage 3 (1967-68) Labour	Zero norm	All criteria of 1965-66 restored	Voluntary (although powers retained to delay wage increases by (i) up to 30 days, (ii) further 3 months while referred to NBPI, and (iii) further 3 months if recommended by NBPI)		Policing the powers of delay

Stage 4 (1968-69)	Labour	Zero norm	3½% average increase as a ceiling for exceptional cases but with no ceiling in 3 cases: (1) genuine productivity bargaining, (2) wage restructuring, and (3) low paid workers, included in an overall agreement which provided for an average increase below the ceiling	Voluntary, with powers of delay with (iii) extended to 8 months		
Stage 5[b] (1969-70)	Labour	2½-4½% norm	As for 1968-69	Voluntary, with powers of delay of (i) 30 days and (ii) 3 months whilst NBPI reported		
1970-72	Conservative	The 'n-1' policy	None	Voluntary, by government example in the public sector	None	None
1972-74 Phase 1 (1972-73)	Conservative	Freeze	None	Compulsory	None	None

Table 10.8 (*cont.*)

Phase 2 (1973)	£1+4% maximum with 12 month rule	None	Compulsory	Pay Board	(i)To ensure the implementation of the pay code, with legal powers (ii) To advise the government on questions relating to pay
Phase 3 (1973-74)	Maximum of 7% or £2.25 plus threshold agreements	None	Compulsory	Pay Board	
1974-77 Social Contract					
Phase 1 (1974-75) Labour	To compensate for price increase between main settlements (less threshold payments) with 12 month rule	None	Voluntary	None	None
Phase 2 (1975-76) Labour	£6 maximum (freeze on incomes over £8,500) with 12 month rule	None	Voluntary	Price Commission	Wage increases which exceeded the norm not allowable in entirety as cost increases
Phase 3 (1976-77) Labour	5% with minimum of £2.50 and maximum of £4	None	Voluntary	Price Commission	

Phase 4	(1977-78)	Labour	10%	Productivity deals and certain pension provisions	Sanctions against companies	Price Commission
	(1978-79)	Labour	5%	Productivity deals and those earning less than £4.50 pw		
	1979 onwards	Conservative	Policy off			

[a] Insisted on by TUC.

[b] This was only a nominal policy.

Source: Tarling and Wilkinson (1977).

of 'wage freezes'. The latter form of pay restraint was adopted by the Conservative government in the middle of 1961 and lasted till April 1962, when it was breached by concessions made by the Electricity Board to its employees. It was adopted again when the Labour government imposed, following the sterling crisis of July 1966, a six-month freeze on wages and prices. Finally, in November 1972, the Conservative government, in response to rising prices, announced a three-month wages and prices freeze.

We have already commented on the fact that both the Conservative governments of 1970 and 1979 were elected on a platform of non-interference with the wage-bargaining process. The Heath government, deterred by economic circumstances and by its lack of commitment to its own ideology, soon reversed its policy. Mrs Thatcher's commitment to, and belief in, her policies has been greater and three and a half million unemployed have not deflected her from her course. However, given the absence of policies to restrain pay, the real incomes of those in employment have grown and this has ensured the government's high standing in the polls. The Labour party, on the other hand, has never had any ideological reservations about attempting to influence the level of pay settlements, and the need for policies on incomes and prices have always been expressed in party documents. One possible reason for Labour's predilection for incomes policies is that such policies can be argued to be an essential component of an economic strategy based on planning, in which the workings of the market economy are subject to the overall supervision of the state.

Apart from the periods of wage freezes discussed above, both Labour and Conservative policies on incomes have taken the form of establishing norms for pay increases. The differences that emerge between the establishing of these norms appear not to be so much inter-party as inter-period. Pay norms in the 1960s were fixed with reference to anticipated rates of increase in aggregate productivity. Thus in 1962–64, the Conservative party's 'guiding light' was a productivity based 2–2½ per cent increase; in 1965 Labour adopted a productivity-based norm of 3–3½ per cent. In the 1970s the norm was established not so much with productivity increases as with target rates of inflation in mind. Correspondingly, along with this change in the basis of the norm, these later policies concentrated on flat-rate increases subject to very few exceptions.

Paralleling the increasing concern of governments with inflation has been the greater reliance on statutory powers to enforce policies on incomes. Up to the Labour government of 1964, pay restraints relied upon a voluntary acceptance of such restraints by unions and their members, although, as in 1961–63, the government did use its position as an employer to influence public sector wages directly. In 1965, for the first time, the Trade Union Congress involved itself in the implementing of incomes policies by setting up a committee to examine the appropriateness of wage claims from affiliated members. This marked a radical departure in that the autonomy of the individual unions was compromised through subservience to the umbrella body. After 1970, however, pay policies depended much more on statutory compliance for their implementation. The Heath government's 1972–74 policy relied upon statutorily enforceable limits on pay increases, and the succeeding Labour government was able to dispense with such legally enforceable limits only because of surrogate policing by the Trade Union Congress.

Given the importance of trade union involvement in policies designed to restrain pay, Lawson (1982) has analysed the conditions required for effective trade union support to be forthcoming. In eliciting such support it is first of all important for the government to persuade union officials and leaders to support its policy, but, in turn, it is as important for union leaders to obtain the consent of rank and file members to their support of government policy. Union officials have only been prepared to support incomes policies when such policies have been part of a wider social programme with which they have had sympathy. Thus the report of the Trade Union Congress to its 1965 Conference argued that 'the justification for trade union participation in an incomes policy lies in the contribution that it will make to the attainment of social and economic policies which will lead to more substantial and lasting benefits for their members'. This would imply that trade unions, with their ideological affiliations to the Labour party, are more likely to support incomes policies which are initiated by a Labour rather than a Conservative government. Indeed this lack of ideological and social *rapport* between the unions and the Conservative party has meant that Conservative-inspired incomes policies have been implemented in the teeth of union opposition and hence have relied for their success on statutory compliance.

Trade union officials may also be persuaded to support Labour-inspired incomes policies if they perceive the successful implementation of such policies as being necessary to maintain the Labour party in power. This was evident in the 1965 conference of the Trade Union Congress when it was felt that Labour could only continue in power with trade union co-operation for its income policies, and it was evident again in 1966–67 and 1975–77, which were both periods of stress for the Labour party.

However, even with the support of union officials, incomes policies have evoked opposition from union rank and file members, essentially because such policies depress their standards of living. This opposition grows with the length of the policy and eventually communicates itself – through increasing strike action – to union leaders, who are then pushed into opposing a renewal of a policy they originally supported. It could plausibly be argued that there is a divergence between the interests of officials and ordinary members of unions. The former have an interest in the continuance in power of the Labour party since this gives them a vicarious taste of power and enhances their status. The ordinary members however are anxious for their standard of living to be protected and are ready to penalise a government of whatever political persuasion which threatens this.

The Social Contract of 1974–75 (produced through co-operation between the Labour party and trade union officials) illustrates this process. The loss in real wages in 1976 and 1977, with no obvious gain in sight, led to successful strikes (for example the lorry drivers against the Road Haulage Association) the pressure for which came from the shop floor. Attempts by the government to impose an incomes policy unilaterally (Stage IV of the Social Contract), to which, by this time, even the Trade Union Congress was opposed, culminated in the so-called 'Winter of Discontent' and the downfall of the Labour government in May 1979.

As Lawson (1982, p. 34) notes, this experience illustrates 'both the need for, and the difficulty of, enlisting the support of rank and file workers for any national economic strategy'. Although it is true of all policies that they cannot work in the face of determined public opposition, it is particularly relevant for incomes policies since opposition to them, by virtue of being relatively easy to organise, can be easily articulated. Workers might accept pay restraints provided they perceive fairly immediate benefits accruing to them from their sacrifice. Without this optimism, they may well regard such self denial (whether voluntary or statutorily imposed) as pointless and react accordingly.

10.8 Conclusions

This chapter has examined the political aspects of the formulation of economic policy in Britain from the perspective of the theory of political economy developed in Chapters 7, 8 and 9. The general approach in this chapter has been to look closely at the institutional framework within which policy is made and also to examine, in greater detail than hitherto, the nature of the policy options available to the government. In doing so we attempted to show that, rather than being the output of a homogeneous entity, a government's economic policy is often the result of a resolution of conflict both within and between departments. In addition, to understand the political influences bearing on policy it is important to examine in detail the instruments of policy that are actually within a government's control.

The main aim of this book has been to show that voting behaviour and government popularity are influenced by economic performance and social class structure (Part I) and that economic policy at a disaggregated level is severely constrained by re-election, ideology and balance of payments considerations (Part II). This research has very serious implications for the view of the government as a benevolent dictator, a view prevalent in the orthodox theory of economic policy. This theory has a *normative* character and explains how a government *ought* to behave in order to attain maximal social welfare. In our view this theory is deficient since governments make efforts to promote their own ideology and to secure re-election. This suggests that an analysis of economic policy needs to account for political factors. This would result in a *positive* theory of political-economic policy, which views the government as a political animal.

What are the implications of this observation for economists advising governments? It would seem to follow that these economists should become politically involved and offer advice to the political party of their choice on how to attain its ideological objectives and secure itself terms in office. This would produce a criterion of *political* welfare, which would resolve the conventional dilemma of the appropriate choice of objective function found in the orthodox theory of economic policy. To a certain extent economists already follow this prescription, as witness the wide variety of economic forecasters and modellers of very different political persuasions. It is not surprising that, in terms of the political-economic framework developed in this book, Mrs Thatcher's government in Britain should have lent, *via* the Social Science Research Council, considerable support to economists closest to her own political persuasions.

It is often suggested that economists should be objective and search for the 'Holy Grail' of optimal social welfare. But, in principle, this could only be done by redesigning the political structure so as to avoid the re-election and ideological effort of politically-motivated governments. However Arrow's (1951) 'impossibility theorem' for social choice demonstrates that it is impossible to obtain a satisfactory voting process implying a well-behaved social welfare function derived from individual preferences. This supports our view that economists advising governments should abandon their idea of themselves as objective consultants attempting to maximise social welfare and, instead, should advise on the best way of attaining the goals of the interest groups and political parties to which they are allied.

Notes

Notes to Chapter 4

1 The data, the sample period and the choice of economic and electoral variables correspond to the ones used in Pissarides (1980). We are grateful to Dr Pissarides for providing us with his data set.

2 $\bar{R}^2$ is the coefficient of multiple correlation adjusted for degrees of freedom, DW is the Durbin–Watson statistic, s is the estimate of the equation standard error and the subscript -1 denotes a one-period lag. The estimation technique used was that for Seemingly Unrelated Regression Equations (SURE) incorporated into the package SHAZAM developed by K. J. White. The estimate of the covariance between the error terms $\epsilon^{\mathrm{R,O}}$ and $\epsilon^{\mathrm{O,LIB}}$ was -0.003.

Notes to Chapter 5

1 In response to the question 'If there was a general election tomorrow which party would you vote for?'.

2 In response to the question 'How strongly do you approve or disapprove of the way the Government is handling the economy?'.

3 This hypothesis is discussed at length in Chapter 2.

4 A lag of two quarters was the most satisfactory characterisation of unemployment effects (cf. Chapter 4).

5 Except when there was a change in the ruling party, when the values were 10, 9, 8 . . . Both electoral variables were used by Pissarides (1980).

6 The employed estimation technique is Zellner's (1962) method for Seemingly Unrelated Regression Equations (SURE) with the appropriate cross-equation restraints imposed. This technique is appropriate for equation systems which are not simultaneous, but which may nevertheless be interrelated through their respective error terms or cross-equation restraints. The estimation was carried out using K. J. White's SHAZAM program.

7 Unless otherwise stated the tests used are likelihood ratio tests with $2 \log (L^{\mathrm{U}}/L^{\mathrm{R}})$ distributed as $\chi^2(r)$; where L^{U} is the likelihood of the sample in the absence of restrictions, L^{R} is the likelihood of the sample with the restrictions imposed and r is the number of restrictions. The probability of Type I error in all tests is 0.05. For further details see Silvey (1970, Chapter 7).

8 Figures in parentheses are t-ratios.

Notes to Chapter 6

1 The derivation of (6.4.4) assumes a two-party framework. This study therefore restricts choice to two political parties only. This is not very serious, because in the British election of 1966 over 90 per cent of the voters chose Conservative or Labour. In fact the 177 constituencies examined in this paper excluded the major areas of Liberal support, hence in the estimations the Liberal vote is ignored.

2 When one combines the time-series approach (constant $\mathbf{y}_j$) adopted in Chapter 5 with the cross-section approach (constant $\mathbf{x}^k - \mathbf{x}^s$) adopted in this chapter, one obtains the model (6.4.8) with differences in economic performance of the political parties varying over time and attributes varying across constituencies.

3 Census 1966. *U.K. General and Parliamentary Constituency Tables*, HMSO, London, 1969.

4 Figures in parentheses are t-ratios, s is the equation standard error and $\bar{R}^2$ is the coefficient of multiple correlation adjusted for degrees of freedom.

5 The logarithmic lead evaluated at the mean was 0.355 and gives rise to 58.8% of the votes going to Labour and 41.2% to the Conservative party.

6 How the restricted version of equation (6.6.6), for analysing voting within classes, compares with the general uniform model (6.4.9) may be analysed with reference to the master model with explanatory variables $\{1, w_j, u_j, h_j, h_j w_j\}$, since both specifications may be derived as a special case of this master model. That is, the restricted version of (6.6.6) obtains upon deletion of the variable h_j and (6.6.9) obtains upon deletion of $h_j w_j$. Since the t-ratio on $h_j w_j$ is significant (4.04) and the t-ratio on h_j is insignificant (0.82) at the 5% level, one rejects the general model with three attributes (6.4.9) in favour of the model of voting within occupational classes.

7 This statement may be formally tested with the powerful J-test for non-nested hypotheses (Pesaran, 1974; Davidson and MacKinnon, 1981). Under the null hypothesis that the model with no class differentials (i.e. $(\alpha_w, \boldsymbol{\theta}'_w) = (\alpha_m, \boldsymbol{\theta}'_m)$) is true, the alternative hypothesis that the restricted version of (6.6.6) is valid cannot be rejected as the relevant t-ratio is 0.83. On the other hand the model with no class differentials is rejected, assuming the restricted version of (6.6.6) is true, since the relevant t-ratio is 26.93. Hence, the restricted version of (6.6.6) is preferred over the model with no class differentials.

Notes to Chapter 7

1 When there is a two-party system (government and opposition), equation (3.3.1) may be changed to

$$p_t^s = F(M_t^s - M_t^k) + \epsilon \qquad (3.3.1')$$

where $F(\,.\,)$ denotes the cumulative density function of the bias terms and ϵ_t denotes an error term to allow for political events of the moment (e.g. World Cup, Falklands crisis, etc.). The probability of party s winning an election equals

$$\text{prob}\{p_t^s > 0.5\} = 1 - F_\epsilon\{0.5 - F(M_t^s - M_t^k)\}$$

where F_ϵ is the cumulative density function of the error term ϵ_t. Since both $F(\,.\,)$ and $F_\epsilon(\,.\,)$ are monotonic increasing functions, the probability of winning an election is a monotonic increasing function of the number of votes cast in favour of the government.

2 In the language of econometricians there seems a case of *observational equivalence* of competing hypotheses regarding the behaviour of a government.

3 Van Winden (1983) focuses on four major interest groups: capitalists, private sector workers, state sector workers and dependents on the state.

4 The Marxist view seems to assign a weight of 100 per cent to the preferences of capitalists (especially during the boom period), although it is not unlikely that the workers will get represented ('stabilization policy') during a depression. In Minford and Peel (1982) a Conservative (Labour) government gives no weight at all to the staunch Labour (Conservative) voters and concentrates on representing both the Conservative and floating voters.

If a government were interested only in maximising votes it would not represent the interests of its own already-committed voters, so that if it does this represents an element of ideology.

5 A particularly illuminating illustration of this conflict between bureaucrats in ministries and politicians is provided by the popular BBC programme 'Yes Minister'.

Notes to Chapter 8

1 All variables are indicated by capital letters, whereas the coefficients, such as c_i^d and c_i^m, are denoted by small letters and are always assumed to be positive.

2 The Mexican government adopted this policy during the early part of 1982 in an attempt to keep the relative prices in Mexico and the USA constant.

Notes to Chapter 9

1 This literature assumes that the objective functions of politicians and bureaucrats differ. The politicians aspire to equalise marginal cost and marginal political benefit, since then the surplus to politicians is highest. The bureaucrats, however, do not care about the financial sacrifice politicians have to make and merely wish to maximise the size of their office, salary, prestige, etc. They simply ensure that total real costs are covered by the Budget. In practice the actual outcome will be determined by a bargaining procedure, but a good approximation is to assume that the bureaucrats win.

2 The adopted formulation implies that the partial derivatives for each of the $U_i(\,.\,)$ are positive.

3 Were we to have a conflict model (e.g. van der Ploeg, 1982e), we could model the conflicting interests between capitalists and workers by separating the group of active private sector agents into these two component groups.

4 Pareto-optimality occurs, in our context, when it is impossible to improve the interest of any group, say group i, without worsening the other groups, $j \neq i$. This may be formalised by

$$\operatorname*{Max}_{\tau} U_i(\tau)$$

subject to the constraints

$$U_j(\tau) \geqslant \bar{U}_j, \quad j \neq i$$

where $\bar{U}_j$ denotes the fixed (arbitrary) *status quo* elementary utility of group j. The associated Lagrangian function is

$$U_i(\tau) - \sum_{j \neq i} \lambda_j (U_j(\tau) - \bar{U}_j)$$

where the λ_j denote the Kuhn–Tucker multipliers at the optimum

$$\lambda_j = \frac{\partial U_i}{\partial \bar{U}_j} \leqq 0, \quad j \neq i$$

The λ_j are also known as the imputed shadow costs, since they indicate how much group i loses out when the *status quo* of group j increases by a marginal amount. The power parameters may now be related to the shadow costs as follows

$$\rho_i = \left[1 - \sum_{j \neq i} (\lambda_j)\right]^{-1} \geqq 0 \quad \text{and} \quad \rho_j = -\lambda_j \rho_i \geqq 0$$

where $\Sigma_i\, \rho_i = 1$.

5 The remaining proportion represents material expenditures of the government bought from the private and foreign sectors.

6 For the extreme case $\xi = i_1^d = m_g = 0$, we find

$$\frac{\partial Y_s}{\partial \tau} = b_3 \mu_2^g Q(1 - c_1^d)(1 - \tau)^2$$

which is always positive.

7 A Labour government might find it easier to increase the fiscal deficit than the tax rate, since the former does not damage the interests of the private sector workers as much (see Subsection 9.3.2).

8 The reader may wish to compare this result with van Winden and van Velthoven (1982) who obtain for the optimal tax rate

$$\tau = \rho_4/(\rho_1 + \rho_4)$$

by ignoring bureaucrats.

9 The partial derivatives of B^{**} will be larger than of B^* due to the expansionary implications of endogenous government spending.

10 The dynamics of purely economic systems has been investigated many times before (e.g. Turnovsky, 1977), so that here we focus exclusively on the dynamics of the reaction functions.

11 The formal proofs of these (in)stability results are presented in the appendix to this chapter.

12 This criterion for determining the stability of a particular assignment of the instruments, tax rate and state spending, to the targets, ideology and popularity, is not unlike the principle of effective market classification developed for decentralized decision making in an open economy (e.g. Mundell, 1962). However the discontinuous nature of the policy rules represent a major extension of this early literature.

Note to Chapter 10

1 Throughout this chapter, the term 'general government' refers to central government and local authorities. The 'public sector' refers to general government and public corporations. The terms 'general government' and 'public authorities' are also used synonymously. However, both the central government and local authorities constitute a part of the elected component of the public sector and, in terms of the definitions given in Chapter 9, constitute part of government. The bureaucrats constitute the non-elected component of the public sector.

Bibliography

Alford, R. R. (1963). *Party and Society. The Anglo-American Democracies*, John Murray, London.
Alt, J. E. (1979). *The Politics of Economic Decline*, Cambridge University Press, Cambridge.
Amemya, T. (1981). 'Qualitative response models: a survey', *Journal of Economic Literature*, vol. 19, pp. 1483–1536.
Ando, A. K. and F. Modigliani (1963). 'The life-cycle hypothesis of saving: aggregate implications and tests', *American Economic Review*, vol. 53, pp. 55–84.
Arcelus, F. and A. H. Meltzer (1975). 'The effects of aggregate economic variables on congressional elections', *American Political Science Review*, vol. 69, pp. 1232–1240.
Arrow, K. J. (1951). *Social Choice and Individual Values*, John Wiley, New York.
Bailey, M. J. (1956). 'The welfare cost of inflationary finance', *Journal of Political Economy*, vol. 64, pp. 93--110.
Begg, D. (1982). *The Rational Expectations Revolution in Macroeconomics*, Phillip Allen, Oxford.
Blinder, A. S. and R. M. Solow (1972). 'Does fiscal policy matter?', *Journal of Public Economics*, vol. 2, pp. 319–338.
Bloom, H. S. and H. D. Price (1975). 'Voter response to short-run economic conditions: the asymmetric effect of prosperity and recession', *American Political Science Review*, vol. 69, pp. 1240–1254.
Boddy, R. and J. Crotty (1975). 'Class conflict and macro-policy: the political business cycle', *Review of Radical Political Economics*, vol. 7, no. 1, pp. 1–19.
Borooah, V. K. and F. van der Ploeg (1982a). 'British government popularity and economic performance: a comment', *Economic Journal*, vol. 92, pp. 405–410.
Borooah, V. K. and F. van der Ploeg (1982b). 'The changing criteria of economic success: performance and popularity in British politics', *Manchester School of Economic and Social Studies*, vol. 50, pp. 61–78.
Borooah, V. K. and F. van der Ploeg (1982c). 'Economic conditions, class and voter behaviour', *The Scottish Journal of Political Economy*, vol. 29, pp. 206–214.
Brittan, S. (1964). *The Treasury under the Tories 1951–1964*, Pelican, London.
Brittan, S. (1969). *Steering the Economy*, Secker and Warburg, London.
Brittan, S. (1978). 'Inflation and democracy', in F. Hirsch and J. H. Goldthorpe (eds), *The Political Economy of Inflation*, Martin Robertson, London.
Bryson, A. E. and Y. C. Ho (1969). *Applied Optimal Control*, Blaisch Waltham, Cambridge, Mass.
Buiter, W. (1980). 'The macro-economics of Dr. Pangloss: a critical survey of the New Classical Macroeconomics', *Economic Journal*, vol. 90, pp. 34–50.
Burton, J., M. J. Hawkins and G. L. Hughes (1981). 'Is liberal democracy especially prone to inflation? An analytical treatment', in D. A. Hibbs and H. Fassbender (eds), *Contemporary Political Economy*, North-Holland, Amsterdam.
Bush, W. C. and A. T. Denzau (1977). 'The voting behaviour of bureaucrats and public sector growth', in T. E. Borcherding (ed.), *Budgets and Bureaucrats:*

The Sources of Government Growth, Duke University Press, Durham, North Carolina.
Butler, D. and A. King (1966). *The British General Election of 1966*, Macmillan, London.
Butler, D. and D. Stokes (1974), *Political Change in Britain*, Macmillan, London.
Caves, R. E. and L. B. Krause (eds) (1980). *Britain's Economic Performance*, Brookings Institution, Washington, D.C.
Census (1966). *U.K. General and Parliamentary Constituency Tables*, HMSO, London.
Chrystal, K. A. and J. Alt (1979a), 'Endogenous government expenditure: Wagner's law or Götterdämmerung', in P. Jackson and S. Cook (eds), *Recent Developments in the Theory of Fiscal Policy*, Martin Robertson, London.
Chrystal, K. A. and J. Alt (1979b). 'Public sector behaviour: the status of the political business cycle', Discussion Paper no. 128, Department of Economics, University of Essex.
Chrystal, K. A. and J. Alt (1981a). 'Some problems in formulating and testing a politico-economic model of the United Kingdom', *Economic Journal*, vol. 91, pp. 730–736.
Chrystal, K. A. and J. Alt (1981b). 'Politico-economic models of British fiscal policy', in D. A. Hibbs and H. Fassbender (eds). *Contemporary Political Economy*, North-Holland, Amsterdam.
Comanor, W. S. (1976). 'The Median Voter Rule and the Theory of Public Choice', *Journal of Public Economics*, vol. 5, pp. 177–88.
Converse, P. E. (1958). 'The Shifting Role of Class in Political Attitudes and Behaviour', in E. E. Maccoby, T. M. Newcomb and E. L. Hartley (eds), *Readings in Social Psychology*, Methuen, London.
Cyert, R. M. and M. H. De Groot (1974), 'Rational expectations and Bayesian analysis', *Journal of Political Economy*, vol. 82, pp. 521–536.
Cyert, R. M. and J. G. March (1963). *A Behavioural Theory of the Firm*, Prentice-Hall, Englewood Cliffs, New Jersey.
Daganzo, C. (1980). *Multinomial Probit*, Academic Press, New York.
Daniel, W. W. (1974). *A National Survey of the Unemployed*, Political and Economic Planning Broadsheet, London.
Daniel, W. W. (1975). *The PEP Survey on Inflation*, Political and Economic Planning Broadsheet, London.
Daniel, W. W. (1981). *The Nature of the Current Unemployment*, British-North American Research Association, (Occasional Paper 6), London.
Davidson, J. E. H., D. F. Hendry, F. Srba and S. Yeo (1978). 'Econometric modelling of the aggregate time series relationship between consumers' expenditure and income in the United Kingdom', *Economic Journal*, vol. 88, pp. 661–692.
Davidson, R. and J. G. MacKinnon (1981). 'Several tests for model specification in the presence of alternative hypotheses', *Econometrica*, 49, pp. 781–793.
Davis, O. A., M. J. Hinich and P. C. Ordeshook (1970). 'An expository development of a mathematical model of the electoral process', *American Political Science Review*, vol. 64, pp. 426–48.
Doel, H. van den (1979). *Democracy and Welfare Economics*, Cambridge University Press, Cambridge.
Downs, A. (1957). *An Economic Theory of Democracy*, Harper and Row, New York.
Duesenberry, J. S. (1948). *Income, Savings and the Theory of Consumer Behaviour*, Harvard University Press, Cambridge, Mass.
Fair, R. C. (1975). 'On controlling the economy to win elections', *Cowles Foundation Discussion Paper*, no. 397, Yale University, Yale.
Fair, R. C. (1978). 'The effect of economic events on votes for President', *The Review of Economics and Statistics*, vol. 60, pp. 159–173.
Fassbender, H. (1981). 'From conventional IS–LM to political-economic models',

in D. A. Hibbs and H. Fassbender (eds), *Contemporary Political Economy*, North-Holland, Amsterdam.
Feiwel, G. R. (1974). 'Reflections on Kalecki's theory of the political business cycle', *Kyklos*, vol. 27, pp. 21–48.
Finney, D. (1971). *Probit Analysis*, Cambridge University Press, Cambridge.
Fiorina, M. (1981). 'Short- and long-term effects of economic conditions on individual voting decisions', in D. A. Hibbs and H. Fassbender (eds), *Contemporary Political Economy*, North-Holland, Amsterdam.
Fischer, S. (1977). 'Long-term contracts, rational expectations and the optimal money supply rule', *Journal of Political Economy*, vol. 85, pp. 191–206.
Frey, B. S. (1974). 'The politico-economic system: a simulation model', *Kyklos*, vol. 27, pp. 227–253.
Frey, B. S. (1978a). 'Politico-economic models and cycles', *Journal of Public Economics*, vol. 9, pp. 203–220.
Frey, B. S. (1978b). *Modern Political Economy*, Martin Robertson, Oxford.
Frey, B. S. (1978c). 'Keynesian thinking in politico-economic models', *Journal of Post-Keynesian Economics*, vol. 1, pp. 71–81.
Frey, B. S. and H. Garbers (1971). ' "Politico-Econometrics" – On Estimation in Political Economy', *Political Studies*, vol. 19, pp. 316–320.
Frey, B. S. and L. J. Lau (1968). 'Towards a mathematical model of government behaviour', *Zeitschrift für Nationalökonomie*, vol. 28, pp. 355–380.
Frey, B. S. and H. J. Ramser (1976). 'The political business cycle: a comment', *Review of Economic Studies*, vol. 43, pp. 553–556.
Frey, B. S. and F. Schneider (1978a). 'A politico-economic model of the United Kingdom', *Economic Journal*, vol. 88, pp. 243–253.
Frey, B. S. and F. Schneider (1978b). 'An empirical study of politico-economic interaction in the U.S.', *Review of Economics and Statistics*, vol. 60, pp. 174–183.
Frey, B. S. and F. Schneider (1981). 'Central Bank behaviour. A positive empirical analysis', *Journal of Monetary Economics*, vol. 7, pp. 291–315.
Frey, B. S. and F. Schneider (1982). 'Politico-economic models in competition with alternative models: which predict better?', *European Journal of Political Research*, vol. 10, pp. 241–254.
Friedlaender, A. F. (1973). 'Macro-policy goals and revealed preference', *Quarterly Journal of Economics*, vol. 86, pp. 25–43.
Friedman, M. (1957). *A Theory of the Consumption Function*, Princeton University Press, Princeton.
Friedman, M. (1961). 'The lag in the effect of monetary policy', *Journal of Political Economy*, vol. 69, pp. 447–466.
Friedman, M. (1968). 'The role of monetary policy', *American Economic Review*, vol. 58, pp. 1–17.
Gärtner, M. (1981). 'A politico-economic model of wage inflation', *De Economist*, vol. 129, pp. 183–205.
Goldthorpe, J. H., D. Lockwood, F. Bechhofer, and J. Platt (1968). *The Affluent Worker: Political Attitudes and Behaviour*, Cambridge University Press, Cambridge.
Goodhart, C. A. E. and R. J. Bhansali (1970). 'Political Economy', *Political Studies*, vol. 18, pp. 43–106.
Goodman, S. and G. H. Kramer (1975). 'Comment on Arcelus and Meltzer, The effect of aggregate economic conditions on congressional elections', *American Political Science Review*, vol. 69, pp. 1255–1265.
Goodwin, R. M. (1967). 'A growth cycle', in C. H. Feinstein (ed.), *Socialism, Capitalism and Economic Growth* (essays in honour of Maurice Dobb), Cambridge University Press, Cambridge.
Gudgin, G. and P. J. Taylor (1979). *Seats, Votes and the Spatial Organisation of Elections*, Pion Ltd., London.

Haavelmo, T. (1945). 'Multiplier effects of a balanced budget', *Econometrica*, vol. 13, pp. 311–318.
Hausman, J. A. and D. A. Wise (1978). 'A conditional probit model for qualitative choice: discrete decisions recognizing interdependence and heterogeneous preferences', *Econometrica*, vol. 46, pp. 403–426.
Hibbs, D. A. (1976). *Economic Interests and the Politics of Macroeconomic Policy*, MIT Center for International Studies, Cambridge, Mass.
Hibbs, D. A. (1977a). 'Political parties and macroeconomic policies', *American Political Science Review*, vol. 71, pp. 1467–1487.
Hibbs, D. A. (1977b). *Trade union power, Labor militancy and wage inflation: a comparative analysis*, MIT Center for International Studies, Cambridge, Mass.
Hibbs, D. A. (1982a). 'On the demand for economic outcomes: macroeconomic performance and mass political support in the United States, Great Britain and Germany', *The Journal of Politics*, vol. 44, pp. 426–461.
Hibbs, D. A. (1982b). 'Economic outcomes and political support for British governments among occupational classes: a dynamic analysis', *The American Political Science Review*, vol. 76, pp. 259–279.
Hibbs, D. A. and H. Fassbender (eds) (1981). *Contemporary Political Economy*, North-Holland, Amsterdam.
Hicks, J. R. (1937). 'Mr. Keynes and the Classics', *Econometrica*, vol. 5, pp. 147–159.
Hotelling, H. (1929). 'Stability in competition', *Economic Journal*, vol. 39, pp. 41–57.
Ito, T. (1980). 'Disequilibrium growth theory', *Journal of Economic Theory*, vol. 23, pp. 380–409.
Jennings, I. (1961). *Party Politics, II: The Growth of Parties*, Cambridge University Press, Cambridge.
Kahn, R. F. (1931). 'The relation of income investment to unemployment', *Economic Journal*, vol. 41, pp. 173–198.
Kaldor, N. (1971). 'Conflicts in national economic objectives', *Economic Journal*, vol. 81, pp. 1–16.
Kalecki, M. (1943). 'Political aspects of full employment', *Political Quarterly*, October/December, pp. 322–331. Also reprinted in *Essays on the Dynamics of the Capitalist Economy, 1933–1970*, Cambridge University Press, Cambridge.
Kalecki, M. (1971). *Selected Essays on the Dynamics of the Capitalist Economy*, Cambridge University Press, Cambridge.
Kernell, S. and D. A. Hibbs (1981). 'A critical threshold model of presidential popularity', in D. A. Hibbs and H. Fassbender (eds), *Contemporary Political Economy*, North-Holland, Amsterdam.
Keynes, J. M. (1936). *The General Theory of Employment, Interest and Money*, Macmillan, London.
Kindleberger, C. (1963). *International Economics*, Irwin, Homewood, Illinois.
King, A. (1968). 'Why all governments lose by-elections', *New Society*, 21 March 1968, pp. 413–415.
Kirchgässner, G. (1979). 'Popularity of the government and the opposition in a 2-party and 3-party system', mimeo, Eidgenössische Technische Hochschule, Zürich.
Koutsoyannis, A. (1979). *Modern Microeconomics*, Macmillan, London.
Kramer, G. H. (1971). 'Short-term fluctuations in U.S. voting behaviour, 1896–1964', *American Political Science Review*, vol. 65, pp. 131–143.
Lawson, N. (1968). 'A new theory of by-elections', *Spectator*, 8 November 1968, pp. 650–652.
Lawson, T. (1982). 'Incomes policy and the real wage rate resistance hypothesis: econometric evidence for the UK, 1955–1979', *Department of Applied Economics*, University of Cambridge (mimeo).

Lepper, S. (1974). 'Voting Behaviour and Aggregate Policy Targets', *Public Choice*, vol. 18, pp. 67–81.
Lindbeck, A. (1976). 'Stabilization policy in open economies with endogenous politicians', *American Economic Review* (*Papers and Proceedings*), vol. 66, pp. 1–19.
Luce, R. D. (1959). *Individual Choice Behaviour*, Wiley, New York.
McCallum, B. T. (1978). 'The political business cycle: an empirical test', *Southern Economic Journal*, vol. 44, pp. 505–515.
McFadden, D. (1973). 'Conditional logit analysis of qualitative choice behaviour', in P. Zarembka (ed.), *Frontiers in Econometrics*, Academic Press, New York.
Mackay, D. I. and G. Reid (1972). 'Redundance, Unemployment and Manpower Policy', *Economic Journal*, vol. 82, pp. 1256–1272.
MacRae, D. (1977). 'A political model of the business cycle', *Journal of Political Economy*, vol. 85, pp. 239–263.
Maddock, R. and M. Carter (1982). 'A child's guide to rational expectations', *Journal of Economic Literature*, vol. 20, pp. 39–51.
Malinvaud, E. (1980). *Profitability and Unemployment*, Cambridge University Press, Cambridge.
Marx, K. (1967). *Capital*, Volumes I, II, III, International Publishers, New York.
Mayer, C. (1982). 'The structure of corporation tax in the UK', *Fiscal Studies*, vol. 3, pp. 121–141.
Miller, W. L. (1977). *Electoral Dynamics*, Macmillan, London.
Miller, W. L. and M. Mackie (1973). 'The electoral cycle and the asymmetry of government and opposition popularity: an alternative model of the relationship between economic conditions and political popularity', *Political Studies*, vol. 21, pp. 263–279.
Minford, P. and D. Peel (1982). 'The political theory of the business cycle', *European Economic Review*, vol. 17, pp. 253–270.
Mosley, P. (1976). 'Towards a satisficing theory of economic policy', *Economic Journal*, vol. 86, pp. 59–72.
Mueller, D. C. (1979). *Public Choice*, Cambridge University Press, Cambridge.
Mundell, R. A. (1962). 'The appropriate use of monetary and fiscal policy for internal and external stability', *IMF Staff Papers*, vol. 9, pp. 70–79.
Musgrave, R. A. and A. T. Peacock (1967). *Classics in the Theory of Public Finance*, Macmillan, New York.
Muth, J. F. (1961). 'Rational expectations and the theory of price movements', *Econometrica*, vol. 29, pp. 315–335.
Niskanen, W. A. Jr. (1971). *Bureaucracy and Representative Government*, Aldine-Atherton, Chicago.
Nordhaus, W. D. (1975). 'The political business cycle', *Review of Economic Studies*, vol. 42, pp. 169–190.
Okun, A. (1970). *The Political Economy of Prosperity*, Norton, New York.
Paldam, M. and F. Schneider (1980). 'The macro-economic aspects of government and opposition popularity in Denmark 1957–1978', *Nationaløkonomisk Tidesskrift*, bind 18, pp. 149–170.
Parkin, F. (1967). 'Working-class Conservatives: a Theory of Political Deviance', *British Journal of Sociology*, vol. 18, pp. 278–290.
Patinkin, D. (1956). *Money, Interest and Prices*, Harper and Row, New York.
Peacock, A. T. and J. Wiseman (1961). *The Growth of Public Expenditure in the UK*, Princeton University Press, Princeton.
Pesaran, M. H. (1974). 'On the general problem of model selection', *Review of Economic Studies*, vol. 16, pp. 153–171.
Pesaran, M. H. (1983). 'The New Classical Macroeconomics: A critical exposition', in F. van der Ploeg (ed.), *Mathematical Methods in Economics*, John Wiley, Chichester (forthcoming).

Phelps, E. S. (1967). 'Phillips curves, expectations of inflation and optimal unemployment over time', *Economica*, vol. 34, pp. 254–281.
Phillips, A. W. (1954). 'Stabilization policy in a closed economy', *Economic Journal*, vol. 64, pp. 290–322.
Piachaud, D. (1978). 'Inflation and income distribution', in J. H. Goldthorpe and F. Hirsch (eds), *The Political Economy of Inflation*, Harvard University Press, Cambridge, Mass.
Pissarides, C. A. (1980). 'British government popularity and economic performance', *Economic Journal*, vol. 90, pp. 569–581.
Ploeg, F. van der (1982a). 'Medium-term planning with a multisectoral dynamic model of the U.K. economy', *International Journal of Systems Science*, vol. 13, no. 1, pp. 57–71.
Ploeg, F. van der (1982b). 'The industrial implications of an optimal reflationary mix for the British economy', *Applied Economics*, vol. 14, pp. 355–373.
Ploeg, F. van der (1982c). 'Government policy, real wage resistance and the resolution of conflict', *European Economic Review*, vol. 19, pp. 181–212.
Ploeg, F. van der (1982d). 'Disposable income, unemployment, inflation and state spending in a dynamic political–economic model', presented to the 1982 Annual Meeting of Dutch Economists, Amsterdam.
Ploeg, F. van der (1982e). 'Economic growth and conflict over the distribution of income', presented to the 1982 European Meeting of the Econometric Society, Dublin, forthcoming in the *Journal of Economic Dynamics and Control.*
Price, R. W. R. (1978). 'Budgetary policy', in F. T. Blackaby (ed.), *British Economic Policy 1960–74*, Cambridge University Press, Cambridge.
Robertson, D. (1975). *A Theory of Party Competition*, Wiley, London.
Rose, R. (1974). 'Britain: Simple Abstractions and Complex Realities', in R. Rose (ed.) *Comparative Electoral Behaviour*, Free Press, New York.
Royal Commission on the Distribution of Income and Wealth (1978). *The Causes of Poverty*, HMSO, London.
Runciman, W. G. (1963). *Social Science and Political Theory*, Cambridge University Press, Cambridge.
Samuelson, P. A. and S. Swamy (1974). 'Invariant economic index numbers and canonical duality: survey and synthesis', *The Review of Economics and Statistics*, vol. 64, pp. 566–593.
Sandford, C. T. and P. N. Dean (1970), 'Public expenditure: the paradox of control', *The Banker*, vol. 120, pp. 377–387.
Silvey, S. D. (1970). *Statistical Inference*, Penguin Books Ltd, London.
Simon, H. A. (1952). 'A behavioural model of rational choice', *Quarterly Journal of Economics*, vol. 69, pp. 99–118.
Smithies, A. (1941). 'Optimum Location in Spatial Completion', *Journal of Political Economy*, vol. 49, pp. 423–39.
Stackelberg, H. von (1952). *The Theory of the Market Economy*, Oxford University Press, Oxford.
Stigler, G. J. (1973). 'General economic conditions and national elections', *The American Economic Review*, vol. 63, pp. 160–167. (See also subsequent discussion by MacCracken, Okin and others.)
Swaan, A. de (1973). *Coalition Theories and Cabinet Formations*, Elsevier, Amsterdam.
Takayama, A. (1969). 'The effects of fiscal and monetary policies under flexible and fixed exchange rates', *Canadian Journal of Economics*, vol. 2, pp. 190–209.
Tarling, R. J. and S. F. Wilkinson (1977). 'The social contract: Post-war incomes policies and their inflationary impact', *Cambridge Journal of Economics*, vol. 1, no. 4, pp. 395–414.
Taylor, M. and M. Laver (1973). 'Government coalitions in Western Europe', *European Journal of Political Research*, vol. 1, pp. 205–248.

Theil, H. (1964). *Optimal Decision Rules for Government and Industry*, North-Holland, Amsterdam.
Tinbergen, J. (1952). *On the Theory of Economic Policy*, North-Holland, Amsterdam.
Tobin, J. (1968). 'A general equilibrium approach to monetary theory', *Journal of Money, Credit and Banking*, vol. 1, pp. 15–29.
Trevithick, J. A. and C. Mulvey (1975). *The Economics of Inflation*, Robertson, London.
Tufte, E. (1978). *Political Control of the Economy*, Princeton University Press, New Jersey.
Turnovsky, S. J. (1974). 'On the role of inflationary expectations in a short-run macroeconomic model', *Economic Journal*, vol. 84, pp. 317–337.
Turnovsky, S. J. (1977). *Macroeconomic Analysis and Stabilization Policy*, Cambridge University Press, New York.
Turnovsky, S. J. (1981). 'The optimal inter-temporal choice of inflation and unemployment: an analysis of the steady state and transitional dynamics', *Journal of Economic Dynamics and Control*, vol. 3, pp. 357–384.
Tustin, A. (1954). *The Mechanism of Economic Systems*, Heinemann, London.
UK Treasury (1978). *Report of the Committee on Policy Optimization*, Cmnd 7148, HMSO, London.
Wagner, A. (1883). *Finanzwissenschaft*, translated and reprinted as 'Three extracts on public finance', in R. A. Musgrave and A. T. Peacock (eds) (1967).
White, K. J. (1978). 'A general computer program for econometric methods – SHAZAM', *Econometrica*, vol. 46, pp. 239–240.
Whiteley, P. (ed.) (1980). *Models of Political Economy*, Sage, London and Beverley Hills.
Winden, F. A. A. M. van (1983). *On the Interaction Between State and Private Sector*, North-Holland, Amsterdam, forthcoming.
Winden, F. A. A. M. van and B. van Velthoven (1982). 'Een eenvoudig politiek-economisch model', *Economisch Statistische Berichten*, vol. 67, pp. 1196–1206. An English version is 'The interest function approach to politics', mimeo. University of Utrecht.
Wright, G. (1974). 'The political economy of the New Deal spending', *Review of Economics and Statistics*, vol. 56, pp. 30–36.
Zellner, A. (1962). 'An efficient method of estimating seemingly unrelated regressions and tests for aggregation bias', *Journal of the American Statistical Society*, vol. 57, pp. 348–368.